1984

Designing for human–computer communication

Computers and People Series

Edited by
B. R. GAINES

The series is concerned with all aspects of man–computer relationships, including interaction, interfacing modelling and artificial intelligence. Books are interdisciplinary, communicating results derived in one area of study to workers in another. Applied, experimental, theoretical and tutorial studies are included.

Designing for human–computer communication

edited by

M. E. SIME

*MRC/SSRC Social and Applied Psychology Unit,
University of Sheffield, Sheffield, England*

and

M. J. COOMBS

*Department of Computer Science, University of
Strathclyde, Glasgow, Scotland*

ACADEMIC PRESS, INC.

(Harcourt Brace Jovanovich, Publishers)

London   Orlando   San Diego   New York
Toronto   Montreal   Sydney   Tokyo

ACADEMIC PRESS INC. (LONDON) LTD
24/28 Oval Road, London NW1 7DX

United States Edition published by
ACADEMIC PRESS, INC.
Orlando, Florida 32887

British Library Cataloguing in Publication Data

Designing for human—computer communication.—
(Computers and people)
1. Man—machine systems   2. Electronic digital
computers
I. Sime, M. E.   II. Coombs, M. J.   III. Series
001.64   QA76.5

ISBN 0-12-643820-X

PRINTED IN THE UNITED STATES OF AMERICA

84 85 86 87   9 8 7 6 5 4 3 2

Contributors

R. G. Ball
Royal Signals and Radar Establishment
B1103, St Andrews Road
Great Malvern
Worcestershire WR14 3PS
England

R. F. Bateman
Royal Signals and Radar Establishment
B1212, St Andrews Road
Great Malvern
Worcestershire WR14 3PS
England

M. J. Coombs
Department of Computer Science
University of Strathclyde
Livingstone Tower
26 Richmond Street
Glasgow G1 1XH
Scotland

P. J. Cruickshank
MRC/SSRC Social and Applied
  Psychology Unit
University of Sheffield
Sheffield S10 2TN
England

R. Davis
Massachusetts Institute of Technology
Room 819, 545 Technology Square
Cambridge, Mass. 02139
USA

M. J. Fitter
MRC/SSRC Social and Applied
  Psychology Unit
University of Sheffield
Sheffield S10 2TN
England

B. R. Gaines
Department of Computer Science
York University
4700 Keele Street
Downsview, Ontario
Canada M3J 1P3

L. R. Harris
Artificial Intelligence Corporation
200 Fifth Avenue
Waltham, Mass. 02254
USA

I. D. Hill
Department of Computing and
  Statistics
Clinical Research Centre
Watford Road, Harrow
Middlesex HA1 3UJ
England

E. H. Mamdani
Department of Electrical and Electronic
  Engineering
Queen Mary College
University of London
Mile End Road
London E1 4NS
England

G. Ord
Royal Signals and Radar Establishment
B1212, St Andrews Road
Great Malvern
Worcestershire WR14 3PS
England

J. Palme
National Defence Research Institute
S-104 SO Stockholm 80
Sweden

M. L. G. Shaw
Department of Computer Science
York University
4700 Keele Street
Downsview, Ontario
Canada M3J 1P3

E. H. Shortliffe
Heuristic Programming Project
Departments of Medicine and Computer
   Science
Stanford University
Stanford, Calif. 94305
USA

M. E. Sime
MRC/SSRC   Social   and   Applied
   Psychology Unit
University of Sheffield
Sheffield S10 2TN
England

J. C. Thomas
International Business Machines
J. Watson Research Centre
P.O. Box 218
Yorktown Heights
New York 10598
USA

M. M. Zloof
International Business Machines
J. Watson Research Centre
P.O. Box 218
Yorktown Heights
New York 10598
USA

Preface

A well reported outcome of the current expansion in the use of computers within all areas of academic, commercial and industrial life, is the growing number of users without formal training in programming or computer technology. Such users wish simply to employ the machine as a tool in their daily work, and are not interested in becoming computer professionals or in understanding the details of their application system. People within this category come from a very wide range of educational and professional backgrounds, each individual ideally requiring a system carefully matched to the technical, psychological and social needs of his occupation. The chapters in this volume are concerned with the satisfaction of this ideal.

In order to design systems which permit an effective relationship between people and computers, it is necessary to focus upon two different problem areas: *the user interface* and *the task interface*. In recent years the term "interface design" has become restricted to the first of these. It is our opinion that this is a mistake, because user interface problems often arise out of errors in the choice of task. We have therefore given equal weight in our selection of chapters to both areas and have devoted considerable space to discussion of the relationship between the user and task interfaces in the introductory chapter.

The primary role of the *user interface* is to support information exchange between user and computer. There have until recently, however, been few well established principles to help the software designer decide upon either the best medium for transacting the exchange or the selection of content. Research topics have thus ranged from the consideration of surface factors such as the effect of a given lexicon or command language syntax on mental load, to the problems of providing a dialog to help users develop accurate and effective mental models of a system. It is our belief that the latter is the priority problem area, the efficiency with which users are able to employ a system being directly related to their understanding of it. The chapters in Part 1 of this volume amplify this interest within a wide variety of applications, including the retrieval of information from databases, air traffic control and knowledge-based problem solving.

Research on the user interface is of comparatively recent origin as is pointed out by Gaines and Shaw in the opening chapter of Part 1. However, the study of the *task interface* discussed in Part 2 has a longer history, being a natural extension of work on the cognitive ergonomics of instrument systems started during the Second World War. The current primary interest in this area, which is reflected in three of the five chapters, is the identification of the most effective distribution of a task between user and computer. Although research in this area overlaps to some extent with work on the user interface, a focus on the task itself raises rather different questions. These have less to do with the enhancement of user–computer communication, than the principles underlying the users' employment of the system and of their expectations of it.

The reader will note that the tone of the majority of contributions in this book is strongly empirical rather than theoretical. This is because the factors involved in the construction of "user efficient" systems are often very diverse, subject to complex interactions and, for their explication, require concepts and methodologies drawn from a number of different disciplines. It is therefore rarely possible to conduct research clearly within a single established theoretical framework. However, we are confident that the reader will find that an empirical approach has produced a number of very effective systems, in addition to a set of design principles which are now available for more structured examination. Moreover, although the main systems discussed in this book originated in the early 1970s, they are all still very much "state of the art" projects awaiting general application. This work should be of wide interest, serving the software industry as models of effective interface design, and stimulating the academic community to develop the conceptual tools and evaluation techniques to enable systems to be designed routinely to achieve human–computer communication—*not* computer–human domination, as may be feared.

We would like to take this opportunity of thanking Mike Fitter and Richard Gibson for many valuable discussions on issues raised in this volume. Richard Gibson has also contributed to the conventions editing of many of the papers: an arduous task which he executed swiftly and accurately.

September 1982

Max. E. Sime
Michael J. Coombs

Contents

Part 2 The task interface

Introduction

MAX E. SIME and MICHAEL J. COOMBS

I. The problem

The practical range of tomorrow's computer applications depends heavily upon the successful development of acceptable user interfaces. Few people, other than researchers or hobbyists, buy computers to program them. Users' interests are not, in general, concerned with programming but with the utility of the end product. This will often depend on how easy the system is to use.

Since the recent revolution in hardware technology changed the economic balance of computing and placed a major emphasis on software costs, there has been an intensified effort to make computers easier to program by providing better programming languages, better program development environments and an array of programming aids. The question "What makes a language better?" has become an important focus of research not only within computer science but from the standpoint of psycholinguistics, cognitive psychology and cognitive ergonomics. The latter, recently emergent, discipline is concerned primarily with discovering the relevant factors which determine "goodness of fit" between the conceptual requirements imposed by a task, such as programming or operating a computer, and human mental capacity and characteristics. Although the bulk of work in this area has to date been empirical, the relevance of theory and models from cognitive psychology and psycholinguistics is evident. The reader who wishes to be acquainted with this research background will find invaluable a collection of some 50 papers in *Human Factors in Software Development* (Curtis, 1982). The present volume, however, is about the characteristics of the products of computer programming, rather than about the process itself.

When considering the requirements of an application system, it is becoming increasingly important to distinguish clearly between programmers and users. The programmers' art is that of employing the "logical

DESIGNING FOR HUMAN–COMPUTER COMMUNICATION
ISBN 0 12 643820 X

bricks" of a general purpose machine to build a tool which performs some useful job. The users are those who need to use the tool. The criterion by which any tool is judged is that it is "worth its salt" in the context of its use, and there is no reason to view the products of computer programming differently.

Naturally, programmers are themselves a major class of user, and depend for their efficiency upon tools which are the products of their own trade. As specialists, however, they tend to be by temperament or training, unusually tolerant of systems which require significant skill and a demanding level of attention to fine detail (James, 1981, pp. 344–346). The exercise of skill can of course be pleasurable in its own right. Just as programming has proved of late to be a popular and seductive pastime for the hobbyist, the serious programmer may well derive satisfaction from his conceptual battle with a demanding system. However, the main objective of the attempt to develop systems which are easy to use is not to reduce the need for human skill, but rather to enhance human potential. One does not fit a crash gearbox in a formula-one car! It is, in any case, quite unlikely that the task of programming (as defined above) will ever be "de-skilled", as the complexity of the projects undertaken will surely expand to the limits of the conceptual power available.

The focus of programming effort will of course continue to change as new programming devices and techniques are developed. Just as higher-level languages have rendered assembly code programming less common, so a programming aid which automatically produces code from flowcharts would reduce the skill and effort required to achieve syntactic accuracy, and emphasize instead the expression of requirements in a (possibly less demanding) diagrammatic notation. Few programming aids render skills redundant without requiring some others to be gained in their place. The criterion of effectiveness rests not upon skill reduction but upon the achievement of a favourable return in power for expended effort.

The power of a computer is useful only to the extent that it is practically usable in any given context and today the "potential" range of applicability far exceeds that in which a practical solution has been achieved. What then stands in the way? The precise requirements of any tool must depend upon the task and the conditions under which it will be performed. Nevertheless, there are a number of common requirements which apply widely.

"Conceptual tools" as opposed to "computer games" are not an end in themselves and so must not incur a gratuitous mental load by imposing spurious demands upon the user. They should not, for example, demand excessive syntactic precision, or make obscure responses when precision is not achieved. Nor should they impose the need for a user to handle more than the minimum of concepts which are not directly related to the task for which the tool is employed. A doctor who wishes to make use of a computer aid, perhaps during a consultation, needs to think about doctoring, not data structures. A tool which requires him to consider computing concepts in parallel with those of his own discipline might well be judged to have costs in excess of its benefits. This point is discussed in some detail by Fitter and Cruikshank in Chapter 9.

A synthesis of principles for achieving effective man–computer communication is presented by Gaines and Shaw in the first chapter of this volume. They argue that there now exists over 20 years experience at designing interactive computer systems, yet there are still no production techniques for dialog design on a fully specified, scheduled, quality-controlled basis. A central principle for successful design was recognized a considerable time ago (Petri, 1962) but has never been thoroughly implemented. This is, that man and computer should be regarded as a system, with man as the main focus of the design process. The computer should be regarded as subservient to human needs, "emancipating" the user by extending his memory and reasoning powers. The problem, however, is to be able to clearly characterize both the task that the user wishes the system to perform, and his preferred way of conceptualizing about it. Gaines and Shaw propose a number of concrete techniques for achieving these objectives (e.g. the use of grid analysis techniques (Kelly, 1955) for representing a user's understanding of command verbs). Grid techniques are discussed extensively in an earlier book in this series (Shaw, 1980).

A central principle proposed by Gaines and Shaw is that the designer should "use the user's model". Just as a programmer would not expect to require an intimate knowledge of computer hardware, he should not expect the user of his own products to need more knowledge of programming than is absolutely necessary. The attitude of "This is what computers are like, so if you want the benefits you had better learn!", is not likely to commend itself to users, be they typists, managers, doctors, air traffic controllers, etc., who want help to do an already demanding job; not an additional workload. In any case it ducks the real challenge to computer science, which is to solve the communication problem not by relying on human adaptability but by complementing (and sometimes perhaps by emulating) human capacities.

In recent years a new subject area has developed with the objective of exploring principles and methods for fitting computer systems to human needs. The area is as yet immature with no simple title, and no well established repertoire of concepts and techniques. The subject is frequently designated by such terms as "interface design" and "dialog engineering". Gaines and Shaw (Chapter 1) list a number of books in this area. However, although immature, there are already clear points of focus, two of which we have used to provide the main divisions of this book. There is, however, considerable overlap in the content of chapters within these divisions. Papers have been grouped according to their dominant theme.

The first division is that of the **user interface**. Here we are concerned with processes involved in the support of information exchange between user and computer. Practical considerations in this area are centred on the design of command languages, the selection of communication devices and the generation of systems messages, including error messages. Research topics range from consideration of surface factors, such as the effect of a given command language syntax on mental load (e.g. Barnard *et al.*, 1980), to the issues involved in helping users to develop accurate and effective mental models of a system (e.g. de Boulay and O'Shea, 1981, p. 184). The second division is that of the **task interface**. There are two groups of issues in this area. The first is concerned with the mapping of computer processes on to the user's natural conceptualization of a task, and the second with the most effective distribution of the work task between user and computer. There is also a third interface area relevant to "designing for human–computer communication" which is not considered in detail in this volume. This may be termed the **organization interface** and covers factors related to the effects of a given class of system on the quality and structure of relationships within a work organization. Such issues enter to some extent into the discussions of Palme (Chapter 5), Fitter and Cruikshank (Chapter 9), Shortliffe (Chapter 8) and Ball and Ord (Chapter 10). Readers interested in this area are also directed to Rasmussen (1980), de Brabander *et al.* (1981) and Damodaran and Eason (1981).

II. The user interface

A. User language

Users, like programmers, need to be able to instruct the machine on their requirements and to do so needs some form of "language". The discourse universe which must be encompassed by the user's language will naturally depend upon the task being undertaken and the vocabulary of the language is likely to reflect the structure and content of the task. The typist using a word-processor will need to make statements in some language about setting margins, inserting and deleting characters, moving sections of text and printing or storing records. Statements about flight paths, arrival times, etc., would be meaningless in this language, although possibly of central importance in a system to be used by a booking clerk or air traffic controller. The universe of discourse to which "general purpose" computing languages apply comprises of basic computing concepts and operations. These, although essential for the construction of a computer aid, are rarely relevant to the task of operating it. Even in applications where the user requires the power to modify the tool he is using by augmenting the commands, information displays, or even the decision rules upon which it operates, this need may be better met by a language which reflects the concept domain of the task rather than one which mirrors the basic constructs of computer programming.

The special purpose language provided for a user is often described as a "command language". Its most obvious use is to allow commands to be given to the computer to perform some operation, such as to find and divulge given information. To consider such a language simply as a set of legal commands would be, however, much too narrow a view of things and would, in all but the simplest systems, be quite misleading. The language must be viewed as the total set of communications which can occur between the user and the device. Equally important to issuing commands or requests is knowing that they have been correctly understood when they have, and knowing what they have been taken to mean when they have not. Even in minimally interactive systems, communication is a two-way process. The user needs information and assurance about system states in order to be able to maintain orientation in the "control space". In devices of even modest complexity, such as word-processors, a command which is meaningful whilst the system is in one mode of operation might have quite unwelcome consequences if applied in some other mode. On the device which I am using to type this paper the "single keypress command" labelled **RETURN** will, in one mode of operation, move the typing head to the left-hand margin. In another mode, it will issue a complaint that I have not provided an argument to say how many line feeds I want, and in yet another context it will cause the previous line I have typed to be treated as a command.

A theme discussed by Gaines and Shaw and echoed throughout the book is that an interface language should do more than simply provide a list of commands which may be issued to the computer. The design process should ensure that the language is capable of supporting the full range of conceptual operations that the user requires for a given range of tasks. For example, given the ubiquity of errors in programming, the language should ideally be capable of generating error messages which are meaningful both in the sense of identifying the cause of the error in terms of the users mental model of the system and in the sense of indicating an appropriate response. The language should also provide an adequate range of constructs to prevent panic and frustration: when a command causes the VDU screen to go blank, how may one know whether the machine is engaged on an onerous processing task, is waiting for a further command, or is looping to infinity (until the plug is pulled)?

Gaines and Shaw identify the main difficulties in defining and supporting a full range of language functions, and suggest some solutions. Communication between a system analyst and potential users may be improved from the outset. To achieve this, the user would benefit by gaining active experience of a similar system and the designer would benefit by using such tools as grid analysis (Shaw, 1980) to, for example, assess the user's understanding of language terms. On the other hand, these writers recognize that a user's understanding of a system, and his language requirements, will change with experience. The implication is that at the very least there should be facilities for the designer to add new commands and structures without destroying the integrity of the earlier system. Palme (Chapter 5) and Bateman (Chapter 6) describe implementations of such facilities. Another solution might be for the system to model and monitor its users, automatically adjusting to them as required. Such possibilities are not just in the realm of science fiction. At the lowest level, the system could collect statistics on pre-selected functions, e.g. **ABORT**, **DELETE**, and take appropriate action when values reach some critical point. At a more sophisticated level, a knowledge-based interface (Waterman, 1979) could be used to model both the users and their processing task, and to employ such knowledge to provide a flexible computer response, e.g. decide on the appropriate level of "help" a user requires. The work by Davis (Chapter 4) goes some way in this direction within the environment of a knowledge-based investment advisor.

When viewing user language it is important not to confuse the "power" of the language itself with an enhancement of *user power*. The issue is not what a user *could* do had he the time to learn and the need to do it, but rather how the facility enhances the work he *in fact* wants to do. The date-set, month, year, time-zone adjustment, optional alarm tone selection, 24-h clock readout option plus chronograph with lap recording and night light, all set up and operated by four tiny buttons, tend not to enhance humour or performance in the twilight hours when one wishes merely to adjust the alarm to get an hour more or less sleep. Without an exceptional memory for the unmemorable one might be tempted to abandon the pride of microchip technology on one's wrist in favour of the older machine which has a comforting tick and a more limited command set. A colleague of ours who suffered a persistent alarm bleeb whilst attending an Elizabethan concert feels quite strongly on this point. The fact that he is a professional in man–machine systems research did little to help him quieten it quickly, or to lessen his embarrassment. It did however lead him to design an augmented state-transition notation to help describe his watch's "command language" (Green, 1982).

By the same token, the sales manager who desires a quick glance at the performance of his sales force might be impressed, but not well served, by a high technology query language offering the power not only to extract from the explicit contents of his database but also to infer facts implied by the stored data. Not at any rate if this involves him in learning an extensive formal syntax and attending a brush up course on logic to use it. Similarly the power to express queries of indefinite complexity ceases to be useful at the point where it is easier for the user to formulate a series of simple queries, the subsequent ones possibly referring to the output from those preceding them.

The design of languages to achieve the seemingly straightforward task of retrieving information from databases has proved to be considerably more difficult than anticipated. The problem is mainly that the logical formalisms which prove most effective for designing the actual databases are psychologically "unfriendly". They are therefore unsuitable for direct use by non-programmers. However, the consequences of such unfriendliness prove to have even deeper implications, in that the difficulty humans experience in handling logical quantification, disjunction and partially overlapping sets (Thomas, Chapter 7) means that the underlying logical structure of the database system will tend to remain opaque. There will be no easy way of providing the user with a model of the system's control structure which will help him to generate correctly formulated queries and to understand errors. The value of designing systems with an understandable control structure is illustrated by the range of user aids which Davis (Chapter 4) is able to provide for his "expert system" on investment. The fact that he can be confident that users will be able to handle an AND/OR decision tree, allows him to develop debugging and development facilities based on the relations present in the structure.

Given the difficulty users' experience in employing information retrieval languages based on formal logic (Thomas, Chapter 7) designers have been forced to adopt one of two alternative strategies. The first is illustrated by Zloof (Chapter 11) who designed a system "Query-by-Example" based upon the "natural" control structures a user would have acquired for handling the objects commonly used in business, e.g. tables, charts, etc. Query-by-Example allows a user to program by putting symbols in the named columns of tables. With appropriate operators, it is possible to represent all the database actions of a more demanding logical language in this way, including projection, union, join, intersection, difference and selection. In addition, it is even possible to provide facilities for electronic mail and report writing. Moreover, experimentation has shown that novices are capable of learning to use the system very quickly and with considerable accuracy, again in contrast to conventional logic languages (Thomas, Chapter 7).

A second strategy is to take the task of translating a query into a formal query system completely out of the hands of the user. Query-by-Example does this to some extent via table notation (for example, filling in two columns in the same row of a table implies conjunction and entering a variable under a column implies existential quantification). However, another approach is to allow some form of natural language query specification, and leave the system to do the interpretation. Harris (Chapter 3) describes such a system (INTELLECT) which uses a natural language interface. This interface has considerable power, being able not only to correctly translate clearly formulated queries of considerable complexity (e.g. five ANDED properties, one containing an embedded OR—see Harris, Chapter 3) but also able to interpret queries with many convaluted subordinate clauses. The power is achieved largely by capitalizing upon the restrictions in meaning imposed by the subject domain. For example, if the system is asked to "Name all bakers in the file", the system will be aware of an ambiguity, the term "baker" being present as a surname and as the name of an occupation. It will therefore be able to return to the user with a request to resolve the ambiguity. However, it would not consider attempting to list all the "bakeries" in Bradford, PA.

Finally, whilst it would be a mistake to imagine that with "good command language" and "good information" displays all problems which exist in matching mechanized to human information processing would be solved, it is not an unreasonable place to start. Providing, that is, we can discover what is "good" about a language. This is a less simple matter than it at first appears and the problem is relieved very little by replacing the word "good" by "natural", "user friendly", etc. Our best intuitions are likely to need substantial empirical testing for the forseeable future and certainly until there emerges a strong theoretical structure upon which to base design.

B. Natural communication

Most of us find it fairly easy to have ourselves understood and understand others in our native tongue. There are times of course when conversation can be difficult, but the problems seem usually to stem from discrepant assumptions, intrusive emotions, or concealed motives, rather than with the ability to handle language, and although language has to be learned, most of us feel comfortable with it by the time we get around to using computers. Perhaps, of course, tomorrow's home computing trend will bring "keyboards in the cot" at a pre-speech stage of user developments; as there seems to be no accounting for the extremes of parental endeavour to progress their offspring. In general, however, we can assume natural language and observe that the process of learning and using our mother tongues appears to match the characteristics of our brains in a way that is not true of the formalized language of today's computers.

It would not seem unreasonable therefore for a user to ask "Why can't a computer be more like me?" Perhaps we should view the development of natural language computing as the natural solution to the user communication problem. Of course we must accept that for the moment there is no practical way of achieving such a target in full; of providing a computer with the wealth of contextual knowledge and the mechanism of inference which is taken for granted in everyday discourse. Even the limited objective of programming a machine to converse generally in a "knowledgeable" way about the semantic structure of a tiny "building block" world has been shown to be, although achievable, a significant problem (Winograd, 1972). But such problems can be overcome and there is little doubt that with the advance of artificial intelligence techniques the potential for constructing close approximations to natural language systems is growing.

Modern parsing systems are already very powerful (e.g. LIFER—Hendrix, 1977) and work on text understanding has shown that with appropriate knowledge, computers are capable of displaying very high levels of natural language comprehension (e.g. Schank and Abelson, 1977; Lehnert, 1978). However, there are many problems, both practical and theoretical, to using such systems for routine applications. The main practical problem is that such systems are of necessity very large and slow. Schank's system, for example, requires considerable processing power, and used as a front-end to an application program would require a fair sized computer to itself. On the theoretical front, the "frame" and "semantic network" formalisms used in text understanding systems are not fully adequate for dealing with logical constructs such as quantification. However, the area is developing fast in tackling these problems (e.g. Hendrix (1979) on the extension of semantic networks to encompass logical quantification) and there are often ways round them when working in restricted domains (see Harris, Chapter 3).

On the above point alone, it is important to make the distinction between the problem of building a general natural language understanding system and the provision of a natural language interface for some limited problem solving domain, e.g. a database retrieval system. In the former it is necessary for the system to be able to cope with a very wide range of vocabulary and grammatical constructions of arbitrary complexity, referring to any topic and without user feedback. Such systems make heavy use of sophisticated methods of knowledge representation and a range of specialized processing strategies. Successful flexibility is bought at the cost of considerable complexity. However, in the latter case, many problems of syntactic, semantic and structural ambiguity can be solved by capitalizing on restrictions in the subject domain and a restricted format for representing knowledge (Davis, Chapter 4) or data facts (Harris, Chapter 3).

The system described by Harris is an example of what can already be achieved within a defined area of discourse and where the operations are limited to extracting information from a database. The "TEIRESIAS" system of Davis, also indicates the feasability of mechanisms which allow a user to share and communicate about the semantics of a task domain and receive meaningful feedback about the machine's "reasoning".

Given that a good approximation to natural language might be achieved, how far would this resolve the casual user's problems? Our authors diverge somewhat on this issue and Hill (Chapter 2) argues strongly that where precision is required, plain language would often serve us less well than a formal language. Certainly, although tolerant of syntactic deviations, the extraction of meaning from plain language is very dependent on context and shared background knowledge. It would be a mistake to imagine, however, that analogous problems do not occur with the syntactically precise language of computers. Where a user's assumptions about how a machine works are wrong, the chances of confusion resulting are not much reduced by a well defined syntax. Recently a medical receptionist, wishing to access a patient's record, typed in the name and initials as instructed, only to receive the reply "not known". She knew that the computer stored patients' addresses and used them to find records in cases where there was more than one patient with the same name. Not unreasonably, therefore she proceeded to type in the patient's address, to help the computer in its search. Again the reply was "not known", so she concluded that if the computer could not find the record with all that information, it could not be there and she must be dealing with a new patient. She had in point of fact misspelled the name and the record she wanted was in store. But how was she to know that the computer would not search on the basis of the address until it had found the name?

Whether the above case indicated the need for better training or for a better search algorithm is not the point. The fact that a computer accepts an input does not mean that it "understood it" in the way that a user meant it. Nor may its reply mean what a user thinks it means should any discrepancy in assumptions exist. Perhaps these problems are at their worst with systems which seem to be clever but are not as clever as they seem. Users can be lulled into expecting more sense and understanding from a system than it is designed to offer. This is analogous to the problem of

"English-like" syntax not backed up with the intelligence its appearance implies. It can give the illusion of being easy to learn and use but may be no less demanding in this respect than less cosmetic language; and more seriously, can sometimes seem to mean what it does not (see Harris, Chapter 3). It is equally important that the limitations of a system be apparent to a user and that he is aquainted with its power (Plum, 1977).

Of course achieving "natural" communication is not just a matter of providing tolerant and familiar syntax. The freedom to use linguistic constructions appropriate to the task is equally important. We encountered an interesting example some years ago of users being both surprised and frustrated by a system which, although allowing them to say what they needed to say, prevented them from doing so in a way that seemed natural to them. In fact it seemed to inhibit seriously their performance of the task. We were experimenting with a procedure which we called "progressive automation" at the time (Fitter and Sime, 1980), where non-programmers were, in the course of performing a schedulling test, able to pass on their methods to the computer which would thereafter perform them automatically. The rules, or "productions", they could pass on were of the form, "If such and such is the case do such and such"; e.g. "If long queue at machine one use machine two". They could not however express rules of the form "If long queue at machine one don't load any jobs there". Computer programmers, of course, are not unduly worried that most programming languages fail to provide facilities for telling the machine *not* to do something, as machines are not strong on personal initiative.

The reverse is, of course, true of human beings, this being a fact which is often ignored by writers of both system and error messages. Software designers ignore the "action" orientation of natural language (Grice, 1975), the effort after meaning displayed by even the most naive user usually ensuring that the most obscure system message is giving some interpretation (see Gaines and Shaw, Chapter 1). The ICL 1900 George editor, for example, prints out the message "**????FILE NAME REQUIRED????**" when the user misses the filename parameter off an editor call. There are no similar marks on other messages, and the additional symbols in this context increase its apparent importance. However, in one sense it is the least complex or problematic message printed by the editor. But when confronted by it, naive users have been known to abandon an edit and start again. Some preliminary investigations were made into the origin of the question marks, the explanation proving to be quite straightforward. The message is actually generated by the system itself which uses a convention of ******** for general information and **????** for errors. The designer has simply passed the message through to the user with no change, so leading the user to infer more than is intended (Alty, 1980).

III. The task interface

Although there is a level of understanding at which a user has no more need
to know how his program works than a viewer of television needs to know
electronics, there is another level where such understanding can be crucial.
As Gaines and Shaw (Chapter 1) point out, a user's view of a system will
tend not be static but will change with experience. The change in view will
not merely amount to tighter or more appropriate conceptionalizations of
the systems for the performance of existing tasks. With experience, the user
will perceive new processing possibilities, perhaps extended into new
application areas. Even formal languages are to some extent "living" in that
the user may create new structures out of old. To successfully use a
computer in "creative mode" an understanding of the underlying system
will be important, and perhaps necessary.

Computer systems would ideally be constructed to be fully "understandable" within the concepts the user requires to complete his work task.
Learning to use a new system would thus require a minimum of effort, and
errors, at least those originating from the user, would be perceived in a
context which was transparent both in its implications for the task and in
methods of corrections. However, it is often impossible to make the
requisite mappings at the task interface perfect, with a consequent risk of
incomprehension.

These problems have directed considerable research attention to the
design of the task interface, the present book containing sample solutions
within the areas of commercial databases, air traffic control, medical
diagnosis and medical history taking. One of the central problems of this
area is that of designing an interface system which supports a dialog within
the domain of the task and which smoothly interrelates with other human
task activities. There are two major problems. First, the activities
undertaken by the system should ideally form a "module", being relatively
complete within themselves and having a simple relationship with external
task activities. However, it is unusual for work activities to conveniently
decompose in this way. A system for entering information on a patient's
medical history may be required to be used in a single pass, if the doctor is
using it for routine purposes, and in a random manner, if the doctor is using
it to help him focus in on a particular disease. Secondly, the processing
capabilities of a module are often hard to predict. These problems are
particularly well illustrated wtih reference to the rule-based systems
described by Davis (Chapter 4) and Shortliffe (Chapter 8).

Having decided upon some decomposition of the task and on the roles to
allocate to the computer (following some period of task analysis), the
designer needs to develop a "user image", embodying the required

mapping between the expected user view of the task and the system representation. One of the major difficulties of defining such an image is that there is a tendency for languages which are simple and consistent, and so easy to learn, to highlight certain classes of information at the expense of others. For example, flow charts emphasize sequential relations and therefore make it easy to express and retrieve order information. However, this will be at the expense of a means of expressing and retrieving information about the states which can exist concurrently within a system, such as might be required to make fast decisions on the basis of states (Fitter and Green, 1981; Green *et al.*, 1981). For most complex tasks the designer will have to develop a task language which emphasizes the requisite relations and allows them to be processed efficiently. It will often be very difficult to achieve this goal because of the side effects of emphasizing a particular class of relation; a common problem is writing general program modules in that variable names which help to emphasize the "meaning" of the procedure in one context, interfere with understanding in another context.

Computers are increasingly being used in situations where the decision logic involved cannot be specified with the certitude of mathematics and where the validity of outputs cannot be assumed as might be the solution to a physical equation. A program for allocating housing or for determining welfare entitlements, based on the wording and interpretation of legislation, would yield outputs which themselves remain subject to evaluation and interpretation. The rules by which a society is governed are rarely sufficiently detailed and precise as to cover every contingency (Palme, Chapter 5). Not only do conclusions based on such rules need to be evaluated; in a civilized society they need to be explained. "Because the computer said so!", has never been an appropriate level of explanation, which probably accounts for its popularity in computer jokes. Were one to receive it as a reason for being denied a benefit which others in similar circumstances were allowed one would not be impressed.

In the above situation the issue of "de-skilling" takes on a different significance. Where decision procedures, for reasons of economy, speed or accuracy, are transferred from person to machine, it is important that the consequences of the transfer for overall system function, including supervision and monitoring, be considered. It should not be assumed, for example, that peoples' ability to evaluate or explain outputs will still remain unimpaired after the task of processing the data has been taken from them. Where it is intended that someone will supervise, evaluate, possibly override, explain or take responsibility for the outputs of an automated process, special measures may be called for to ensure that the conditions obtain to make this task realistic. The problem which this requirement presents can vary depending on the nature of the task, from the trivial to the exceedingly complex.

Whereas a simple task such as computing a payroll, automated for speed and convenience rather than to augment conceptual power, is unlikely to present serious problems of supervision, a complex computation indicating, say, a dangerous convergence of aircraft, flight paths, requiring rapid correction in a crowded air space, could be quite another matter. Ball and Ord (Chapter 10) discuss this issue in considerable detail. The detection of any error assumes the existence of a standard of comparison against which its output is judged. In a constantly changing situation this would seem to require a parallel computational model generating "expectations". In the case of an air traffic controller a conflict between his expectations, based on his "in head" appreciation of the state of the air space and a computer recommendation, would face him with a serious problem and little time to resolve it. The decision whether to accept or override such computer "advice" raises a number of questions which have an important bearing on the design of the "task interface".

Clearly in such a situation social and psychological factors relating to the consequences of a wrong decision could influence and possibly impair human judgement. It is one thing to make a well informed decision and in the event be proved wrong; it is quite another thing to decide against a course of action which has been indicated by a "presumably well validated", computer model. In such a situation a wrong decision could, in addition to its potential for personal remorse, leave one in an ambiguous legal situation. Issues of status, responsibility and liability need to be defined (Fitter and Sime, 1980).

Perhaps it must be accepted that there will be a range of situations where human monitoring and control in any instrumental sense will simply not be practical. A totally automated air traffic control system might well handle levels of traffic which, should it fail, would be too much for people to cope with, even with computer aids. There is nothing irrational about placing human lives in the hands of machines in this way, providing the track record of the machines is such as to justify the risk. After all we trust our lives to machines every day; to aircraft engines, elevators, roller coasters, traffic lights and many other man-made systems. We race through a green light with no less confidence than we show when waved on by a traffic policeman. Be that as it may, when we do choose to maintain human monitoring and control we must ensure that the conditions exist to make the task possible.

There is nothing unique about the air traffic control situation. The problem could be as well illustrated with reference, say, to an automated steel rolling mill, or any other application in process control where there is a rapidly changing environment controlled by machine but requiring occasional human intervention. The pace of change of traffic in an air space, and the irreversability of aircraft flight paths, does however highlight the difficulty of gaining enough time to re-evaluate a situation where computer or other advice appears wrong-headed to the human monitor. The work reported by Ball and Ord illustrates an ingenious approach to this problem using a computer model to predict future states of an air space and thus increase the available decision time. This technique of "prediction simulation" could in principal be applied irrespective of whether the decision making is left in human hands, or automated, but monitored by people.

The use of computer models to explore future states, or potential consequences of proposed decisions is of course well utilized in the sphere of planning and design. Reliable models can readily be achieved where the rules governing the environment to be simulated can be precisely stated.

This is not always the case, however. For many, even very complex tasks, stating the rules presents no problem, but for other, often seemingly simple tasks, the problem defeats us. People do many things with no apparent effort but cannot say precisely how. We conclude that "John is trustworthy" or that "Jane is the wife for me", without being able to tell a computer how to arrive at that conclusion. Perhaps we should not be too disturbed by this limitation. Part of being human is to be fallible and there are areas of experience where the aid of infallible robots might be better dispensed with. There are, nevertheless, between the extremes of algorithm and intuition, a range of problems where solution procedures are difficult to specify in full but where substantially reliable rules and guidelines exist. And these, augmented by human judgement, can be invoked towards a solution. Problems in medical diagnosis, interpretation of legislation, planning and scheduling investment decisions, etc., appear to be of such a character. In such cases we might well lack confidence in a totally automated solution procedure, but still wish to avail ourselves of the power of a computer program to reveal the consequences of complex rules when applied to complex data.

Where a substantial degree of computer aid or support is involved, the responsibility for the efficient conduct of a task is likely to remain with the user of the computer rather than with those who built or programmed it. The doctor, for example, who is offered a computer to support him in diagnosis will still, most likely, remain answerable for the decisions he takes. For this to be at all reasonable the rationale of any computer generated information or "advice" must be apparent to him, the system must be made "transparent".

Recent years have seen an important extension in the use of computers for information processing which has emphasized the transparency problem. This extension involves a shift of focus from the database computer, where simple factual information is stored for easy retrieval (Thomas, Palme, Zloof in this book), and from fundamentally numerical processing, as in the air traffic control work of Ball and Ord (Chapter 10), to the use of computers to process "propositional information" in order to simulate the intelligent activities of a highly trained expert. The systems discussed by Shortliffe (Chapter 8) and Davis (Chapter 4) are of this type. These activities typically include:

(1) diagnostic problem-solving using the data stored in the system;
(2) the addition of knowledge to the database;
(3) communication with the user in a flexible way to give a solution, explain a solution, or to acquire additional knowledge directly from the expert.

Such knowledge-based programs have become termed "expert systems" and have expanded the potential applications of computers. For example, the same basic program structure could be used to make technical advice accessible in a number of places where no expert is available, and to do so within the language and subject context of a particular class of user, as well as providing a tool to help an expert understand the structure of his own knowledge. Expert systems achieve this flexibility by seeking to process the "rules of convenience" used by experts in problem solving. Within a diagnostic problem-solving situation such as that described by Shortliffe (MYCIN, Chapter 8), the rules are activated to relate chains of evidence in order to reach a given response. This may be a request for further information from the user, or a particular problem solution.

The range of processing possibilities achieved by using "rules of convenience" or "heuristics" as they are termed, is considerable. It is possible to achieve acceptable diagnostic results with knowledge which is incomplete and, with the aid of some statistical additions to the rules, or "Fuzzy Logic" discussed by Mamdani (Chapter 12), to handle uncertain evidence. A program for diagnosing faults with a car might contain such questions as "How certain are you that the spark plug had a black deposit? Please answer by typing a number from -5 (definitely not) to $+5$ (certain)". With an appropriate interactive user interface for the addition and deletion of rules, exploration of the decision tree, and explanatory play-back of a particular decision path, it is possible to use what is basically a diagnostic aid as a learning system, the user being able to explore his own understanding of the relations inherent in the data and the consequences of his rules.

Using an heuristic approach to programming, however, carries its own difficulties. By definition, heuristics cannot be guaranteed to result in the best solution to a problem; or even to give a solution at all. Additionally, it is well known that because of limitations in short-term memory, users find it very difficult to hand-simulate the processing of rules to test implications. Lists of "condition-action" type rules, whilst making explicit the circumstances which must obtain for any given action to be performed, offer little help in inferring the route through which a program might have progressed to achieve these conditions. When a user is "surprised" at some outcome, he needs some support in asking "*Why?*". Such "explanation" facilities˙are available in an elementary form in MYCIN (Shortliffe, Chapter 8), while TEIRESIAS (Davis, Chapter 4) is specifically designed to provide user support. Using the question **WHY**, the user may obtain information on possible solution paths (i.e. how evidence combines to produce the solution); the question **HOW** traces the evidence collected towards a particular conclusion during the current session. It turns out that fundamentally the same facilities are required for the tutorial use of an expert system as are required for supporting its diagnostic application.

Davis's system TEIRESIAS (Chapter 4) is a significant attempt to design a comprehensive user support system. In doing so he highlights many of the "pragmatic" requirements that follow from the interface principles listed by Gaines and Shaw (Chapter 1), Thomas (Chapter 7) and by other writers throughout this book. Perhaps the most important of these is that the designer should establish an explicit and rigorously defined "image" for the system, which is both complete (in that all system behaviour can be explained and *predicted* from it) and clearly congruent with a given application (system behaviour can be understood in terms of the user's conceptualization of the task). Within the context of a diagnostic knowledge-based system, the central structure of an AND/OR decision tree, processed as production rules, and with a simple property list format for the representation of individual data items, approaches all of the above criteria.

Davis points out that the design criteria would be more difficult to satisfy with systems that mixed different types of control and data structures. However, the work again points the way towards techniques for designing "test" programs which take some user input and give a trace of execution which makes explicit the relationships between input, processing control and processing products. The important advance on traditional trace facilities, is that the explanation and debugging aids aim to produce a high-level account of processing, and in a way that will direct the user's attention towards appropriate corrections. A comprehensive user support system would thus include:

(1) facilities for providing relevant and comprehensible systems information on request;
(2) facilities for computer-aided guidance of the user;
(3) facilities for evaluating the adequacy of user guidance and system messages;
(4) a software vehicle which allows the system to adapt to the user and to evolve with increasing knowledge of system problems and user needs.

IV. Prospects

The rapid expansion in the use of interactive computers in the mid-1960s, has led to many of the problems of human–computer communication discussed in this book, predominantly arising from

(1) the abstract nature of the general purpose machine underlying information handling;
(2) fundamental differences in the way computers and humans process information (Wason and Johnson-Laird, 1976).

Many of these problems have still not been subject to general solution. Nevertheless, significant conceptual advances have been made throughout the area and several successful practical approaches are illustrated by projects in this book.

Considerable effort has been invested by manufacturers in making their systems more "user-friendly" by following the principles that (a) the software should address the user in his own terms, and (b) wherever possible, the software should *prevent* the user from making errors. While on the surface these may seem very sound objectives, they have proved to be hard to implement in systems of any generality. For example, even with a straightforward stock-control system, it is unlikely that the designers will be able to anticipate all major sources of error, or to achieve the lesser objective of selecting variable names that are unambiguous to all levels of users. This is because it is usually impossible for a client to specify his requirements in detail without actual experience with the system designed to fulfil them. Computer systems tend to be used in practice in ways that the designer could never have anticipated and by people whom the designer could never have considered (Edmonds, 1981).

Given the above problems, the ideal of user-friendly software is difficult to achieve. However, systems often maintain a façade of understanding and friendliness by being "chatty", while maintaining a high degree of computer control. While this has proved a successful strategy with systems for users having no knowledge of computing and working at simple, well defined tasks, there can also be significant disadvantages. Chatty user interfaces may often induce misunderstanding by mixing technically precise terms with informal language; they may also become irritating for the experienced user who knows exactly what he wants to do and would like to do it using the minimum number of command symbols with the minimum of computer prompting. Excessive computer control can also be undesirable, even for the novice users of complex, general systems, because they may prevent him from developing a full and accurate mental model of the system.

A more realistic objective for system designers is the production of what may be termed "user-efficient software", the fundamental principles of which are that:

(1) the user should be helped to achieve his processing goal within a range of acceptable error, and
(2) the user should be helped to learn from his mistakes.

A more realistic aim for user-efficient software is not to make error impossible but to help the user reduce it through understanding. The principles thus place a new emphasis upon the quality of the dialog the software is capable of maintaining with the user, and techniques for assessing and sustaining high quality interaction.

V. References

Alty, J. L. (1980). An approach for improving system dialogues and error messages for non-computer professionals. *Research Report No. 123*. Computer Laboratory, University of Liverpool.

Barnard, P. J., Hammond, N. W., Morton, J., Long, J. B. and Clark, I. A. (1980). Consistency and compatibility in human/computer dialogue. *Research Report*. IBM UK Laboratories Ltd., Hursley Park, Winchester.

Curtis, B. (1982). *Human Factors in Software Development*. IEEE Computer Society, Los Angeles.

Damodaran, L. and Eason, K. D. (1981). Design procedures for user involvement and user support. *In* M. J. Coombs and J. L. Alty (Eds), *Computing Skills and the User Interface*. Academic Press, London and New York.

de Boulay, B. and O'Shea, T. (1981). Teaching novices programming. *In* M. J. Coombs and J. L. Alty (Eds), *Computing Skills and the User Interface*. Academic Press, London and New York.

de Brabander, B., Vanlomme, E., Deschoolmester, D. and Lgder, R. (1981). The impact of computer use in organization structure. *In* B. Schakel (Ed.), *Man–Computer Interaction: Human Factors Aspects of Computers and People*. Sijthoff and Noordhoff, Alpher aan den Rijn.

Edmonds, E. A. (1981). Adaptive man–computer interfaces. *In* M. J. Coombs and

J. L. Alty (Eds), *Computing Skills and the User Interface*. Academic Press, London and New York.

Fitter, M. J. and Green, T. R. G. (1981). "When do diagrams make good computer languages?" *In* M. J. Coombs and J. L. Alty (Eds), *Computing Skills and the User Interface*. Academic Press, London and New York.

Fitter, M. J. and Sime, M. E. (1980). Responsibility and shared decision making. *In* H. T. Smith and T. R. G. Green (Eds), *Human Interaction with Computers*. Academic Press, London and New York.

Green, T. R. G. (1982). Pictures of programs and other processes, or how to do things with lines. *Behaviour and Information Technology* 1, 3–36.

Green, T. R. G., Sime, M. E. and Fitter, M. J. (1981). The art of notation. *In* M. J. Coombs and J. L. Alty (Eds), *Computing Skills and the User Interface*. Academic Press, London and New York.

Grice, A. P. (1975). Logic and conversation. *In* P. Cole and J. L. Morgan (Eds), *Syntax and Semantics III: Speech Acts*. Academic Press, New York and London.

Hendrix, G. G. (1977). The LIFER manual: a guide to building practical natural language interfaces. *Technical Note 138*. Artificial Intelligence Centre, SRI International Inc., Menlo Park, CA.

Hendrix, G. G. (1979). Encoding knowledge in partitioned networks. *In* N. V. Findler (Ed.), *Associative Networks: Representation and Use of Knowledge by Computers*. Academic Press, New York and London.

Lehnert, W. G. (1978). *The Process of Question Answering: A Computer Simulation of Cognition*. Lawrence Earlbaum Associates, Hillside, N.J.

James, E. B. (1981). The user interface: how we may compute. *In* M. J. Coombs and J. L. Alty (Eds), *Computing Skills and the User Interface*. Academic Press, London and New York.

Kelly, G. A. (1955). *The Psychology of Personal Constructs*. Norton, New York.

Petri, C. A. (1961). *Kommunikation it Automaten*. Dissertation, Universität Bonn.

Plum, T. (1977). Fooling the user of a programming language. *Software-Practice and Experience* 7, 215–221.

Rasmussen, J. (1980). The human as a systems component. *In* H. T. Smith and T. R. G. Green (Eds), *Human Interaction with Computers*. Academic Press, London and New York.

Schank, R. C. and Abelson, R. P. (1977). *Scripts, Plans, Goals and Understanding. An Inquiry into Human Knowledge Structures*. Lawrence Erlbaum Associates, Hillside, N.J.

Shaw, M. L. G. (1980). *On Becoming a Personal Scientist*. Academic Press, London and New York.

Wason, P. C. and Johnson-Laird, P. N. (1976). *Psychology of Reasoning: Structure and Context*. Batsford, London.

Waterman, D. A. (1979). User-oriented approach to capturing expertise: a rule-based approach. *In* D. Michie (Ed.), *Expert Systems in the Micro-electronic Age*. Edinburgh University Press, Edinburgh.

Winograd, T. (1972). *Understanding Natural Language*. Academic Press, New York and London.

Part 1

The user interface

1. Dialog engineering

B. R. GAINES AND M. L. G. SHAW

Department of Computer Science, York University, Downsview, Ontario, Canada

I. Introduction

Thirty years ago a technological revolution took shape as the first stored-program computers stumbled through their early calculations. Fifteen years later computer systems had become sufficiently reliable for a second revolution to take place as the first time-shared *interactive* systems began to offer their services. The MIT MAC system (Fano, 1965) in 1963, the RAND JOSS system in 1963–1964 (Shaw, 1968) and the Dartmouth College BASIC system in 1964 (Danver and Nevison, 1969), pioneered a new style of computing in which users at remote teleprinter terminals were in direct communication with the computer. No longer did the user have to prepare all his programs and data meticulously in every detail in advance for submission to a queue of jobs eagerly awaiting the magic moments when the computer was actually working. Titles of books in the mid-1960s give some indication of the dramatic impact of this *Transition to On-Line Computing* (Gruenberger, 1967) through *The Challenge of the Computer Utility* (Parkhill, 1966) using *Conversational Computers* (Orr, 1968) to offer *Computer Augmentation of Human Reasoning* (Sass and Wilkinson, 1965). However, for many years to follow the majority of users still continued to use batch-processing systems.

Now, another fifteen years on, the continuing decline in computer costs and increase in reliability has made hands-on, interactive use of computers a commercial reality for all users (Gaines, 1978a). Conversational computing will become increasingly the normal mode of operation for the majority of computer users. We have previously emphasized the important role of *personal computers* not just as a change of technology but as a new force in the relationship between the individual and society (Shaw and Gaines,

1981b); a point argued more dramatically by both De Bono (1979) in *Future Positive*, and Toffler (1980) in *The Third Wave*. This presupposes the possibility of a close relationship developing between people and computers akin to that which Licklider (1968) calls *man-computer symbiosis*.

Despite the recognized importance of this transition to *conversational* and *personal* computing the study of the design of man–machine dialogs has only recently gained recognition as a field for the development of computer science and technology. It is interesting to examine the history of this growth of interest in the user interface at a cognitive rather than solely ergonomic level. The Klerer and Reinfelds (1968) collection of some 45 papers on *Interactive Systems for Experimental Applied Mathematics* already contains studies such as Fried's (1968) *On the user's point of view* emphasizing "direct user control" and "development of individual user systems", and Patton's (1968) on *A message system for interactive dialog* emphasizing a state-determined branching dialog structure as a standard interface to all interactive programs. Hansen (1971) at the Fall Joint Computer Conference appears to have made the first attempt to tabulate some *user engineering principles* for the design of interactive systems.

The key significance of the growing community of non-computer-oriented users of interactive systems was emphasized by Wasserman (1973) at the National Computer Conference two years later in his paper entitled *The design of idiot-proof systems*. The search for a more pleasant terminology for this key class of people, the *non-professional, naive* or *casual* users, continues today. They are only thus in relation to their technical knowledge of the inner workings of the computer and the need for such terminology is a significant message about the history of computers: the early users were necessarily computer technicians; the next generation of users had to go through these technicians in order to access the computer (Gaines, 1978e); and it is only now that computer usage has become potentially completely open. The motorist is not non-professional nor naive because he does not understand the internal combustion engine and the motor trade takes pride, and profit, in making him an expert user without needing to have that knowledge. The computer trade will only attain its full potential when there is similar pride, and profit, in making computer power readily available to users whose expertise is in their usage, not in their knowledge of bits, interrupts and DO-loops.

The first book on the topic of dialog programming was Martin's *Design of Man–Computer Dialogues* in 1973, followed in 1977 by Gilb and Weinberg's *Humanized Input*. Both books give a wealth of anecdotal experience and a variety of recommended techniques, but neither was then in a position to give a systematic account of what constitutes good dialog programming. In the mid-1970s we were in the same position with *programming man–computer interaction* as we were with hardware design 30 years ago and software design 10 years ago—we were reliant on un-systematized *craft* skills passed on erratically through fortunate *apprentice-ships*. Through evolution many systems had become reasonably satisfactory in their basic dialogs and these could be copied in similar situations, but we had no production techniques for *dialog engineering* on a specified, scheduled, quality-controlled, reliable basis. The effects of this were starkly stated at the 1974 National Computer Conference:

> the lowered cost of computer access and the proliferation of on-line systems produced a new breed of users, people whose expertise was in some area other than computer technology. As their initial fascination with conversational computing wore off, users reported experiencing feelings of intense frustration and of being 'manipulated' by a seemingly unyielding, rigid, intolerant dialogue partner, and these users began disconnecting from time-sharing services at a rate which was very alarming to the industry. (Walther and O'Neil, 1974)

These remarks were still echoed by Nickerson (1981) recently in his paper *Why interactive computers are sometimes not used by people who might benefit from them.*

In the mid-1970s there was an increase in studies of man–computer interaction commencing with attempts to give: rules for "well-behaved" interactive procedures by Kennedy (1974); a systematic *Dialog specification procedure* by Pew and Rollins (1975) at Bolt Beranek and Newman; and systemic guidelines with theoretical and psychological underpinning by Gaines and Facey (1975). Thereafter the literature on man–computer dialog design grew rapidly and began to form the basis of overall appraisals such as that in Shneiderman's (1980) book on *Software Psychology* where the work already mentioned, together with that of Cheriton (1976), Gebhardt and Stellmacher (1978) and Turoff *et al.* (1978) is tabulated and discussed. Various collections of papers have also been published recently on *Human Interaction with Computers* (Smith and Green, 1980), *Methodology of Interaction* (Guedj *et al.*, 1980), *Man–Computer Interaction* (Shackel, 1981) and *Computing Skills and the User Interface* (Coombs and Alty, 1981). It is often forgotten that Petri's (1962) work on net representations of concurrent systems arose from his studies of the dynamics of complete systems including the users. Dehning *et al.* (1981) have recently published a wide-ranging presentation of *User requirements in dialogs* based on petrinet concepts.

Naturally the many sources of guidelines are not always mutually consistent and Maguire (1982) has given a coherent account of them and suggested resolutions of conflicting guidelines. Some of the apparent inconsistencies are themselves significant—we have suggested elsewhere (Gaines, 1980) that "the opposite of a statement worth making is also a statement worth making". There is a further analogy from the motor trade where the instructor will initially tell a trainee driver to "let in the clutch very gently" in order to avoid stalling the engine. Later, when the semi-experienced trainee is letting the engine race excessively, the instructor will tell him to "let in the clutch rapidly". These guidelines apparently conflict only if they are taken as universal generalities rather than rules appropriate to different stages of knowledge of the trainee. It is this discrimination and refinement in the engineering of man–computer interaction that we can see becoming significant in the 1980s.

In reviewing the next stages of development in man–computer communication (Gaines, 1978e), we stressed the need to consider both the internal models of the *worlds* within man and computer when setting up and analysing communication, and also the mutual models that the computer and man have of one another (Shaw and Gaines, 1981a). We have also emphasized the short-term practical role that developing a *technology of interaction* has for business applications of minicomputers in the next decade, and placed a *dialog processing module* on par with other fundamental modules for *database control*, *document production* and so on (Gaines, 1978a). This chapter may be seen as a more specific attempt to take that framework of mutual modelling and generate within it detailed characteristics for dialog engineering.

It would be rash to pretend any work at this stage can approach a complete formulation of the techniques for *dialog engineering*. In particular, the rapid change in interface technology requires constant re-interpretation of the guidelines, possibly even their fundamental modification if they are not systematically stated. The advent of *intelligent terminals* in which a local microprocessor gives very flexible control over a visual display, the availability of graphics as well as textual display, the capability to recognize handwriting and, perhaps soon, speech—all of these change the man–computer interface and require a re-appraisal of dialog engineering techniques. However, the rules given in this chapter do represent some further steps in the direction taken by the work noted above in beginning to systematize the rules for programming man–machine interaction through the engineering of formal dialogs.

II. Programming interaction

First let us make it clear what kinds of conversation and dialog are under consideration in this chapter. Natural language dialog with computers has been the goal of much *artificial intelligence* research, and Weizenbaum's (1967) ELIZA with its *cocktail party* capability to maintain a conversation *without understanding*, and Winograd's (1972) SHRDLU that used its *understanding* of a narrow domain to allow facile manipulation of language, both gave hope that the goal was achievable. Petrick's (1976) survey of work on natural language-based systems demonstrates the increasing capabilities of such systems, and database query systems such as Hendrix's (1977) LIFER and Harris's (1977) ROBOT are very impressive in their abilities to maintain meaningful and useful dialogs with a wide range of real users. Indeed, natural language communication itself can now be seen as available technology limited in its application by more fundamental defects in our database systems (Gaines, 1979).

However, there are a number of reasons why such truly *natural language* systems will probably not play major commercial roles for some years to come:

(1) They still require large programs in powerful machines for their operation.
(2) The typing by the user to generate complete English sentences is too great—one day speech recognition (Cox and Martin, 1975; Woods *et al.*, 1976) may change this, but for the moment *unnatural* dialogs minimizing user typing activities are essential.
(3) In many applications where the computer replaces or mimics the clerk in an office the *natural* dialog is already highly formalized because it has evolved to carry information clearly and concisely—we have a formal *battle language* that is purely functional, resistant to noise and corruption, and readily assimilated by newcomers.

It is these more formal dialogs with which we are concerned in this chapter—they form the major requirement in current commercial systems, but their programming is still too much a *hit and miss* affair. However, most of the points made are basic systemic and psychological requirements that carry over to the free form natural language dialog that may one day become possible and desired. Figure 1 gives a sample of the type of dialog under consideration—in this case a data entry sequence in a securities dealing system. The line numbers are for reference only—user input follows the last colon on each line, lines 4, 7 and 8 offer default options, line 12 is validation before entry.

Seven years ago we attempted to analyse lessons learnt in a wide range of experience of *Interactive system development and application* (Gaines and Facey, 1975) in a variety of medical, industrial and commercial projects. One section of this paper was entitled *The programming of interaction*, and at the second draft we decided to make it rather more pointed by phrasing

```
 1   GDR:E
 2   Item:S
 3   Stock number:85
 4   Full name: Treasury :Exchequer
 5   Issue date:6/7
 6   Type (SMLTN):S
 7   Dividends/year: 2 :
 8   Final div date : 1/1 :5/8
 9   Redemption years(s):81
10   Coupon:3 1/4
11   Number of calls: 0 :
12     85:Exchequer   3 1/4   1981   5/8   S   6-Jul-77 OK?:Y
13   GDR:
```

Fig. 1.   Typical dialog sequence.

the lessons learnt as a set of eleven *rules*. Whilst tightly formulated *rules of dialog* were undoubtedly at that stage of the game still pseudo-science, it has been invaluable in further development of dialog programming techniques to have a set of well-defined and precise guidelines with which to work. Having a defined set of rules has already led to suggestions for further rules and amendments to the first ones in the light of others' experience and these were published by Gaines (1978b, 1981). In the next section further developments of these rules are reiterated and expanded with a brief comment on each, and later sections use them as a basis for formalizing dialog programming, and refine them further. To complete this section we wish to establish some very basic guidelines for the objectives of actually having man–computer interaction to start with, and for the relative roles of man and computer in such systems. This is clearly a fundamental aim of a book such as this, to establish why man should wish to communicate with the computer, and on what terms he does so.

There are three remarks that for us epitomize our objectives in designing interactive systems: James Martin in his book on the *Design of Man–Computer Dialogues* states:

> man must become the prime focus of system design. The computer is there to serve him, to obtain information for him and to help him do his job. The ease with which he communicates with it will determine the extent to which he uses it. Whether or not he uses it powerfully will depend upon the man–machine language available to him and how well he is able to understand it. (Martin, 1973, p. 3)

Walter Doherty, Manager of the in-house systems at IBM's Thomas J. Watson Research Laboratories, remarked in a seminar at Essex University in September 1977:

The computer is a tool to extend man's memory and reasoning power—these are the key bases on which technical advances should be evaluated.

And John Cleary at EUROCOMP 74 in discussing the role of such new system concepts as the *virtual machine* said:

The only virtual machine of interest to a user is one that has abolished all lower levels of system and presents an *understandable* and *sympathetic* face to its user.

Doherty's remark brings out the role of the computer as a *tool* aiding a person in coping with their mental workload—in an interactive system the machine should do all that is possible to minimize unnecessary activity on the part of the user—it has an *emancipatory* role (Gaines, 1978d,e). Cleary's remark emphasizes that the interactive interface seen by the user is actually to a *virtual machine*—one which Krammer (1980) has termed the *attention processor*. Too often dialog programming is treated in an ad hoc fashion that takes no account of the fact that what the user is seeing is the highest level in a hierarchy of virtual machines (Gaines, 1975, 1976c) and that the rigour with which we treat the definition of the lower levels (in terms of procedures, languages, instruction sets, microprograms, etc.) can, and should, be applied at the dialog level—that is one objective of this chapter. Cleary then goes on to say that the virtual machine should have an "understandable" and "sympathetic" face, two apparently non-technical terms which may however be given quite definite meaning in terms of the comprehensibility of the virtual machine and the availability of helpful aids to the user. Much of what follows is concerned precisely with these two requirements.

In the next section we review basic rules for dialog engineering and explain them systemically, psychologically and through examples. In the following section we extend them to more general dialogs, particularly those through visual display units with local intelligence and graphics. We continue with a discussion of language support and implementation requirements and techniques for these rules.

III. The basic rules

This section gives an extended set of dialog programming rules based on those in Gaines and Facey (1975). The rules are classified into four categories: those concerned with systems analysis and development; those concerned with the user's adaptation to the system; those concerned with minimizing the mental load on the user; and those concerned with error detection and correction.

A. Systems analysis and development

The first rule previously proposed is concerned with the initial design of the dialog. In performing the systems analysis that precedes dialog design it is easy to forget how little conception potential users have of the interactive use of computers if they have never experienced it:

> *Rule 1. Introduce through experience*: interactive systems should be experienced not talked about. Get prospective users onto a terminal on a related, or model system before discussing their expected relationship to their own system.

This first rule is worth emphasizing if only because it does not occur in other guidelines in the literature and is prior to the presuppositions they make. However, it highlights a major pitfall into which we will all occasionally fall since the phenomenon of assuming that what we personally know and have experienced is *obvious* is a common one for all human behaviour. We cannot understand the output of a speech synthesizer and cannot understand how others can do so. Suddenly it becomes clear and we are able to comprehend each word. Thereafter we are surprised when others have the same problem in understanding initially what is, for us, now transparently clear material. We have always to remember the need for experience and learning on the part of others before we can have a meaningful discussion with them about topics they have never previously encountered.

Our second rule relates back to Hansen's (1971) first principle, "know the user", and is really a warning to the systems analyst who attempts to impose a new framework on an already existent and satisfactory situation:

> *Rule 2. Use the user's model*: use a model of the activity being undertaken which corresponds to that of the user, and program the interactive dialog as if it were a conversation between two users mutually accepting this model.

This second rule may be seen as asking the systems analyst to listen and learn the user's vocabulary—not to impose a new language unnecessarily in an existing situation. We use the word *model* deliberately, however, to emphasize that there is rather more than a vocabulary involved. We have to consider the way in which the words are being *used* to achieve some desired change in the world. It is an action-orientated, Gricean view of language (Bennett, 1976) that we have to take in order to make all aspects of the dialog, its vocabulary, its sequence, its consequences, appear natural to the user.

In this respect, the axiomatic, conventialist psychology developed by Kelly (1055) in terms of *personal constructs* has a significant role to play in formalizing the processes of systems analysis for dialog engineering. As he notes:

Man looks at his world through transparent patterns or templets which he creates then attempts to fit over the realities of which the world is composed (p. 8). . . . A person's processes, psychologically speaking, slip into the grooves which are cut out by the mechanisms he adopts for realizing his objectives. (p. 49)

It is the "grooves" created by the construct structures of the users determining their vocabulary in communicating with one another that we have to reproduce. Kelly himself developed a means for eliciting such construct structures through his *repertory grid,* and in recent years his technique has been automated and substantially extended by Shaw (1980, 1981) in the *PEGASUS* and *FOCUS* systems. We have linked these techniques elsewhere with Checkland's (1981) *soft systems methodology,* and shown how they may be applied in systems analysis (Shaw and Gaines, 1982). Techniques for the interactive elicitation of personal construct structures may now be seen as essential tools for the dialog engineer in his preliminary analysis of the activities and requirements of a new user community. There are fascinating possibilities also, not yet exploited, of building such construct-elicitation processes permanently into a system to expedite some of the continuing system development called for in Rule 3 below.

The first two rules can also be given more context by noting that, in some sense, "the computer is itself in the situation of a new person coming into the office and adjusting to its procedures" (Gaines *et al.,* 1976). Rule 1 then says that before you decide how to deploy someone with new ways and skills take the opportunity to become familiar with them, or someone similar. Rule 2 says that if you are a newcomer in an office then try and slip into the familiar ways and jargon expected in that office—the new colleague who tries to impose new ways of performing existent tasks and new vocabularies for old conversations will not be welcome.

This animistic view of the computer is a very useful one if not overdone—at times of doubt the question, "well, what would I do?", is a good one. Indeed, one early qualm about computer systems, that they would depersonalize tasks through their lack of personality, is very rapidly dispelled as soon as one notes that interactive programs *do* have personality—usually some partial replica of that of their designer. This is unfortunate if the designer has hidden sadistic tendencies that surface in his programs. More usually it is the erratic human nature of the designer that comes over, being extremely helpful at one moment and then forgetting the obvious the next. We have suggested (Gaines *et al.,* 1974) that the personality one should attempt to project is that of a *servant*—a very Dickensian one with wit and intelligence rather than servility, but a servant dedicated to his master's ends. This role may be an unfamiliar one for the modern technologist but it provides a sure logical foundation for many of the essential features of a good interactive system.

The model of the interactive computer as a newcomer in an office also suggests the next rule, since one vital characteristic of a person is their *adaptability*. If you as a newcomer have behaviour patterns which do not fit well into those of the office then social pressures soon lead you to conform (or leave). The natural mechanism for such pressures to have effect is ready adaptability to criticism, overt or covert. If what you do is not liked then you adjust rapidly until you gain approval, often through mimicry. At the current state of the art it is clearly the system designer who has to provide the interactive system with its adaptability. Fortunately, an interactive system can, and should, also be interactively programmable at the same location, probably at the same terminal, as the user. This enables the designer to set up a three-part dialog between himself, computer and user in which the effects of changes in programming the interaction can be made immediately apparent to the user and his evaluation received:

> *Rule 3. Design never ceases*: use the interactive capabilities of the system for programming also, so as to close directly the adaptive loop between system and user through yourself as designer.

This is not intended to say that interactive dialog *design* should take place at a terminal. Like any programming activity there is a need for thoughtful preparation away from the machine, and the best mode of working depends on the programmer. It is certainly to say, however, that the skill of rapid system modification at an interactive terminal is a very valuable one that should be developed, particularly in the current context.

Clearly the designer cannot remain an integral part of the system forever—even if an attractive role, with the declining costs of hardware relative to liveware, it is too expensive an option for most customers. However, Rule 3 does really mean *never* and provision has to be made both for the designer to play a continuing, but decreasing role in the adaptation of the system to changing circumstances and changing users, and also for the reversal of roles that will take place once the computer is the *old hand* rather than the *newcomer*. When the computer system is established and accepted we do then have to make provision for it to evaluate its users' behaviour patterns and inform them of reasons for their difficulties. Fortunately, one of the easiest things to program an interactive system to do is to keep records of its own activities:

> *Rule 4. Log activities*: use the computer to maintain selective records of system and user activities and provide programs to analyse these in terms of, for example, errors, broken down by user and by dialog sequence.

One golden rule is that logging without purpose is useless—the analysis programs must be designed as part of the logging procedure and their applications defined as well as any other on the system. Unnecessary actions on the parts of users are one obvious activity to trace—deletions, line cancellations, transaction aborts, and so on. If one user is producing excessive quantities of these he clearly needs guidance. If one section of the dialog is producing excessive quantities it clearly needs re-design. Proper long-term quality control of this nature is rarely found in current systems and yet the benefits are obvious, both for short-term system improvement and for long-term development of improved design techniques. We suspect the lack of proper dialog instrumentation is not due nearly so much to the commercial pressures commonly adduced as to the lack of appropriate dialog technology.

It seems probable that the logging recommended here will be subject to legislative constraints under pressure from labour organizations. In so much as it generates information about individuals, it would seem simplest to deal with it by analogy with other records of personal information, i.e. generally to allow free access to the individual concerned. In many ways it is tragic that it should be necessary to take legislation that far, and it is symptomatic of the (proper) fear of the use of computers in what Habermas (1972) calls a *technical cognitive* mode. In practice, if we wish to shape the behaviour of cooperative users (and if we wish to make all users cooperative ones), the most effective technique is to use the computer in *emancipatory cognitive* mode to portray to a user the structure and consequences of his own behaviour (as done by Mulhall (1977) in his clinical studies of personal relationships). Again one can envisage that advanced dialog processing systems will provide facilities for users themselves to access analyses of their own behaviour. In human terms it is the ability to look up and ask, "how am I doing", that an effective logging system can provide.

B. User adaptation to the system

One of the advantages of close man–computer interaction is that one may program the system to minimize the mental workload on the man. In so doing one concentrates upon the weaknesses of the human mind, taking into account limited short-term memory capacity, inaccuracy of calculation, etc., and it is easy to begin to think of the computer as the senior partner which must somehow compensate for the inadequacies of its weaker partners. A natural development of this "senior" role is to attempt to program the system to identify the weaknesses of particular users and to call up compensating facilities to cope with them, e.g. more guidance in the dialog, closer error-checking, tutorial messages, and so on. This was, for example, part of the philosophy of many of the early computer-aided instruction systems, where *individualized* instruction was intended to be generated dynamically by the computer through the infinite wisdom of its programmer. In later developments there has been a swing towards *learner-controlled instruction* (Bunderson, 1974), because the on-line identi-fication of human characteristics required for computer-controlled in-dividualization proved unrealistic to implement.

Part of the problem is that in concentrating on the weaknesses of the person we forget their strengths, one of which is the modelling of the environment. There is a general phenomenon at work here which is summed up in the following rule:

> Rule 5. *The user will model the system*: do not assume that the user is a passive static system to be controlled, modelled and directed by the computer. Evaluate all actions of the system in terms of their effect on an actively changing user who is attempting to comprehend the system.

People automatically form internal models of their environment regardless of their naivety or intelligence. The mind is all the time searching out patterns of cause and effect—Michotte (1963) has shown that much of this activity takes place at a fairly low level and, like the perception of optical illusions, it is not under conscious control. The models formed by users may vary widely and have many connotations that arise from their previous background experience and bear no direct relation to the system. Referring back to Cleary's remark quoted in section II, we may say that to make the system *understandable* is to maximize the possibility of the user forming, with the minimum of effort, a model of the system which aids his effective use of it. Recently there have been some interesting studies of user models in some computational situations (Card *et al.*, 1980; Mayer and Bayman, 1981; Young, 1981).

Another danger of attempting to program adaptation to the user within the system is that the user is not only coming to comprehend the system but also to adapt to it himself. We have a control-theoretic situation in which two coupled systems are each attempting to adapt to one another and instability may result:

> Rule 6. *User should dominate computer*: either the computer or the user should dominate interaction or there will be instability. If the computer is to dominate it must be programmed to, and have sufficient information to model the user. If the user is to dominate then the computer system must be simple to understand. At the present state of the art the user should dominate the system.

It is worth emphasizing the grounds for this rule which are not *soft* ones relating to the proper role of computers in society. The channel of communication from person to computer just does not provide a sufficient flow of information for on-line identification of the characteristics of the person. As mentioned previously in Rule 4, it is possible to gather specific useful information about individual users if this is designed into the original system, but the time-constant of doing this will be too long for immediate action within the interactive dialog. A similar phenomenon has been noted in investigations of adaptive process control—the normal channels of control only rarely provide a sufficient information rate about the plant characteristics for on-line adaptation to be feasible. Recently there have been some careful studies of the design of self-adaptive dialog interfaces avoiding these problems (Edmonds, 1981; Innocent, 1982).

One key rule that we proposed previously that arises out of the requirement to make the computer system understandable to the user is:

Rule 7. Avoid acausality: make the activity of the system a clear consequence of the user's actions.

This rule sums up a variety of phenomena in interactive dialog. The basis for it is one that we have developed in system theoretic terms in a number of publications (Gaines, 1976a,b, 1977): the identification of an acausal system (involving non-deterministic behaviour) is very much more difficult than that of a deterministic system; people seem to pre-suppose determinism in the world but one may show (Gaines, 1976a) that if this supposition is false they will generate highly elaborate, "superstitious" models. We have suggested this as an explanation of the relative difficulty of using a time-shared computer rather than a dedicated single-user system. The hesitancies of the shared system due to activities that are deliberately hidden from the user have no apparent cause but this does not mean that the user will not continue, both at conscious and unconscious levels, to invent one. The importance of hesitancy patterns in the perception of speech (Goldman-Eisler, 1961) suggests that use of such information is, like the Michotte illusions, *wired-in* to the person and unavoidable.

Since Miller (1968) first suggested that there might be an *optimum* non-zero response time there have been many empirical studies ranging from large-scale statistical analyses of productivity showing optimum response time to be zero (Thadhani, 1981), through multivariate studies of controlled response time situations (Goodman and Spence, 1981) to laboratory studies of rates of information presentation (Bevan, 1981). There is no clear-cut result from such studies but they suggest that the objective of having short response times which are consistently related to user activity is a desirable one.

All this emphasis on the system being static suggests that one must under-utilize the capabilities of the computer to offer different dialogs under different circumstances, e.g. a highly tutorial dialog to the naive user but a rapid, terse dialog for the experienced user. This is not the case—just that such changes should be under user control. The next section contains some consideration of minimizing the effort by the user in exerting such control, but there is one simple technique that has proved very effective in practice that we have previously noted:

> *Rule 8. Parallel-sequential trade-off*: allow the user maximum flexibility to make his responses holistically (in parallel) or serially (in sequence) according to his wishes.

Figure 2 shows the same sequence as that in Fig. 1 but with the user grouping his responses into clusters rather than making one at a time in sequence. At line 1′, the user puts in what were previously three separate inputs, E, S and 85. The system finds it has the responses to what were previously prompts 2 and 3 as well as that to 1 (in Fig. 1), and goes straight on to prompt 4′. Similar groupings occur in response to 5′ and 8′, and the

```
 1′   GDR:ES85
 4′   Full name: Treasury :Exchequer
 5′   Issue date:6/7S2
 8′   Final div date: 1/1 :5/8 81 3 1/4 0
12′      85:Exchequer  3 1/4  1981  5/8  S  6-Jul-77 OK?:Y
13′   GDR:
```

Fig. 2. Dialog sequence with grouped responses.

overall dialog is much terser. As far as the user is concerned, the advantage is not just in reducing the verbosity of the system, but also in that he comes to *think* in terms of the clustered responses so that the dialog really is mentally shortened, i.e. ES85 is the unitary *sentence* "Enter Stock 85". Such groupings of basic actions together to form single unitary sequences is a major characteristic of the formation of any skill, and it is very natural for the user to adapt his actions in this way. Note, as emphasized previously, that the change in the way the system is being used is entirely under user control—the dialog is adapting to the user's increasing skill and the system is programmed to allow such adaptation, but it is still the user who dominates the interaction by deciding when to group his inputs.

There are clearly some syntactic constraints upon responses that may be grouped in this way but they are rarely severe in practice.

C. Minimizing the mental load on the user

It is common to find systems in which much effort has been put into user aids but this effort has not been enforced and so, occasionally, the aids are not available. Similarly one finds that dialog terminologies or command structures are similar throughout a system except for a few particular modules. In both cases the user becomes familiar with certain features of the system and then occasionally finds that what he has learnt does not always apply. This not only puts an additional memory load on the user but can also be devastating psychologically when a naive user has at last gained confidence in his familiarity with a system and then suddenly finds that his trust in himself (and system and its designer) is misplaced. This leads to the following rule:

Rule 9. Uniformity and consistency: ensure that all terminology and operational procedures are uniformly available and consistently applied throughout all system activities.

This is clearly a particularly important rule for the naive user becoming familiar with the system. However, we have also found it important for skilled users *transferring* to a new system—a good standard dialog technology has the same impact as a good standard programming language—users can transfer experience from one situation to another. This has been a focal point for many designers of standardized dialog systems in recent years (Barnard *et al.*, 1981; Moran, 1981; Robertson *et al.*, 1981; Guest, 1982; Treu, 1982).

One of the most important facilities to make consistently and uniformly available is a good "help" command that enables a user to obtain selective advice from the system at any point in the dialog. There is nothing more daunting to a naive user (or any of us) than a thick user manual with masses of fine detail about the nuances of every transaction. Yet such documentation clearly should exist and there are times when particular details in it are required. In practice there is a close connection between the state of a transaction and the information that may be relevant from the user manual, and the system itself may be used to make the relevant parts of the manual available as the user requires them. This basically corresponds to the "help" facility available on many systems whereby the user can request information and advice as he goes through a transaction. The difficulty with this is to know what advice would be most valuable to the user at any point: sometimes a list of possibilities; sometimes an example; sometimes an explanation of what will result from an input, and so on. We have developed a technique that enables a simple user command structure to control a multi-level help facility:

Rule 10. Query-in-depth: distribute information and tutorial material appropriately throughout the dialog system to be accessed by the user through a simple uniform mechanism. Organize the material so that the user accesses brief memory aids first at any point but has further access to more detailed expansions.

We use a question-mark, ?, as the command which is always available to the user to obtain help. It may be typed as reply at any point of a dialog and immediately elicits a short note of the main actions available at that point, or an example of data that could be entered. Typing a question mark again drives the help system to greater depth so that it gives a full range of options and their effects. Typing a further question mark may lead to further expansion or, more probably, to a manual reference. Figure 3 shows query-in-depth in action during the dialog sequence of Figs 1 and 2. The successive question marks at lines 1, 3, 10 and 27 show questioning in depth as do those at lines 38 and 40.

Sometimes the queries which the user wishes to make may involve the generation of information, perhaps through access to system utilities such as directory listing programs. In this event it is very important that the mainstream of the dialog is not interrupted and that the user is returned exactly to the point that he left with no change in the state of the environment.

The extensive use of query-in-depth may be seen as a way of embedding a *manual* interactively within the system such that is always "open" at the right page when required by the local context. This may be viewed as a means of avoiding the need to write user manuals altogether and indeed we have found that users readily transfer to new systems without using manuals. However, when a manual is written, it is certainly a rationale for linking the text back to the query-in-depth and not creating yet another level of discourse with which to confuse the user. This leads to the rule:

> *Rule 11. User manuals should be based on actual user dialog*: illustrate the use of the system in action by showing actual dialog sequences that achieve specific objectives. Illustrate the structure of the system through dialog sequences where question marks are typed to elicit information about the system.

Thus in practice, rather than distributing a manual through the system using query-in-depth, one inserts the appropriate material and then creates a manual from an existing system by using query-in-depth to generate the text.

The availability of query-in-depth is a very great aid to on-system training and we have found that new users can most rapidly acquire knowledge of the system through actual experience of it rather than formal training. This leads to the rule:

> *Rule 12. Train through experience*: get users interacting with an actual system as their initial training and introduce them to the system facilities such as query-in-depth.

```
 1   GDR:?
 2     B (buy), S (sell), I (invest), L (list)
 3   GDR:?
 4     E (enter), R (remove), L (list)
 5     B (buy), S (sell), I (invest), M (modify)
 6     D (vary dates), C (vary commission rates)
 7     V (vary VAT rate)
 8     SUM (summarize deals), SYS (system status)
 9     INIT (initialize GDR)
10   GDR:?
11     E    enter a stock, client, dealer or jobber
12     R    remove a stock, client, dealer or jobber
13     L    list stocks, clients, dealers, jobbers
14     total files, records, or free closing
15     B    buy a stock
16     S    sell a stock
17     I    invest an amount in a stock
18     M    modify an incorrect record of a deal
19     D    vary date to update back records
20     C    commission rate entry and listing
21     V    VAT rate change
22     SUM    summarize all deals for day
23     SYS    give system status
24     INIT    reinitialize this system as if just starting
25     :   abort GDR
26     \   exit to GDR: command level
27   GDR:?
28     See Gilt Dealing Records User Manual p.12
29   GDR:E
30   Item:?
31     Item to be entered: S (stock), D (dealer),
32     J (jobber), C (client)
33   Item:S
34   Stock number:?
35     Number of stock in range 10–99
36   Stock number:85
37   Full name: Treasury :Exchequer
38   Issue date:?
39     e.g. 7/5/87 or 6-MAY-77
40   Issue date:?
41     Date at which stock issued
42     e.g. 30/8/64 or 30-AUG-64
43   Issue date:
```

Fig. 3. Examples of query-in-depth in dialog.

Many of the rules so far may be seen as techniques for avoiding the need for explicit training. Through Rule 2 we are "using the user's model" so that the activity and terminology itself is natural to the user. Through Rule 9 we are ensuring "uniformity and consistency" to aid the transfer of experience from one part of the system to another. Through Rule 15 on p. 42 we are enabling the user to make errors freely knowing he can avoid the consequences using a clean "reset" facility. *Training* is something that we have to put great effort into when we have a poorly designed system that is unnatural to the user. We can measure our success in system design by the degree to which explicit user training is unnecessary. In cases where we have installed a number of systems in succession over a period of years it has been gratifying to note that users who have learnt to operate one system have been completely happy to transfer to a new one having very different functions without explicit training, relying on the query-in-depth and reset facilities to allow them to learn about the new system through their own unguided efforts.

The dialog examples have all shown the user inputting short codes for commands rather than full English words. This is desirable to minimize typing effort since most users are not trained typists nor ever will be. However, the use of short codes increases the possibility of error in command sequences and it is important to give the user feedback as soon as possible as to what action he has actually requested. In particular, dialog sequences for different activities which go through the same initial dialog may reinforce the user's opinion that he used the right command, and the effect of finding the error later when the sequences diverge is much more devastating since it is unexpected and the user has to look back for the source of error. Hence we formulated the rule:

> *Rule 13. Make the state of the dialog observable*: give the user feedback as to the state of the dialog by making an immediate unambiguous response to any of his inputs which may cause the dialog to branch. The response should be sufficient to identify the type of activity taking place.

For example, if the prompt "Item:" could follow a command other than E, then it would be better to qualify it appropriately, e.g. "Item to be entered:". Note how this requirement interacts, however, with the previous rule 8, because the dialog of Fig. 2 bypasses the prompt "Item:". In this case the dialog programmer may either decide that it does not matter since the user is skilled (or, what amounts to the same thing at this level of discourse, is pretending to be skilled—we should not be too paternalistic towards users), or if the possibility of error at this step is very significant (e.g. a little-used command) the observability prompt may be made an output in response to the initial command:

1 GDR:E
2 Stock Entry Sequence
3 Item:

Fig. 4. Immediate feedback of state of dialog.

which will not be bypassed by a grouped initial command like ES85. However, such messages should not be used too freely or the dialog will become annoyingly pedantic—it is like the listener who repeats each sentence back at you.

Many of the prescriptions of the section can be subsumed under what Thimbleby (1980) calls *dialogue determination*, i.e. that a dialog should be neither over- nor under-determining. An under-determining dialog is one that leaves the user excessive freedom with too little information to use it, breaking Rule 13 on observability and probably Rule 10 on the capability to query for possible actions; Thimbleby notes that the user will be *mystified* by such a dialog. An over-determining dialog is one which unnaturally constrains the user, breaking at least Rule 6 and probably others requiring flexibility such as Rule 8. There are useful systemic concepts that can be seen as generative principles for several of the rules.

D. Error detection and correction

One of the significant reasons for using interactive data entry systems is to have on-line validation at source. In the light of the preceding discussion validation of data entered may be seen as part of the process of informing the user about errors in the transaction. We have found that absolute validation involving complete rejection of data is a dangerous procedure— it is rare that sooner or later some data does not come up that lies outside the prescribed "norms" and yet must legitimately be entered. It is far better to *query* suspect data, asking the user if that is really what he meant, rather than reject it. However, too frequent queries also disrupt the dialog and it is best to set norms reasonably wide so that queries are infrequent but have a final validation just before the transaction is accepted. This happens at line 12 of Fig. 1, and the clarity of the procedure is very apparent. The user knows that he is coming to a natural checkpoint where action will be taken when such validation is requested. Up to that point he is assured of being able to abort the transaction with no side effects. He also sees the overall transaction in a global fashion that was not apparent before and, because the print-out can be a standard one used for normal documents from the system, it can be a familiar form of output where errors will be most obvious. The rule is:

Rule 14. Validate data on entry by checking syntax and values, but beware of rejecting data or querying too much as being outside norms. Have the user himself revalidate major updates before acting upon them.

Errors in dialog are not essentially key problems to be avoided at all costs. Naive users should feel free to make errors as part of their exploration of the system—even highly skilled users will make errors because they will only devote to the dialog that part of their channel capacity necessary to maintain the error rate to an acceptably low level for them. In both cases the users need the *sympathetic* system noted by Cleary—they should be able to make most errors with absolute confidence that they can readily escape the consequences—or at least all but the administrative chore of going back and doing it correctly. This led us to the rule:

Rule 15. Provide a reset command that cleanly aborts the current activity back to a convenient checkpoint. The user should be able at any stage in a transaction to abort it cleanly with a system command that takes him back to a well-defined checkpoint as if the transaction had never been initiated.

We used the colon, :, as a uniformly available command to abort a transaction—it is easy for users to remember, "If you don't want to continue, type back to the computer the last character of its prompt to you, i.e. the colon". Thus one might get the sequence:

```
1   GDR:ES85
2   Full name: Treasury ::
3   GDR:
```
Fig. 5.   Use of reset command.

This rule is a very important one for the user, but often the most difficult to implement for the system programmer. There may well be transactions involving many resources on a time-shared system where the "roll-back" required to allow such free aborting is almost impossible to implement. This is a very good example where making the system simple and understandable to the user may involve great complexity in the programs—however, this is clearly the right division of labour.

The user may realize that he has made errors part way through a transaction, or at the final validation and wish to go back to correct them. This is not an easy operation to offer to an unskilled user and, if such action is rarely required, it may be better to recommend that they use the abort facility of Rule 15 and go through the transaction again. Another alternative is to provide a good record update and correction facility as discussed in the next paragraph and advise users to complete the incorrect entry and then correct it as a separate activity. We have found it useful to provide a backtrack facility that allows users to unwind the dialog in reverse order on the assumption that the error will be in the immediately preceding sequence:

> *Rule 16. Provide a backtrack facility* that allows a user to return through the dialog sequence in reverse.

We use the "up-arrow" character as a backtrack request:

```
 1   GDR:E
 2   Item:S
 3   Stock number:85
 4   Fullname: Treasury :¯
 5   Stock number:58
 6   Full name: Treasury :
 7   Issue date:6/7
 8   Type (SMLTN) :¯
 9   Issue date:¯
10   Full name: Treasury :¯
11   Stock number:57
12   Full name: Treasury :
13   Issue date:6/7
14   Type (SMLTN):
```

Fig. 6.   Correction by backtracking.

where at line 4 the user backtracks once to change the stock number entered and then at lines 8, 9 and 10 does so three times to change the number again.

The updating and correction of records is just as important as their original entry. We have learnt to assume that any field whatsoever in a record may require updating—people seem to change their name, sex and age far more frequently than one might reasonably expect. To avoid the user having to master another dialog sequence for record correction, it is possible to use exactly the same sequence as for data entry but print out field values after the prompt and take a RETURN input alone as meaning that the value has not changed. This is a particularly rapid way of modifying even a single field at a visual display terminal. The rule is:

> *Rule 17. Make corrections through re-entry:* use the entry dialog with default field print-outs from a record as a means of correcting the record.

For example, in terms of Fig. 1, if we re-enter stock 85:

```
 1  GDR:E
 2  Item:S
 3  Stock number:85
 4  Full name: Exchequer :
 5  Issue date: 6-Jul-77 :
 6  Type (SMLTN): S :
 7  Dividends/year: 2 :
 8  Final div date : 5/8 :6/8
 9  Redemption years(s): 81 :
10  Coupon: 3 1/4 :
11  Number of calls: 0 :
12     85:Exchequer  3 1/4  1981  6/8  S  6-Jul-77 OK?:Y
13  GDR:
```

Fig. 7.   Correction of record through entry sequence.

At lines 4–7 and 9–11 the user just presses the RETURN key to indicate field unchanged. At line 8 he types in a correction input. Note how the stored record in this sequence appears exactly as do the default values in Fig. 1.

IV. Extending the rules to other dialog situations

The rules described in the previous section have been targeted around the kind of formal dialog situations shown in Figs 1–7. There are many variants of man–computer dialog, however, which are still formal, or semi-formal, that go outside this framework. In this section we briefly consider some of these and the implications of the rules for them.

Chris Evans led a number of studies of computers in use to supplement human interviewing in such areas as general medicine (Card and Lucas, 1981) and experimental results suggested that the computer terminal was more acceptable than the person for many patients (Card *et al.*, 1974). The approach Evans took to making systems *user-friendly* included the use of *encouraging phrases* such as "Thank you. You are managing to answer my questions very well." Spiliotopoulos and Shackel (1981) report experiments to determine the effect of such phrases on the acceptability of computer interviews. Clearly the random emission of relevant remarks to provide a friendly halo to a conversation is a valid technique in that it corresponds to a level of human behaviour that is significant in interpersonal relations. It goes against Rule 7 to some extent, to avoid acausality, but it may be consistent with Rule 2, in that the user's model in some contexts may include the expectation of friendly phrases with little semantic content.

The examples given in this chapter have all been based on a sequential *prompt-and-response* style of dialog which treats the interaction as a one-dimensional stream. The availability of low-cost visual displays with cursor addressing and their extension recently to high-resolution graphics has led to the developments of different forms of dialog. At the simplest level are the *menu* techniques in which the options available to a user are displayed as a table on the screen and he makes a selection from this table. In some systems this corresponds only to the table being part of a large prompt string—one is taking advantage of the speed of the display to give more information. In other systems the menu itself is accessed directly, for example by using a *mouse* to move a graphic cursor to it on Lisp Machines (Weinreb and Moon, 1981a) or by touching the screen itself on the PLATO system (Sherwood, 1977). The same rules of dialog discussed previously apply to such systems—by making more direct forms of interaction available they are highlighting the poor interface provided by the QWERTY keyboard itself for many users.

When a high resolution graphic screen is available for interaction, say with 1000×1000 pixels resolution, then a wide variety of new techniques become available. These have been exploited in program development systems such as that of Teitelman (1979) which allow multiple documents to appear on the screen together, some of which portray the state of ongoing processes and some of which are interactive dialog windows. Such systems are now readily implemented with the technology available (Weinreb and Moon, 1981b) but can become very complex in use. The rules given continue to apply and do not seem to require additions specifically for such systems. The new facilities do, however, allow improved implementation of some features, for example *query-in-depth* is now implementable through a separate *help* document that does not interfere with the ongoing dialog.

V. Implementing the dialog programming rules

Enforcing the dialog programming rules detailed in the previous section is best done through a standard dialog procedure which is written once and used thereafter as the only means of interacting with the user. The main programming language feature necessary for such a feature is the capability to handle variable length strings as data items and particularly as parameters to procedures. Languages such as Snobol and Lisp are ideal in the facilities they provide but even Fortran and Pascal are generally provided with some form of primitive string data type and processing facilities. BASIC has good string handling facilities but very poor procedural modularity with its lack of parameter passing and local variables. Guest (1982) discusses the use of specialist software tools in dialog design.

The systems described in this chapter were written in the interactive systems programming language Basys II (Gaines, 1976d, 1978c; Gaines and Facey, 1977), which provides special facilities for string processing. These are based on the *compiler–compiler* (Brooker and Morris, 1962) language constructs for string analysis incorporated in a BASIC-like language that is extended to have procedure calls with parameters and local variables. The standard Basys II operating system has a dialog processing procedure embedded in it and all dialog, including that of the operating system job control language, goes through this procedure.

The procedure is called with parameters giving the prompt string, query-in-depth replies, and branches for reset and backtrack. Its operation is most readily understood by considering how each rule is implemented in turn:

Rules 1, 2 and 3 do not require any special features in the procedure. Rule 2, *Use the user's model*, implies ease of decoding strings returned by the procedure in an arbitrary format natural to the user, and this is particularly simple in Basys II. Rule 3, *Design never ceases*, implies some form of interactive programming language with a modular structure and again Basys II satisfies this requirement. However, other languages offer equally good string handling or can be provided with suitable procedures.

Rule 4. *Log activities*, is the first where the dialog procedure itself should provide facilities. One of the parameters that can be passed to it is the name of a log-file procedure. This may default either to no action or to logging the complete dialog. However, it is also possible by this mechanism to provide selective logging of the dialog at points which require study or are dependent on other parameters such as the identity of the user.

Rules 5, 6 and 7, in the context of the dialog procedure, are warnings not to make it too "clever" in its actions.

Rule 8, *Parallel-sequential trade-off*, is readily implemented. The string returned by the dialog procedure is in a global variable and the calling routine extracts what items it wants from it. When the dialog procedure is next called it checks the global variable and only if it is null does it go to the user for input. Thus the user may input several items at the same time and they will be passed to the appropriate callers of the dialog procedure.

Rule 9, *Uniformity and consistency*, is primarily ensured by requiring all dialog to go through the standard procedure.

Rule 10, *Query-in-depth*, is implemented by passing to the procedure a table of strings which are used to reply to each successive question-mark.

Rules 11, 12, 13 and 14 depend on how the procedure is used rather than its own characteristics.

Rule 15, *Provide a reset command*, is implemented through the procedure returning not to its normal address but to the branch passed as the reset parameter. This branch can usually be set up as a default for a dialog sequence and should be the code which cleans up any actions taken during the course of the dialog before returning to the top-level program.

Rule 16, *Provide a backtrack facility*, is implemented in a similar way to Rule 15 except that the abnormal branch is to the parameter passed which will usually be the previous call on the dialog procedure or any parameter calculations immediately preceding it.

Rule 17, *Make corrections through re-entry*, is implemented by passing to the dialog procedure a computed prompt string which contains the previous value of the item requested.

Thus most of the key rules may be implemented simply and automatically through a dialog procedure. It is useful also to incorporate in the procedure facilities for diagnostic purposes and for taking the input from a command file rather than a terminal.

VI. Conclusions

This chapter has proposed an approach to *dialog engineering* which has been used in a wide range of interactive systems in the last 15 years. It has proved very successful in allowing naive users to cope rapidly and adequately with complex interactions whilst not frustrating highly skilled users. The rules proposed are intended as guidelines rather than absolutes and each is substantiated by arguments based on both theory and practice. Some aspects of the rules are specific to the particular style of dialog discussed but they are basically systemic and general to all forms of interaction. We hope that this presentation will not only act as a guide to those attempting to create effective interactive systems but also as a stimulus to others to improve, vary, and generally develop both the rules and the entire domain of dialog engineering.

VII. Acknowledgements

We are grateful to Peter Facey, John Gedye and John Sams for their collaboration in the work reported in this chapter, and to Harold Thimbleby and Martin McGuire for access to their work.

VIII. References

Barnard, P. J., Hammond, N. V., Morton, J., Long, J. B. and Clark, I. A. (1981). Consistency and compatibility in human–computer dialogue. *International Journal of Man–Machine Studies* **15**, 1, 78–134.

Bennett, J. (1976). *Linguistic Behaviour*. Cambridge University Press, Cambridge.

Bevan, N. (1981). Is there an optimum speed for presenting text on a VDU? *International Journal of Man–Machine Studies* **14**, 1, 59–76.

Brooker, R. A. and Morris, D. (1962). A general translation program for phrase structure languages. *Journal of the Association for Computing Machinery* **9**, 1–10.

Bunderson, C. V. (1974). The design and production of learner-controlled courseware for the TICCIT system: a progress report. *International Journal of Man–Machine Studies* **6**, 4, 479–491.

Card, S. K., Moran, T. P. and Newell, A. (1980). The keystroke-level model for user performance time with interactive systems. *Communications of the ACM* **23**, 7, 396–410.

Card, W. I. and Lucas, R. W. (1981). Computer interrogation in medical practice. *International Journal of Man–Machine Studies* **14**, 1, 49–57.

Card, W. I., Nicholson, M., Crean, G. P., Watkinson, G., Evans, C. R., Wilson, J. and Russell, D. (1974). A comparison of doctor and computer interrogation of patients. *International Journal of Bio-Medical Computing* **5**, 175–187.

Checkland, P. (1981). *Systems Thinking, Systems Practice*. John Wiley, Chichester.

Cheriton, D. R. (1976). Man–machine interface design for time-sharing systems. *Proceedings of the ACM National Conference*, pp. 362–380.

Coombs, M. J. and Alty, J. L. (Eds) (1981). *Computing Skills and the User Interface*. Academic Press, London and New York.

Cox, R. B. and Martin, T. B. (1975). Speak and the machines obey. *Industrial Research*, pp. 1–6.

Danver, J. H. and Nevison, J. M. (1969). Secondary school use of the time-shared computer at Dartmouth College. *AFIPS Spring Joint Computer Conference* **34**, 681–689. AFIPS Press, New Jersey.

De Bono, E. (1979). *Future Positive*. Maurice Temple Smith, London.

Dehning, W., Essig, H. and Maass, S. (1981). The Adaption of Virtual Man–Computer Interfaces to User Requirements in Dialogs. *In* G. Goos and J. Hartmanis (Eds), *Lecture Notes in Computer Science*, p. 110. Springer-Verlag, Berlin.

Edmonds, E. (1981). Adaptive man–computer interfaces. *In* M. J. Coombs and J. L. Alty (Eds), *Computing Skills and the User Interface*, pp. 389–426. Academic Press, London and New York.

Fano, R. M. (1965). The MAC system: a progress report. *In* M. A. Sass and W. D. Wilkinson (Eds), *Computer Augmentation of Human Reasoning*, pp. 131–150. Spartan Books, Washington D.C.

Fried, B. D. (1968). On the user's point of view. *In* M. Klerer and J. Reinfelds (Eds), *Interactive Systems for Experimental Applied Mathematics*, pp. 11–21. Academic Press, New York and London.

Gaines, B. R. (1975). Analogy categories, virtual machines and structured programming. *In* G. Goos and J. Hartmanis (Eds), *GI—5. Jahrestagung. Lecture Notes in Computer Science*, pp. 691–699. Springer Verlag, Berlin.

Gaines, B. R. (1976a). On the complexity of causal models. *IEEE Transactions on Systems, Man & Cybernetics* SMC-6, **1**, 56–59.

Gaines, B. R. (1976b). Behaviour-structure transformations under uncertainty. *International Journal of Man–Machine Studies*, **8**, 3, 337–365.

Gaines, B. R. (1976c). Human factors in virtual machine hierarchies. *Proceedings Colloquium on the Influence of High Level Languages on Computer System Design*, IEE, London.

Gaines, B. R. (1976d). Interpretive kernels for microcomputer software. *Proceedings Symposium Microprocessors at Work*, pp. 56–69. Soc. Electronic & Radio Technicians, University of Sussex.

Gaines, B. R. (1977). System identification, approximation and complexity. *International Journal General Systems*, **3**, 145–174.

Gaines, B. R. (1978a). Minicomputers in business applications in the next decade. *Infotech State of Art Report on "Minis Versus Mainframes"*, pp. 51–81. Infotech International, Berkshire.

Gaines, B. R. (1978b). Programming interactive dialogue. *Pragmatic Programming and Sensible Software*, pp. 305–320. Online Conferences, Uxbridge, Middlesex.

Gaines, B. R. (1978c). A mixed-code approach to commercial microcomputer applications. *Microprocessors in Automation and Communications*. IERE Conference Proceedings No. 41, pp. 291–301.

Gaines, B. R. (1978d). Computers in World Three. *Proceedings of the International Conference on Cybernetics and Society*, Tokyo, III, IEEE 78CH-1306-0-SMC, pp. 1515–1521.

Gaines, B. R. (1978e). Man–computer communication: what next? *International Journal of Man–Machine Studies* **10**, 225–232.

Gaines, B. R. (1979). Logical foundations for database systems. *International Journal of Man–Machine Studies* **11**, 4, 481–500.

Gaines, B. R. (1980). General systems research: quo vadis? *In* B. R. Gaines (Ed.), *General Systems*, **24**, 1–9. Society for General Systems Research, Louisville, Kentucky.

Gaines, B. R. (1981). The technology of interaction—dialogue programming rules. *International Journal of Man–Machine Studies* **14**, 1, 133–150.

Gaines, B. R. and Facey, P. V. (1975). Some experience in interactive system development and application. *Proceedings IEEE* **63**, 155–169.

Gaines, B. R. and Facey, P. V. (1977). BASYS—a language for processing interaction. *Proceedings Conference Computer Systems and Technology (IERE No. 36)*, pp. 251–262. University of Sussex.

Gaines, B. R., Facey, P. V. and Sams, J. B. S. (1974). An on-line fixed-interest investment analysis and dealing system. *Proceedings European Computing Congress, EUROCOMP* **74**, 155–169.

Gaines, B. R., Facey, P. V. and Sams, J. B. S. (1976). Minicomputers in security dealing. *Computer* **9**, 9, 6–15.

Gebhardt, F. and Stellmacher, I. (1978). Design criteria for documentation retrieval languages. *Journal of the American Society for Information Science* **29**, 4, 191–199.

Gilb, T. and Weinberg, G. M. (1977). *Humanized Input*. Winthrop Publishers, Cambridge, Mass.

Goldman-Eisler, F. (1961). Hesitation and information in speech. *In* C. Cherry (Ed.), *Information Theory*, pp. 162–174. Butterworths, London.

Goodman, T. J. and Spence, R. (1981). The effect of computer response time variability on interactive graphical problem solving. *IEEE Transactions on Systems, Man and Cybernetics* SMC-11, 3, 207–216.

Gruenberger, F. (Ed.) (1967). *The Transition to On-line Computing*. Thompson Book Co., Washington D.C.

Guedj, R. A., tenHagen, P. J. W., Hopgood, F. R. A., Tucker, H. A. and Duce, D. A. (Eds) (1980). *Methodology of Interaction*. North-Holland, Amsterdam.

Guest, S. P. (1982). The use of software tools for dialogue design. *International Journal of Man–Machine Studies* **16**, 3, 263–285.

Habermas, J. (1972). *Knowledge and Human Interests*. Heinemann, London.

Hansen, W. J. (1971). User engineering principles for interactive systems. *Proceedings of the Fall Joint Computer Conference* **39**, 523–532. AFIPS Press, New Jersey.

Harris, L. R. (1977). User oriented data base query with the robot natural language query system. *International Journal of Man–Machine Studies* **9**, 6, 697–713.

Hendrix, G. G. (1977). Lifer: a natural language interface facility. *Proceedings Second Berkeley Workshop on Distributed Data Management and Computer Networks*, TID-4500-R65, pp. 196–201.

Innocent, P. R. (1982). Towards self-adaptive interface systems. *International Journal of Man–Machine Studies* **16**, 3, 287–299.

Kelly, G. A. (1955). *The Psychology of Personal Constructs*. Norton, New York.

Kennedy, T. C. S. (1974). The design of interactive procedures for man–machine communication. *International Journal of Man–Machine Studies* **6**, 309–334.

Klerer, M. and Reinfelds, J. (Eds) (1968). *Interactive Systems for Experimental Applied Mathematics*. Academic Press, New York and London.

Krammer, G. (1980). On computer problem-solving interaction. *In* R. A. Guedj, P.

J. W. tenHagen, F. R. A. Hopgood, H. A. Tucker and D. A. Duce (Eds) (1980). *Methodology of Interaction*, pp. 279–292. North-Holland, Amsterdam.

Licklider, J. C. R. (1968). Man–computer symbiosis. *In* W. D. Orr (Ed.), *Conversational Computers*, pp. 3–5. John Wiley, New York.

Maguire, M. (1982). An evaluation of published recommendations on the design of man–computer dialogues. *International Journal of Man–Machine Studies* **16**, 3, 237–261.

Martin, J. (1973). *Design of Man–Computer Dialogues*. Prentice-Hall, New Jersey.

Mayer, R. E. and Bayman, P. (1981). Psychology of calculator languages: a framework for describing differences in user's knowledge. *Communications of the ACM* **24**, 8, 511–520.

Michotte, A. (1963). *The Perception of Causality*. Methuen, London.

Miller, R. B. (1968). Response time in man–computer conversational transactions. *Proceedings Spring Joint Computer Conference* **33**, 267–277. AFIPS Press, New Jersey.

Moran, T. P. (1981). The command language grammar: a representation for the user interface of interactive systems. *International Journal of Man–Machine Studies* **15**, 1, 3–50.

Mulhall, D. (1977). The representation of personal relationships: an automated system. *International Journal of Man–Machine Studies* **9**, 315–335.

Nickerson, R. S. (1981). Why interactive computer systems are sometimes not used by people who might benefit by them. *International Journal of Man–Machine Studies* **15**, 4, 469–483.

Orr, W. D. (Ed.) (1968). *Conversational Computers*. John Wiley, New York.

Parkhill, D. F. (Ed.) (1966). *The Challenge of the Computer Utility*. Addison-Wesley, Reading, Mass.

Patton, G. C. (1968). A message system for interactive dialog. *In* M. Klerer and J. Reinfelds (Eds), *Interactive Systems for Experimental Applied Mathematics*, pp. 271–283. Academic Press, New York and London.

Petri, C. A. (1962). *Kommunikation mit Automaten*. Dissertation an der Universitat Bonn.

Petrick, S. R. (1976). On natural language based computer systems. *IBM Journal of Research and Development* **20**, 314–325.

Pew, R. W. and Rollins, A. M. (1975). Dialog specification procedure. *Report No. 3129*. Bolt, Beranek & Newman, Cambridge, Mass.

Robertson, G., McCracken, D. and Newell, A. (1981). The ZOG approach to man–machine communication. *International Journal of Man–Machine Studies* **14**, 4, 461–488.

Sass, M. A. and Wilkinson, W. D. (Eds) (1965). *Computer Augmentation of Human Reasoning*. Spartan Books, Washington D.C.

Shackel, B. (Ed.) (1981). *Man–Computer Interaction: Human Factors Aspects of Computers and People*. Sijthoff and Noordhoff, The Netherlands.

Shaw, J. C. (1968). JOSS: experience with an experimental computing service for users at remote consoles. *In* W. D. Orr (Ed.), *Conversational Computers*, pp. 15–22. John Wiley, New York.

Shaw, M. L. G. (1980). *On Becoming a Personal Scientist*. Academic Press, London and New York.

Shaw, M. L. G. (Ed.) (1981). *Recent Advances in Personal Construct Technology*. Academic Press, London and New York.

Shaw, M. L. G. and Gaines, B. R. (1981a). The personal scientist in the community of science. *In* W. J. Reckmeyer (Ed.), *General Systems Research and Design : Precursors and Futures*, pp. 59–68. Society for General Systems Research.

Shaw, M. L. G. and Gaines, B. R. (1981b). The personal computer and the personal scientist. *In* R. D. Parslow (Ed.), *BCS'81 : Information Technology for the Eighties*, pp. 235–252. Heyden, London.

Shaw, M. L. G. and Gaines, B. R. (1982). Eliciting the real problem. *In* H. Wedde (Ed.), *International Working Conference on Model Realism*. Bonn, Federal Republic of Germany.

Sherwood, B. A. (1977). *The TUTOR Language*. Control Data Education Company, Minneapolis.

Shneiderman, B. (1980). *Software Psychology*. Winthrop, Cambridge, Mass.

Smith, H. T. and Green, T. R. (Eds) (1980). *Human Interaction with Computers*. Academic Press, London and New York.

Spiliotopoulos, V. and Shackel, B. (1981). Towards a computer interview acceptable to the naive user. *International Journal of Man–Machine Studies* **14**, 1, 77–90.

Teitelman, W. (1979). A display oriented programmer's assistant. *International Journal of Man–Maching Studies* **11**, 2, 157–187.

Thadhani, A. J. (1981). Interactive user productivity. *IBM Systems Journal* **20**, 4, 407–423.

Thimbleby, H. (1980). Dialogue determination. *International Journal of Man–Machine Studies* **13**, 3, 295–304.

Toffler, A. (1980). *The Third Wave*. Bantam, New York.

Treu, S. (1982). Uniformity in user-computer interaction languages: a compromise solution. *International Journal of Man–Machine Studies* **16**, 2, 183–210.

Turoff, M., Whitescarver, J. and Hiltz, S. R. (1978). The human machine interface in a computerized conferencing environment. *Proceedings of the IEE Conference on Interactive Systems, Man and Cybernetics*, pp. 145–157.

Walther, G. H. and O'Neil, H. F. (1974). On-line user–computer interface—the effects of interface flexibility, terminal type, and experience on performance. *Proceedings of the National Computer Conference* **43**, 379–384. AFIPS Press, New Jersey.

Wasserman, T. (1973). The design of idiot-proof interactive systems. *Proceedings of the National Computer Conference* **42**, M34–M38. AFIPS Press, New Jersey.

Weinreb, D. and Moon, D. (1981a). *Lisp Machine Manual*. Massachusetts Institute of Technology, Cambridge, Mass.

Weinreb, D. and Moon, D. (1981b). Introduction to using the window system. *Artificial Intelligence Laboratory Working Paper 210*. Massachusetts Institute of Technology, Cambridge, Mass.

Weizenbaum, J. (1967). Contextual understanding by computers. *Communications ACM* **10**, 8, 474–480.

Winograd, T. (1972). *Understanding Natural Language.* Edinburgh University Press, Edinburgh.

Woods, W., Bates, M., Brown, G., Bruce, B., Cook, C., Klovstad, J., Makhoul, J., Nash-Webber, B., Schwartz, R., Wolf, J. and Zue, V. (1976). Speech understanding systems. *BBN Report Number 3438.* Bolt, Beranek & Newman, Cambridge, Mass.

Young, R. M. (1981). The machine inside the machine: user's models of pocket calculators. *International Journal of Man–Machine Studies* **15**, 1, 51–85.

2. Natural language versus computer language

I. D. HILL

Clinical Research Centre, Watford Road, Harrow, Middlesex, England

I. Levels of language

At the lowest level, communication with a computer may be made in pure binary notation. The only time, nowadays, that such communication is at all likely is in the setting of handswitches in a "bootstrapping" operation to load an operating system. At a slightly higher level we have assembly code languages, where each instruction corresponds to a single computer instruction but so coded as to be more convenient for the human. Most programming, however, is now done in high-level languages that are specifically designed with the human rather than the machine in mind. The machine has to have an interpreter, or a compiler, to translate to its own language before such a program can be executed.

High-level languages, in spite of their aim of human convenience, are highly stylized, with exact rules that must be learnt and followed. It has sometimes been argued that such restrictions are undesirable; that all that should be necessary should be for the human to give instructions to the computer in whatever form comes naturally, just like giving instructions to some other person, and that the computer should be able to translate these and execute them.

The questions that arise are whether this is possible and if so whether it would be desirable. In a previous article (Hill, 1972) I argued that the answer to both questions was "No". Bemer (1972), similarly, has written

Without intent to put programmers on a par with philosophers, we observe a certain similarity, if one recalls the Philosophers' Stone that was supposed to have power to turn base metals into gold. For many years we have lived in the dream world where the Programmers' Stone, under the guise of using

DESIGNING FOR HUMAN–COMPUTER COMMUNICATION
ISBN 0 12 643820 X

English (or some other "natural language") is supposed to have power to turn programming drudgery into an easy task. Those who believe it have not convinced us who do not, but, alas, neither have we been able to shake their faith.

Now, ten years later, has anything occurred to change the opinions of those of us who wish to demolish the "Programmers' Stone"? It must be made clear that we do not oppose the use of natural words within an exactly specified programming language, where these help to make things easier either to learn or to use. Nor do we seek deliberately to keep things complicated; on the contrary, an important reason for opposing the use of ordinary language is that it would make things, not easier, but much more difficult. This is because English (or any other "natural" language), while excellent for conversational purposes, is far too ambiguous and uncertain when it comes to the precise specification of instructions to be carried out, and indeed this is so whether the instructions are for computers or for humans.

II. Ambiguity in natural language

To take a simple example, suppose that someone is paid £50 a week, and you obey the instructions:

  (1) increase the pay to £100 a week
and a little later:
  (2) now make the pay £50 a week again.

All seems clear, but let us change the wording slightly to specify the same operations:

  (1) make the pay twice as much
and a little later:
  (2) now make the pay half as much again.

But "half as much again" has a special meaning, so what happens? Does the pay end up at £50 a week or £150 a week? Such ambiguity could not arise in a formal programming language.

A. Multiple negatives

If we allow programmers to give their instructions in a non-formal manner, we are bound to come up against the difficulty of interpreting double, or multiple, negatives. It may be relatively easy for a computer to interpret such things *literally*, but that is not the requirement. The human mind is remarkably good at knowing when to interpret literally and when not. When a BBC interviewer asks a passer-by "Do you think that correct grammar is important in everyday English?" and gets the reply "Yes. I can't speak it no other way" we know at once what is meant. Similarly, when the Opposition spokesman on employment refers in Parliament to "the demonstration which took place yesterday, which no one except a Government as naive as this one, could not possibly have believed would not lead to violence", it would be quite the wrong approach to attempt to work out literally whether or not he actually said what he evidently intended. On the other hand, when the Under Secretary of State for the Environment "moved a further amendment to reverse a decision which removed a provision for the termination of decontrol of tenancies" we know that we do have to work at it literally if we wish to understand it. Can anyone specify the rules, to tell a computer how to discover when to interpret such things literally, and when not?

Difficulties can arise with the rules of Boolean algebra—the mathematics of truth and falsehood. Perhaps it is unfair to quote the judge who said that he took into account the defendant's lack of commercial experience "but it takes no training to distinguish between the false and that which is untrue", but ignoring such slips of the tongue the difficulties remain formidable. In a programming language **not false** can always be replaced by **true** (and, similarly, **not true** by **false**), but this is not so in English. "If this is not false then that must be" cannot be changed to "If this is true then that must be", without reversing the meaning.

B. Further ambiguity

Precisely similar wording can have totally different meanings. Consider a restaurant wine list (some years ago, when prices were lower) including:

> Sherry from the wood.
> Liqueurs from 30p.

So much of the interpretation of words depends upon the precise context in which they are used, and not merely on the immediate context of the words but on all the scattered information that we carry around in our heads concerning the wider context. The High Sheriff of Essex, reporting on the conditions in Chelmsford Prison, says that "in the vocational training section, prisoners were being taught the art of copper beating"; while in Manchester they wished to take a new road through a cemetery, provided that they could get approval from "the various bodies concerned".

If you look in the *Dictionary of National Biography* for information about a certain girlfriend of King George III called Hannah Lightfoot, you find the entry "Lightfoot, Hannah—See under George III".

Given the difficulties of writing any algorithm that could specify the rules for interpreting such things, the surprising thing is not that nobody can succeed in doing it at present, but that the human mind should be capable of interpreting them so easily—usually indeed without even realizing that it is doing anything non-trivial. The amount of background information that has to be called in from storage, the relevant bits selected and processed, is almost past belief. Yet we do it all the time. Should we conclude that given enough storage, enough speed, and sufficiently cunning programming, a computer could do it? Or must we conclude that the processes are different in kind? Could it be that consciousness is a necessary ingredient for success? To produce a conscious machine seems a very unlikely achievement at present. (I take it for granted that other people do have consciousness and that computers do not, but there is no way of proving either of these things.)

C. Misinterpretation

Even the conscious human mind sometimes slips up, with perfectly reasonable misinterpretation that had been completely unenvisaged by the originator of the message. A few years ago a computer user was using a terminal with 31 characters on the keyboard. Knowing that $2^5 = 32$, and that the code was likely to be binary, 32 seemed a more logical number and he asked could he not have a thirty-second character available? The request passed through several hands before he got a puzzled message back asking what was this "half-minute character" that he wanted.

D. "WHEN" and "IF"

There are distinctions between instructions that have to be obeyed at once, and those that are merely to be noted, to be obeyed later. In a programming language this distinction is quite clear—an instruction in the main program is different from one in a sub-routine that remains inactive until the sub-routine is called into action. Furthermore, in a programming language a conditional instruction is always clearly expressed as such with the condition explicitly stated. Consider, however, a conference at which, for the final session, the following had been written on the blackboard:

> Please sign list for a taxi.
> Please hand in your key.
> Sit near the front.

Study of the intention of these instructions shows that the first may be done later (but not too much later) and only if you want a taxi. The second is to be done later and is really unconditional although "Please" literally implies otherwise. The third is to some extent conditional on the individual's wishes (in spite of no "Please") but applies at once. Could an automated English language interpreter ever manage to reach those conclusions with certainty?

III. Logical thought

Computer programs are often troubled by "bugs" and very troublesome they can be, but usually they are caused not by the use of particular programming languages but by the absence of sufficiently logical human thought, often in not realizing the special circumstances that may arise. Many examples can be quoted to show that such bugs can arise just as easily in natural language. For example, the border between western Canada and the USA is expressed in the Treaty of Washington as following the 49th parallel "to the middle of the channel which separates the continent from Vancouver Island". It did not occur to the authors of the treaty that this would lead to the absurd situation whereby Point Roberts consists of just six square miles of the USA separated from the rest of the nation by 32 miles of Canadian road—see Fig. 1.

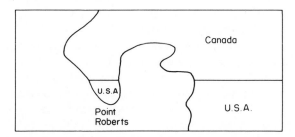

Fig. 1. Location of Point Roberts.

Another set of instructions, whose reasonableness had not been sufficiently considered, occurred in a pamphlet issued some while ago by London Transport which gave "programs" for travelling between each pair of London railway termini and to various other places of interest. To get from Marylebone to Lord's Cricket Ground it said:

> Bakerloo Line from Platform 2 to Baker Street, then by Bakerloo Line (Wembley Park or Stanmore train) from Platform 9 to St. John's Wood.

Now that one branch of the Bakerloo Line has become the Jubilee Line the instructions could be simplified, but that is not the point. The trouble is that the walk from St. John's Wood to Lord's (plus the walks necessary to and from the platforms at each end, and changing at Baker Street) is equal in distance to the walk from Marylebone to Lord's! It is not programming languages that cause difficulty; it is lack of sufficient thought about the object of the program.

A. Legal language

It is precisely because the use of undisciplined language leads to endless trouble when it is used in documents that have to be precisely interpreted, that the legal profession has developed its own artificial rules of language. In a letter to *The Times* a few years ago a correspondent wrote

> The insurance cover on my contact lenses excludes "loss damage or destruction directly or indirectly occasioned by happening through or connected with Earthquake Volcanic Eruption Riot Strike Civil Commotion War Invasion Act of Foreign Enemy Hostilities (whether War be declared or not) Civil War Rebellion Revolution Insurrection or Military or Usurped Power or Looting Sacking or Pillaging following the same".

His question, whether he would be safer without his contact lenses or whether it was just insuring them that might be so dangerous, does not now concern us, but the legal style of the language does. In the first place it is made ugly and difficult by the absence of punctuation. Legal documents, presumably having been bitten in the past by the misplaced comma, now insist on doing without commas altogether. Secondly, while a legal mind may be able to say with certainty what the final two words "the same" refer to, it is far from clear to the rest of us. Do they apply to Pillaging following Sacking? Or to Looting, Sacking or Pillaging following Usurped Power? Or to Looting, Sacking or Pillaging following anything else in the list, or what? And for how long afterwards does "following the same" continue to apply? If lawyers, who have a duty to be unambiguous, can be as vague as this, just imagine what the rest of us can do; but it is my contention that it is time that the lawyers, including the parliamentary draughtsmen, took some lessons from the computer programmers.

I know, and agree with, the arguments that legal language cannot be easy and straightforward because precision, and the absence of ambiguity, are even more important than ease of understanding. But the incorporation of a little bit of mathematical, and algorithmic, notation when appropriate would make things *more* understandable, *more* precise and *more* unambiguous at a stroke. When Value Added Tax was first introduced the regulations included the wording: "tax shall be charged at the rate of 10 per cent ... on the supply of goods or services by reference to the value of the supply as determined under this part of this Act", the value of the supply being found from: "if the supply is for a consideration in money its value shall be taken to be such amount as with the addition of the tax chargeable is equal to the consideration". Surely it would have helped everyone to see what was going on, to give definitions of the terms in English, but to express the relationships symbolically as:

Consideration = Value + Tax
Tax = Rate × Value
(where Rate = 0·1 until further notice).

At a later date, Parliament did make a tentative start in the required direction. The Shipbuilding (Redundancy Payments Scheme) (Great Britain) Order 1978 said, among other things, that there should be paid

to every eligible employee who is dismissed and who on the relevant date is over the age of 62 (if a man) or 57 (if a woman) an amount calculated in accordance with the following formula:

$$£750 + a - b - \frac{c}{24}(£300 + a - b)$$

which, although the newspapers laughed at it (and, of course, misquoted it), is beautifully clear and precise, once we know what a, b and c are. Unfortunately, to discover that we have to descend once more into lawyer's English, and the definitions in their full horror are too lengthy to be quoted here. The definition of c, however, is particularly remarkable being given as:

c is 24 or, if it be lower than 24, the number of calendar months by which his age on the relevant date exceeds 62 (if a man) or 57 (if a woman), part of a month of his age for this purpose being ignored.

I suppose it means that c is either 24, or "the number of months, etc." whichever is less, but what a muddled way of expressing it!

B. Rules of scope

Remarkably the lawyers seem to have no precise rules of scope, in deciding which words are governed by others. Thus the Matrimonial Causes Act 1973 says that a divorce may be refused if "grave financial and other hardship" would be caused to one of the parties concerned. It took the Court of Appeal to decide whether or not the "other hardship" has to be "grave" (it does).

Scope rules are also required to interpret correctly the remarkable statement of a BBC announcer that "The operas *Cavalleria Rusticana* and *I Pagliacci* will be performed simultaneously on Radio 3 and BBC2 television this evening".

C. "And", "or" and "not"

There is also no certainty, in either "natural" English or legal English, as to when "or" is to be interpreted as "inclusive" and when as "exclusive". Sometimes the context tells us: when a mother says to her child "You can have a doughnut or an ice-cream", she certainly intends "exclusive-or"; but when the sign at a railway level crossing, giving special instructions for large or slow vehicles, says "Large means over 55 feet long or 9 feet 6 inches wide or 32 tons total weight" it equally certainly intends "inclusive-or". What an imprecise language! It is also worth noting, in passing, the scope of the word "over" in the last example, which must be intended to apply to all three measurements but it is only the context, not the wording, that tells us so.

Sometimes even the context leaves us in doubt. The Oil in Navigable Waters Act, 1955, says that "If any oil ... is discharged from a British ship ... the owner or master of the ship shall ... be guilty of an offence". It took the highest court in the land, and even then only by a majority of three judges to two, to determine that the "or" here is "inclusive" so that the owner and the master may both be tried. The guilt of one does not imply the automatic innocence of the other.

The use of several "and"s and "or"s in a single phrase can be troublesome. Programming languages define precisely how they are to be interpreted, but when a railway ticket says "via Marylebone or Baker Street and Great Portland Street" does it mean "via Marylebone or (Baker Street and Great Portland Street)"? or "via (Marylebone or Baker Street) and Great Portland Street"? Only knowledge of what route regulations would be sensible on that particular line can tell us.

The scope of the word "not" also causes ambiguity. When a newspaper headline says "Accused not charged because of political views, judge tells jury", does it mean that because of his political views, he was not charged? Or, does it mean that he was charged, but this was not because of his political views?

D. Pronouns

When pronouns are used it is often only context that can tell us what they refer to. No adequate context-free rules of English exist. Rothamsted

Experimental Station once advertised for a statistician "to be responsible for: 1. the analysis of experiments on sheep and pigs, and 2. collaborating in their design." The design of the experiments—or the design of the sheep and pigs?

E. Numbers and arithmetic expressions

Interpreting numbers and arithmetic expressions in natural language is not always simple. If we are told that a distance lies between 30 and 50 miles, it is quite certain that "miles" applies to both the 30 and the 50, but if we are told that a number lies between 30 and 50 thousand it is *not* definite whether the lower limit is 30 thousand or just 30.

If a newspaper headline had said "Rhodesia buys 3 jets from undisclosed source" we should have known that they had purchased three aeroplanes, but when in fact a headline said "Rhodesia buys 707 jets from undisclosed source" they had not purchased seven hundred and seven aeroplanes.

One might think that

$$\frac{\text{II}}{\text{II}}$$

would have the value 1 in any number system whatever. Not so—on a British Rail milepost it can mean $11\frac{1}{2}$ (miles from Paddington). The upper figure is the number of miles in our usual notation; the lower figure is the number of quarter miles, in Roman numerals.

To take a numerical value and simplify it by, for example, cancelling out a common factor is always safe, in mathematical usage, provided that the precise rules are followed. In ordinary English it is not invariably safe to replace "sixth ninths" by "two thirds" for example. Consider: "analysis of all symphonies performed in the Royal Festival Hall during 1972 shows that Beethoven has now soared into the heavens with a score of 28 (including no less than six Ninths)". Should it be objected that the capital N demonstrates a special meaning—I reply that if you punch this on a computer input, it is quite likely to be one of those rotten ones with only a single case of letters available.

If you "add nought" to a figure you presumably leave its value unchanged, but if someone speaks of "adding *a* nought" to a figure he probably means multiplying it by 10.

Even when the numbers themselves are clear it is often only background information that can supply the implied units in which they are expressed. Thus:

Under the offer the basic rate of a driver would go up from £33 to £35·50, a top-rate signalman from £38 to £40·85, and a bottom-grade clerk from £595 to £655.

No mention is made of whether these rates are per week, per month, per year or what, nor of whether or not the same units are to be understood for all three jobs.

Even when we have both the numerical value and the units we still may not be safe without common sense as well. Thus the laws of association football state that the air pressure in the ball "shall be equal to one atmosphere", so if we interpret this literally the ball must not be blown up at all. One atmosphere above the surroundings is evidently intended.

F. The "dangling else"

The "dangling else" has caused trouble in specifying programming languages. The difficulty lies in the construction

if ... then if ... then ... else ...

Does the **else** refer to the first **if-then** or the second? Various languages have taken different solutions to the problem. It can arise just as easily in natural language, where no solution has been defined. A referee's form for a scientific journal says:

> Does the title accurately describe the paper? ... If yes could it be shortened?
> ... If no please give a suggested brief alternative.

Only context, once more, can tell us that "If no" must refer to the first question, not to the second.

IV. Other "natural" and "non-natural" languages

English, of course, is not the only natural language. Could any of the others do any better? I do not have enough knowledge of foreign languages to be able to reply to that in detail, but I strongly suspect that none of them is so logical as to avoid similar troubles.

Evidently languages that use inflexion of word endings, instead of relying on word order so much as English does, could overcome some of the difficulties. But to interpret Latin, for example, common sense is still necessary in spite of all the declensions and conjugations. To consider just a noun of the "first declension", the word endings of the genetive and dative singular and of the nominative and vocative plural are all identical—only context can distinguish them.

When I had to learn Latin I had conversations with my teachers such as:

> "Why is it necessary, for a second declension name, to have different endings for nominative and vocative?"—"So that people can understand whether you are talking *about* him or *to* him".

"Why is it not necessary if his name happens to be first declension?"—
"Well, you can tell by the context".

And yet Latin seems to be constantly spoken of, by its devotees, as a supremely logical language.

Perhaps if we go outside the natural languages to the invented ones, such as Esperanto, we might do better. Esperanto certainly has been suggested in this way. Again I cannot reply in detail, but I suspect that if any language is so logical as to be suitable for computer programming, it is most unlikely to be suitable also for ordinary conversation. The requirements for these different purposes are so dissimilar.

V. An objection

The objection may be made that, while some of the difficulties mentioned above would undoubtedly occur, many of them would not arise in the sort of text that one would wish to use in giving a computer its instructions. I do not accept this objection as valid. A translator worthy of the name has to be ready to tackle anything that is allowed by the language, not only such constructions as are regularly used. Thus a FORTRAN compiler, to the ANSI 1966 standard, would be deficient if it could not handle

IF (I .GT. J) IF (W) 10, 20, 30

even though programmers hardly ever use such a construction (and many of them believe that it would not be legal FORTRAN). Even if an English compiler cannot recognize all possible English constructions well enough to be able to handle them as required, at the very least it needs to be able to recognize them well enough to know when it is in trouble and to be able to say so. This is nearly as difficult.

A. Input by voice

The difficulties are magnified further when the desire is to be able to communicate by voice rather than in writing. The human mind can usually sort out the ambiguities of the spoken word by context, but not always. A solicitor who dictated to his secretary a letter starting

Dear Sir,
    With regard to your heirship …

was surprised by what the secretary typed.

Consider also the two different times of the day that may be expressed as "22.10" and as "20 to 10".

VI. Some existing programs

Well before this point some readers may have been saying "But are there not existing programs that accept English input? Can we not even now converse with computers to some extent?" To some extent, yes, but experience seems to indicate that they are so fragile, when faced by any user who really wishes to test their capabilities, as to leave the aim as far away as ever.

In seeking to test their capabilities, the rules of the game should be that it is perfectly fair for the user to be a little obtuse in hoping to mislead the machine, provided that what he does would have no real chance whatever of similarly misleading a human. For example, if the machine asks "What is your name?" as many such programs do, it is certainly permissible to respond "Which of my names would you like?". More likely than not it will then ask "May I call you Which?" or something of the sort. Since no human would have fallen into that trap, you have some indication of the enormous gulf that still separates the particular program concerned from anything close to human intelligence.

A. Weizenbaum's "ELIZA"

Weizenbaum's (1966) program called ELIZA is, in many ways, very impressive. Its method of working consists of having a number of phrases available (such as "Please go on") that can be used without harm in reply to almost anything, together with a number of skeleton phrases which can be clothed with the user's own words and phrases in repeating them back to him, without needing to understand anything. Even after this is known it remains very impressive.

Such articles as I have seen on ELIZA have all made use of the same example to demonstrate its working; it must be said that actual usage shows that it is rare for such a good conversation to result. The best conversation I ever had with it is shown in Fig. 2.

It is remarkable what can be done without actually understanding a word of it. Clearly, however, this technique is not what is required for being able to use English as a programming language. Weizenbaum (1976) himself makes it perfectly clear that it was never his intention that the program should be taken seriously for that, or any other, purpose, and that he has been much shocked by the naivety of those who have so taken it.

The program can also be easily fooled when desired. For example, knowing that one of its tricks is to store any word following the user's use of "MY", for later use in "TELL ME MORE ABOUT YOUR . . .", enables one to say to it, "MY MY YOU ARE BEING DIFFICULT TODAY" and eventually to receive back "TELL ME MORE ABOUT YOUR YOUR".

B. Winograd's "Understanding natural language"

Winograd's (1972) work that resulted in his book called *Understanding Natural Language* caused a considerable stir among the workers in artificial intelligence when it appeared; more recently it has become widely known through Hofstadter's glorious book (1979). His program manipulates only a very limited world containing a table top, and a number of building blocks of various shapes, sizes and colours. This world exists as pictures on a television screen, and one can give the program instructions, in plain English, for building operations and see them performed on the screen.

The examples given in the book (Winograd, 1972) are certainly remarkable, as is the description of how it is all done, but it is all tied to such a limited context, that to think that we are now ready to advance to tackle the general problem seems rather like having taught a computer to play noughts and crosses and deciding that we are now ready to teach it chess. I have no experience of using the program, so I cannot guess how robust it might be when faced by difficulties.

This is not in any sense an attempt to decry Winograd's work. To accept it as a work of genius only strengthens my argument. If it takes work of that calibre, to make the machine do something so limited compared with what a human can do without any noticeable mental effort at all, there is clearly little hope of a program that can "understand" in any real sense in the foreseeable future.

C. Waltz's "PLANES"

Waltz (1978) reported a program called PLANES that appeared to be comparable to Winograd's pioneering effort, except that it was intended to be useful in a real task instead of being just a research project. It enables casual users to obtain answers from a large database of aircraft flight and maintenance information, by typing requests in English.

Again the context is severely limited—this is not a criticism, that was the intention—and it remains to be seen whether it turns out to be robust and useful in practice, or whether it falls into such problems of scope and of ambiguity, that the effort expended on it would have been better used in teaching its users to be a little more formal in their requests.

It is perfectly possible to admire the great ingenuity and skill that have gone into the programming, and yet to remain doubtful whether it is really heading in the right direction.

VII. Simpler tasks

That problems of language do not yield easily can be seen from the history of the attempts at computer translation from one human language to another. A quarter of a century ago it was being said that this was quite close. Such tasks seem to have a "Hartree constant" of about five years.

HELLO
HOW DO YOU DO. PLEASE STATE YOUR PROBLEM

MY PROBLEM IS UNSTATABLE
YOUR PROBLEM IS UNSTATABLE

THAT'S RIGHT
I'M NOT SURE I UNDERSTAND YOU FULLY

PARTIALLY PERHAPS
YOU DON'T SEEM QUITE CERTAIN

IT'S YOU WHO IS UNCERTAIN
WE WERE DISCUSSING YOU—NOT ME

BUT YOU GOT IT ALL SCREWED UP
OH, I GOT IT ALL SCREWED UP

THAT'S IT. YOU ARE GETTING ON
WHAT MAKES YOU THINK I AM GETTING ON

YOU ARE ALMOST SENILE
DOES IT PLEASE YOU TO BELIEVE I AM ALMOST SENILE

IT DOES
EARLIER YOU SAID—MY PROBLEM IS UNSTATABLE. WHY DO YOU SAY YOUR PROBLEM IS UNSTATABLE

BECAUSE YOU ASKED ME TO STATE MY PROBLEM
DOES THAT SUGGEST ANYTHING ELSE WHICH BELONGS TO YOU

MY PROBLEM IS NOT MINE ALONE
WHAT WOULD IT MEAN TO YOU IF YOUR PROBLEM IS MINE ALONE

("Hartree constant" was defined by Lord Bowden (1953) as "The time which is expected to elapse before a particular electronic computing machine is finished and working. It was Professor Hartree who first pointed out that this estimated time usually remains constant at about six months for a period of several years during the development of a machine" (p. 412). While this definition applies the concept only to hardware, it seems to be just as applicable to software.)

So far no-one has managed even the relatively trivial task of a perfect chess-playing program, although such programs have become much better over the last few years. I am not underestimating the enormous difficulty of

YOU COULD TAKE THE BURDEN FROM ME
WHY DO YOU THINK I COULD TAKE THE BURDEN FROM YOU

WELL IF THE PROBLEM WAS YOURS ALONE I WOULD NOT HAVE IT HANGING AROUND ME
NOT HAVE IT HANGING AROUND YOU WHY NOT

BECAUSE YOU WOULD HAVE IT YOU IDIOT
YOU'RE NOT REALLY TALKING ABOUT ME—ARE YOU

I AM
WHY DO YOU SAY 'AM'

TO ANSWER YOUR QUESTION
WHY ARE YOU CONCERNED OVER MY QUESTION

WHAT DO YOU ASK QUESTIONS FOR IF YOU DON'T WANT ME TO BE CONCERNED OVER THEM
DO YOU THINK ITS LIKELY THAT I DON'T WANT YOU TO BE CONCERNED OVER THEM

I DO NOT BUT YOU IMPLIED THAT IT WAS
WOULD IT SURPRISE YOU IF YOU DO BUT I IMPLIED THAT IT WAS

WOULD IT SURPRISE YOU
WHAT ARE YOUR FEELINGS NOW

CONFUSED—HOW ARE YOURS
WHY DO YOU ASK

YOU STARTED IT
WE WERE DISCUSSING YOU—NOT ME

etc.

Fig. 2. A conversation with ELIZA. The first line of each pair is human input; the second line is computer output.

programming good, let alone perfect, chess; I claim only that it is *relatively* trivial. Perfect information at every stage, and precisely defined rules, must make it so.

It has been pointed out to me (and I am happy to agree) that it may be unfair to criticize advances in chess programs because little research has been funded in this area and most progress has been made in people's spare time. On the other hand there is so much publicity and prestige in chess projects, and so much money to be made from successful computer games, that the efforts that have been made are certainly not negligible. Furthermore it is the sort of area where if we ever do get spectacular progress it is more likely to come from the inspiration of an individual than from a highly-funded research team.

A. Understanding programming languages

If our computer linguists and experts in artificial intelligence wish to do something really useful, and much simpler than understanding natural language, they should set out to try to get a computer to understand programming languages better. Since both the context, and the number of constructions, are limited and well-defined this should be very much easier. The end product could be a compiler that would take over all the tasks of a programming advisory service.

At least they should be able to produce something better than the majority of compilers at present available, which, on the rare occasions that they do try to show a little bit of intelligence so often go ludicrously astray in the attempt. One example concerns a FORTRAN compiler containing a rule that said "If a valid number is immediately followed by a valid identifier, assume that a multiplication sign has been omitted between them, and insert it so as to be able to compile the program." The reader is invited to pause at this point and consider what is wrong with that, before reading the next sentence. When by mistake the number 10 is punched as 1O it multiplies the integer 1 by a real variable called O (that, usually, has not been given a value). Any human could see at a glance that that was not the intention.

VIII. Conclusion

It must be admitted that those who write in this sort of way can never win. If, in five years' time, someone has produced a program that does allow computers to read programs in natural language, and perform the intended instructions correctly, then I have lost at least a considerable part of my

Fig. 3. The argument in a nutshell. Thanks are due to Don Mitchell and *Computer Weekly* for the use of this cartoon.

case. If, however, in five years' time no such thing has happened, they will say "Ah! But just wait another five years and see then".

I am prepared to stick my neck out, however, and say that I remain of the opinion that a program that can "understand" natural language well enough to enable it to be successfully used as a general programming language is not attainable in the foreseeable future, and even if it were, this would be a disastrous step backwards compared with the present situation. The difficulty of writing programs, with any certainty of what they would do, would be greatly increased. Perhaps the best summing-up of the situation is that given in Fig. 3.

IX. References

Bemer, R. W. (1972). From the editor. *Honeywell Computer Journal* **6**, 76.

Bowden, Lord (1953). *Faster than Thought*. Pitman, London.

Hill, I. D. (1972). Wouldn't it be nice if we could write computer programs in ordinary English—or would it? *Computer Bulletin* **16**, 306–312. (Reprinted (1972) in *Honeywell Computer Journal* **6**, 76–83.)

Hofstadter, D. R. (1979). *Gödel, Escher, Bach—an eternal golden braid*. Basic Books Inc., New York.

Waltz, D. L. (1978). An English language question answering system for a large relational database. *Communications of the ACM* **21**, 526–539.

Weizenbaum, J. (1966). ELIZA—a computer program for the study of natural language communication between man and machine. *Communications of the ACM* **9**, 36–45.

Weizenbaum, J. (1976). *Computer Power and Human Reason*. Freeman, San Francisco.

Winograd, T. (1972). *Understanding Natural Language*. Edinburgh University Press, Edinburgh.

3. The advantages of natural language programming

L. R. HARRIS

Artificial Intelligence Corporation, 200 Fifth Avenue, Waltham, Massachusetts, USA

I. Introduction

The previous chapter focused on the inherent undesirability of using natural English as a programming language. In this chapter we present the view that there is basically a continuum of ways that people can interact with a computer in natural language. Some of these are not only desirable but also quite feasible within the current technology. At the other end of the spectrum are applications that will quite possibly either never be implemented, or at least not implemented for many, many years. By discussing selected points on this continuum, we hope not only to demonstrate that progress along the continuum is quite plausible, but also show that we have already begun making measurable progress in the journey.

It has been a commonly held belief that natural language processing by a computer was an all-or-nothing proposition. This feeling is often expressed by the saying "when it comes to natural language, you can't do anything until you can do everything". However, holders of this view ignore the fact that many (indeed, nearly all) interactions with computers take place in an extremely restricted environment. As the environment becomes more and more restricted, the problems associated with understanding natural language within that environment become less and less severe. It is not the elimination of specific linguistic phenomena that causes the simplification. It is the restricted semantic environment that means that certain interpretations do not have to be considered. An example arising in database query is the question:

WHO ARE THE NEW YORK EMPLOYEES LIVING IN BUFFALO?

DESIGNING FOR HUMAN–COMPUTER COMMUNICATION
ISBN 0 12 643820 X

There are many possible interpretations of this request. For example, people in the city of Buffalo in the state of New York, or people born in New York now living in Buffalo, or people commuting to work in New York from Buffalo. Under the proper circumstances any good natural language system must consider all of these possibilities. However, the fact that the discourse environment was restricted to querying a database about employees means that the system need not consider the somewhat ridiculous interpretation of New York people devoured by, but not yet digested by, buffalos. In this way the restricted discourse domain simplifies the problem of understanding the user. The point of this example is that the wide range in the restrictiveness of dialog environments implies that there will be varying degrees of difficulty in constructing natural language systems for these environments.

For the purpose of discussion, let us select two different natural language applications of decreasing restrictiveness. By discussing each of these in turn I hope to show that we have indeed already solved for one important natural language environment, and that progressing from one solution to another is quite realistic.

Let us first qualify my use of the word "solved" in the previous sentence. A problem in computer science (let alone artificial intelligence) is rarely, if ever, solved. Improved solutions are almost always forthcoming for any problem. This implies, of course, that every solution is lacking in some way, or else it could not have been improved upon. For this reason I prefer a more operational definition of "solved", meaning that the people originally faced with the problem feel that a satisfactory solution exists for them. In this sense the life-cycle of a problem is that it is initially unsolved. Then at some point it becomes solved for some class of people facing the problem. After this it will almost certainly be refined further, which may solve the problem for some wider class of people.

Note that a corollary of this definition is that the measure of a natural language system should not be "Can you fool it?" but rather, "Can you use it?", or more precisely "Can you use it more productively than a formal system?". The ability to "fool" a system, i.e. push it beyond its limits until it fails, is only one measure of the value of a system—not the only measure. In fact, the measure of whether a system can be fooled is rather unimportant, since all systems, including people, can be "fooled" under certain circumstances. For example, the value of a desk calculator increases as a function of its decimal precision. A calculator with 1 decimal digit would be of little value, whereas calculators with 8 digits have proven to be extremely useful. But no matter what its accuracy, any calculator can be "fooled" by giving it a problem beyond its capacity. Some of us that can carry our arithmetic operations with variable precision may laugh at its stupidity in these cases, but that does not deny its utility in the domain of its expertise. The critical issue is whether it solves a significant subset of the problems that its users are likely to encounter.

With the definition of "solve" clearly understood, we can begin discussing two points on the continuum of natural language applications. The two problem environments I wish to discuss are:

(1) natural language database query, and
(2) natural language programming.

II. Natural language and database query

Natural language database query is the use of a natural language such as English to extract information from a computerized database. This is certainly a non-trivial application of natural language techniques because it is a very real problem facing thousands of people today. The information contained in computerized databases is of little value until it is communicated to a person who can act upon it.

As I see it, there are only three solutions to this problem. They are:

(1) force all such access to go through a human intermediary;
(2) have everyone adapt to the machine by learning a formal computer language; or
(3) have the computer adapt to the people by training it to understand a sufficient portion of natural language.

The first option is clearly sub-optimal. Anyone who has played the children's game of *Telephone* in which each person relays a given message along a chain, knows that the accuracy of information decreases each time humans handle it. This applies to the user defining the problem to the intermediary, as well as the intermediary conveying the answers to the users. Thus, there are four possible outcomes in this situation:

(1) getting the right answer to the right problem,
(2) getting the right answer to the wrong problem,
(3) getting the wrong answer to the right problem, and
(4) getting the wrong answer to the wrong problem.

In order to be utterly convinced of the absurdity of the intermediary solution, consider a doctor querying a medical database on the latest treatment techniques. Apart from the likelihood of errors introduced by the intermediary, there is value lost because the doctor would not be able to follow his instinctive feel for the data as he extracts the information. The synergism that exists between a specialist and his data is completely lost as soon as an intermediary comes between them.

The second option, that of forcing everyone to learn a formal computer language, is the one that many people believe to be the best choice. However, I think that this belief is predicated on the assumption that the natural language option is not feasible. Let us examine the second option on its own merits, putting aside for the moment the feasibility of natural language. Besides the enormous human costs in training all the people involved, there are subtle problems inherent to the formal language approach. We have ample evidence that dealing with computers requires a level of detail considerably beyond other human activities. We simply have to look at the number of errors made by professional programmers. These are people inclined towards this type of precise technical work, and they still make an outrageous number of errors. Can you imagine the problems a person would have if he was not inclined towards this type of work? I cringe at the thought!

But beyond this is a more significant issue. For some reason people naively envisage the user and his formal computer language walking off into the sunset into the land of precision, clarity and error-free communication. Unfortunately the story does not end this way. The fact that there is no ambiguity in the formal language itself does not imply that there is no ambiguity in a person's use of that language. For example, if a sales manager wanted to know how widgets and screws were selling in the northeast region, he might type:

PRINT SUM (SALES) IF PRODUCT = 'WIDGET'
AND PRODUCT = 'SCREW'
AND REGION = 'NORTHEAST'.

This would seem to be a plausible formalization of the request. However, from the perspective of an end-user, the simplistic appearance of the formal request can be deceptive. After looking at a few such examples people begin to believe that they understand the formal language. Unfortunately there is a big difference between understanding requests that were written by someone else, and generating the requests yourself. This is an important point that is often overlooked. There can be a great deal of subtlety in using a formal language.

The above request illustrates this subtlety because it would actually fail for at least three reasons.

(1) The word "and" would be interpreted as logical intersection, thereby insuring that no records would be selected, because a product cannot be both a widget and a screw at the same time. The user should have said "or" instead of "and".

(2) The word 'if' applies the search criteria along an entire path in the database hierarchy. Thus, depending on the internal database structure, there is the possibility that records containing widgets or screws in the northeast may be rejected at a higher level. The user should have used the word "where" instead of "if".

(3) Finally, depending again on the internal database structure, the request may not force the selection logic to the level necessary to apply all of the search criteria. In many hierarchical systems the selection logic is only applied to the levels of the tree from which data is retrieved. If the fields appearing in the selection criteria are below this point in the hierarchy, they will not impact the retrieval at all. Thus the user may get salesmen outside the northeast, or the sales of products other than screws and widgets in the northeast. The user should have requested the printing of some additional piece of information to force the retrieval low enough in the hierarchy. This, of course, requires complete knowledge of the hierarchical structure.

Notice that a formal system would merrily process this bogus request giving incorrect answers with complete confidence that it properly understood the words "if" and "and". This type of failure is the worst kind of mistake a computer system can make. It is better for a computer system to abort than to give wrong answers without warning.

Any natural language system must accept ambiguity as a way of life. The multiple meanings of words and sentence structures must constantly be analysed for ambiguities. Of course, no system will ever detect every possible interpretation in every situation, but at least there is the attempt to deal with the problem, not a pretention that it does not exist. Like everything else, the value of a natural language system will depend on its relative ability to deal with this problem.

But we must consider whether it is feasible to do this with sufficient accuracy to be of value to some group of users. This type of determination is certainly very hard to ascertain. How can we tell when a new technology, such as natural language processing, has reached the point of utility? We could take the word of the "experts". But the problem is that the experts disagree. Natural language has its detractors as well as its proponents. Expert opinions would range from "given the proper technical environment, we could install a usable system tomorrow" to "the use of natural language for database query is both undesirable and not feasible". The point is that when it comes to assessing the utility of a new technology, it is the users of the technology who are the ultimate judges. We should not believe an expert any more than we should believe an accountant who claims that 8-digit calculators are worthless because they cannot balance a bank's books, or an educator who says they are worthless because children should learn to do arithmetic for themselves. While these statements may be true, they do not diminish the value of the calculator for someone who can make effective use of it.

Measuring user satisfaction with a natural language database query system is now possible. There have been several systems that have been tested in certain real-world applications. These systems include: EUFID, of Systems Development Corporation; LIFER, developed at SRI International; PLANES, developed by Dave Waltz at the University of Illinois; and the RENDEZVOUS and TQA systems of IBM. Since my own experiences in this area have been in the development and installation of the INTELLECT system at the Artificial Intelligence Corporation, I can best relate the satisfaction of end-users in terms of their use of INTELLECT.

The user experience we have had with the INTELLECT system indicates that the natural language database query technology does provide significant advantages over both the intermediary approach and the formal language approach. Over 100 copies of INTELLECT have been installed at large commercial installations in the US. Some of these installations have as many as 100 non-technical users of the system. It is an accepted tool, relied on by managers to provide the timely information they require in the decision making process. These users have neither the desire or the inclination to learn a formal language, and why should they? They already have the capability to retrieve directly the information they require by typing ordinary English requests into the INTELLECT system.

The level of sophistication expected by each of these sites is best illustrated by giving examples of the kind of questions posed by their end-users. Each of the following six questions would be successfully processed by the INTELLECT system in these or hundreds of other wordings.

Question 1
List executives in Massachusetts who earn over $40,000, are unmarried, and are older than 50.

> PRINT THE NAME, AGE, JOB, SALARY, AND FAMILY STATUS OF ALL EMPLOYEES WITH FAMILY STATUS NOT MARRIED & SALARY > $40,000 & STATE = MASSACHUSETTS & JOB = PRESIDENT, VICE PRESIDENT, OR ADMINISTRATOR & AGE > 50.

NAME	YEARS OF AGE	PROFESSIONAL OCCUPATION	SALARY	FAMILY STATUS
ALEXANDER	66	ADMINISTRATOR	$49,791	SINGLE
KINGMAN	51	ADMINISTRATOR	$49,153	SINGLE

Question 2
For the northeast salespeople: display 1979 commissions plus 1980 salary.
PRINT THE LAST NAME AND (79 YR ACT COMM + 80 SALARY) OF ALL SALESPERSONS WITH REGION = NORTHEAST.

LAST NAME	79 YR ACT COM +80 SALARY
SMITH	$76,654
JONES	$112,532
ALEXANDER	$70,861
ADAMS	$72,904
BLACK	$127,756
ADKINS	$101,164
AGAN	$95,007

Question 3
How many of our salespeople are older than 50 and unmarried?
COUNT THE SALESPERSONS WITH MARITAL STATUS NOT MARRIED & AGE > 50.
THE NUMBER OF RECORDS TO BE SEARCHED IS 29.

ANSWER: 2

Question 4

Give me a report of names, second quarter sales, and YTD sales for northeast states other than MA, broken down by state.

STATE	LAST NAME	1980 2ND QTR ACTUAL SALES	1980 YTD ACTUAL SALES
NEW HAMPSHIRE	JOCHEM	$614,128	$1,634,404
	JOCHEM	$400,200	$1,062,719
	GOODWYN	$374,859	$998,820
	GOLDSTEIN	$228,875	$605,071
	CONSTAINS	$229,108	$604,001
	CONDIT	$294,274	$780,994
	AUDREY	$371,915	$990,595
	AUDET	$219,740	$593,749
	ADAMS	$228,127	$897,651
	ALEXANDER	$317,815	$856,336
NEW HAMPSHIRE	SUM	$3,389,041	$9,024,340
VERMONT	JOHNSON	$230,354	$616,619
	GOULD	$464,240	$1,236,134
	COOKE	$245,774	$661,563
	AZER	$440,758	$1,160,733
	BLOCH	$576,036	$1,533,272
VERMONT SUM		$1,957,162	$5,207,321
OVERALL SUM		$5,346,203	$14,232,661

Question 5

Display a histogram of salespersons in each state of the midwest region.

STATE

SCALE IS 1"*" PER 2%

ILLINOIS	24 42.10%	|★★★★★★★★★★★★★★★★★★★★★★★ |★★★★★★★★★★★★★★★★★★★★★★★
KANSAS	10 17.50%	|★★★★★★★★★ |★★★★★★★★★
MISSOURI	18 31.60%	|★★★★★★★★★★★★★★★★ |★★★★★★★★★★★★★★★★
NEBRASKA	5 8.80%	|★★★★ |★★★★

Question 6
How many bakers are in the file?
YOUR REQUEST IS AMBIGUOUS, DO YOU MEAN:
NUMBER 1
COUNT THE EMPLOYEES WITH NAME = BAKER.
NUMBER 2
COUNT THE EMPLOYEES WITH JOB = BAKER.
PLEASE ENTER THE NUMBER OF THE INTERPRETATION YOU DESIRE.
2
ANSWER: 46

Based on the experiences with current installations I think it is fair to conclude that both the desirability and the feasibility of natural language database query have already been determined by the only people who can really make such a determination—the users of such a system.

The above examples give some feeling for the kind of natural language processing that is commercially available today. However, it is worthwhile discussing some of the attributes of the INTELLECT system, rather than just showing examples. Let us consider exactly what a natural language system must do to understand a query.

(1) Be able to identify specific fields of data which are to be retrieved.
(2) Isolate criteria for selecting a desired subset of all records in all files.
(3) Determine the analytical and display process required to manipulate the data.
(4) Invoke the required retrieval, analytical, and display processes in the sequence necessary to answer a question.

The range of English understood by INTELLECT is restricted more by the data and available processes than it is by INTELLECT's grammar. INTELLECT can parse a large subset of the English typed by most users. Needless to say, the user can ask only for those data and processes which are available. That is, a query which is meaningless either to the user or in terms of available data and processes will probably be meaningless to INTELLECT.

INTELLECT can handle most declarative and interrogative forms with as many convoluted subordinate clauses as are required to express the sense of the user's questions. A query can consist of several sentences if it seems desirable to break up the input that way.

In addition, INTELLECT allows pronoun reference to previous questions. For example, if the user asks:

WHO LIVES IN THE BIG APPLE?

a list of people's names will result. The next question could be:

SHOW ME THEIR PHONE NUMBERS.

This will produce a list of all those who live in New York City with their telephone numbers.

The user can continue the pronoun reference in subsequent queries asking either for more information on the same group or by further refining the set. For example, the set of people who live in New York City could be further refined by asking:

WHICH OF THEM EARN OVER $50,000?

There are now two pronoun contexts which INTELLECT allows the user to reference:

(1) Those who live in New York City, and
(2) those who live in New York City and earn over $50,000.

The pronoun contexts continue to exist as long as the user asks questions which use one or the other of them. At the point where a question is asked which does not use one of these reference sets, a new pronoun context is established. Thus the INTELLECT understanding of the physical database keeps pace with the user's view of the logical database.

As an example of the robustness of the INTELLECT syntax, consider the following different wordings of an actual request all of which produce identical INTELLECT formalizations.

Total sales for western or northeastern people by region who were over quota in 1981.

PRINT THE TOTAL 81 YTD ACT SALES IN EACH REGION OF ALL SALES PEOPLE WITH REGION = NORTHEAST OR WEST & 81 YTD ACT % QUOTA > 100.00.

Total of northeast and western sales by region for anyone above quota this year.

PRINT THE TOTAL 81 YTD ACT SALES IN EACH REGION OF ALL SALES PEOPLE WITH REGION = NORTHEAST OR WEST & 81 YTD ACT % QUOTA > 100.00.

Over quota people in the northeast and west showing total sales by region.

PRINT THE TOTAL 81 YTD ACT SALES IN EACH REGION OF

ALL SALES PEOPLE WITH REGION = NORTHEAST OR WEST &
81 YTD ACT % QUOTA > 100.00.

Northeast or west people above quota in 1981 total sales by region.

PRINT THE TOTAL 81 YTD ACT SALES IN EACH REGION OF
ALL SALES PEOPLE WITH REGION = NORTHEAST OR WEST &
81 YTD ACT % QUOTA > 100.00.

THE NUMBER OF RECORDS TO BE SEARCHED IS 110

REGION	1981 YTD SALES
NORTHEAST	$1,869,627
WEST	$2,475,799
OVERALL SUM	$4,345,426

III. Natural language programming

Let us now turn our attention to a somewhat less restrictive application of
natural language processing, that of natural language programming. The
argument is often made that natural language would be a horrible
programming language. I must say that within the current mold of
procedural programming languages such as FORTRAN, COBOL, or
PL/L that I basically agree with this statement. However, our notion of
both programming and programming languages is changing. The recent
introduction of non-procedural programming languages such as NOMAD,
RAMIS, INFO and FOCUS have made substantial inroads in what was
once done in COBOL or FORTRAN. Languages like SMALLTALK, that
are based on the notions of processes and communication, are certainly
changing the way we think about programming. Even Backus, the inventor
of FORTRAN, argued in his Turing award lecture that our notion of
programming is outdated and has suggested a new approach.

Whether natural language will make a good programming language in
some future sense of programming is very hard to say. But of all the new
notions of programming the one that has already earned its stripes is the
group of the non-procedural languages. I would argue that natural
language is the ideal non-procedural programming language. Non-
procedural programming languages, by their very nature, do not require
precise step-by-step instructions, but merely a statement of what the
desired result is. In a non-procedural programming language you state
what you want, not how to get it.

Currently, these languages encompass only a portion of the data processing needs of a given organization. But the functionality of these languages is continually increasing and, therefore, continues to encompass more and more of the needs of a typical organization. There is already a very noticeable shift within many US corporations to replace COBOL applications with canned non-procedural specifications. In the near future, I believe that the bulk of routine data processing will be done in this manner. Procedural programming as we know it will be relegated to specialized tasks lying outside the scope of non-procedural languages. The cost-benefits of the non-procedural languages are so overwhelming that most data processing organizations cannot afford not to adopt them. Of course, given the inertia of the large organizations involved, and the retraining of so many people, the conversion to non-procedural languages will come about slowly; but the first steps have already been made. Thousands of applications have already been successfully built within the non-procedural framework. It is only a matter of time.

What does the "non-procedural revolution" have to do with natural language programming? The current capabilities of systems like INTELLECT are subsets of the functionality of the existing non-procedural systems. There was a time when the non-procedural systems were limited to only database query and simple report generation. The original non-procedural system, MARK IV, fits this description. The natural language technology, at least as embodied in INTELLECT, completely encompasses this capability today. In the meantime, of course, the newer non-procedural systems have gone beyond query and simple reporting to data input, hierarchical structures and more complex reporting. This new set of capabilities has already been proven sufficient to cope with a wide variety of intricate data processing applications. The immediate goals for the development of the INTELLECT system are to allow a larger amount of this new functionality to be expressed in natural language instead of a formal language. In as much as this is possible, INTELLECT will allow "natural language programming" for these same applications that are currently amenable to non-procedural programming.

It may not be necessary or even desirable to express all the non-procedural functions in natural language. For example, high volume data input may be best specified by a formal language, since the frequency of the alteration of the input format is very low compared to the frequency of its use. The general trend I am predicting is first, that non-procedural languages will continue to grow both in capability and in widespread acceptance; and secondly, that natural language technology will track this development. Within this scenario I think we can expect to see a substantial amount of "natural language programming" in the not-too-distant future.

IV. Conclusion

It is all too easy to look at the complexity and intricacy of dealing with natural language and become overwhelmed. It is truly a difficult problem that will require many more years of research to solve, if it is ever completely solved. But we should not be so overwhelmed that we become pessimistic about the feasibility of all natural language applications. In this chapter we have tried to show that there is, in fact, good reason to be optimistic about the future of natural language processing. Having just cleared the first important hurdle, database query, this is not the time to despair, but the time to consider the implications of this new technology and plan new ways to take advantage of it in the design of future systems. The use of natural language will set new standards for the easy use of computers.

4. TEIRESIAS: experiments in communicating with a knowledge-based system

R. DAVIS

Massachusetts Institute of Technology, Cambridge, Massachusetts, USA

I. Introduction

In this chapter we view communicating with computers in the light of three motivations:

transparency;
debugging;
knowledge acquisition.

Transparency is a measure of a program's comprehensibility. A "black box", all of whose internal workings are hidden, is the least transparent type of system. We examine some mechanisms that allow a user to "look" inside the machinery of a program to discover both what it is doing and why. This sort of capability offers advantages in terms of both user-acceptance (people are far more likely to accept what they can understand), and possible educational benefit (they may learn from seeing how the program works).

Debugging is of course an inevitable part of constructing a program, and most debugging tools have been designed by programmers for their own use. But what would a debugging tool look like if it were designed instead for use by the user community? We consider here the design and implementation of a facility that allows non-programmers to track down the source of a certain class of bugs in an application program.

Having discovered a bug, it would of course be nice to have a facility that allowed the user to correct it. Our concept of *knowledge acquisition* includes

DESIGNING FOR HUMAN–COMPUTER COMMUNICATION
ISBN 0 12 643820 X

the idea of giving the user a mechanism for adding to (or modifying) the program's store of information in order to improve its performance.

In this chapter we examine the mechanics of setting up communication facilities to achieve these goals. We examine the kinds of communication that are necessary and describe in some detail the machinery we have implemented to make such communication possible.

II. Background

This work has been done in the context of efforts to design and implement a computer-based consultation system. The system is intended to supply near expert-level advice on difficult cognitive problems, and is designed to interact with two classes of user: (a) naive users who are acquainted with the domain of application but are not necessarily skilled in it, and who are requesting advice or instruction; and (b) experts using the system in order to challenge it, uncover weaknesses, and correct those problems by augmenting or revising the system's knowledge about the domain.

In both cases, we are dealing with users who are assumed to be relatively naive with respect to programming. This puts strong constraints on the level, style, and flexibility of communication that we must establish. Unlike experienced programmers used to the idiosyncracies of dealing with computers, this user population is more demanding and requires a much more natural style of interaction.

III. Perspective on communication

Our goal has been to establish two kinds of communication between the consultation program and its users. The results are embodied in a sytem called TEIRESIAS (Davis, 1977a,b; Davis and Buchanan, 1977; Davis and Lenat, 1981) designed to function as a bridge between the user and the consultation program (Fig. 1). There are thus two distinct programs: (i) the consultation program (or more generally any high-performance application program) intended to supply advice in a particular domain, and (ii) TEIRESIAS, which functions as a link between the user and the performance program.

Information flow from right to left is labelled *explanation*. This is the process by which TEIRESIAS clarifies for the user the source of the performance program's results and motivations for its actions. This contributes to the transparency of the system, providing an important human engineering benefit as well as possible educational impact. The

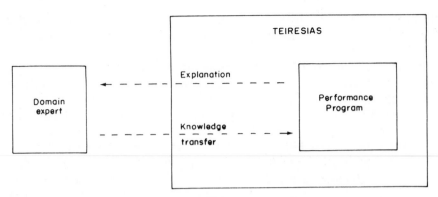

Fig. 1

performance program need no longer be a "black box" whose workings are mysterious to the user and whose results the user must either accept or reject. He can instead (as we will see) uncover the rationale behind them. The explanation facility is also useful as a debugging aid, since it allows an expert to discover what the performance program knows and how it used that knowledge.

Information flow from left to right is labelled *knowledge transfer*. This is the process by which the expert adds to or modifies the store of domain-specific knowledge in the performance program.

Explanations provided for the sake of transparency—making the performance program's inner workings clear to the user—are provided only on request. During a consultation, the performance program takes the initiative, asking questions of the user. If one of those questions seems inappropriate, the user can interrupt and use TEIRESIAS's explanation facilities to find out what's going on. By examining the chain of reasoning that prompted the question, he can find out if the reasoning was motivated by plausible considerations.

The knowledge acquisition facility can use the same mechanism for debugging, and offers as well another explanation and debugging mechanism in which TEIRESIAS takes the initiative. Whichever mechanism is used in knowledge acquisition, the two forms of communication shown above are closely interwoven. This occurs because we view knowledge acquisition as *interactive transfer of expertise*. We see it in terms of a teacher who continually challenges a student with new problems to solve and carefully observes the student's performance. The teacher may interrupt to request a justification of some particular step the student has taken in solving the problem or may challenge the final result. This process may uncover a fault in the student's knowledge of the subject (the debugging phase) and result in the transfer of information to correct it (the knowledge acquisition phase).

There is an important assumption involved in the attempt to establish this sort of communication: we are assuming that it is possible to distinguish between basic *problem-solving paradigm* and *degree of expertise*, or equivalently, that control structure and representation in the performance program can be considered separately from the content of its knowledge base. The basic control structure(s) and representations are assumed to be established and debugged, and the fundamental approach to the problem assumed acceptable. The question of *how* knowledge is to be encoded and used is settled by the selection of one or more of the available representations and control structures. The expert's task is to enlarge *what* it is the program knows.

There is a corollary assumption, too, in the belief that the control structures and knowledge representations can be made sufficiently comprehensible to the expert (at the conceptual level) that he can (a) understand the system's behaviour in terms of them and (b) use them to codify his own knowledge. This ensures that the expert understands system performance well enough to know what to correct, and can then express the required knowledge, i.e. he can "think" in those terms. Thus part of the task of establishing the link shown in Fig. 1 involves insulating the expert from the details of implementation, by establishing a discourse at a level high enough that we do not end up effectively having to teach him how to program.

IV. Design of the performance program

A. Program architecture

To set the context for the work described below, we require a few details concerning the structure of the performance program of the type TEIRESIAS is designed to deal with (Fig. 2). (The performance program described here is modelled after the MYCIN program (Davis *et al.*, 1977a; Shortliffe, 1976), which provided the context within which TEIRESIAS was actually developed. We have abstracted out here just the essential elements of MYCIN's design.) The *knowledge base* is the program's store of task specific knowledge that makes possible high performance. The *inference engine* is an interpreter that uses the knowledge base to solve the problem at hand.

The main point of interest in this very simple design is the explicit

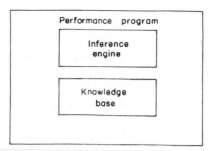

Fig. 2

division between these two parts of the program. This design is in keeping with the assumption noted above that the expert's task would be to augment the knowledge base of a program whose control structure (inference engine) was assumed both appropriate and debugged.

In this discussion we assume the knowledge base contains information about selecting an investment in the stock market; the performance program thus functions as an investment consultant. Since the MYCIN program actually deals with infectious disease diagnosis and therapy selection, the rules and dialog shown later dealt with that subject initially. The topic was changed to keep the discussion phrased in terms familiar to a wide range of readers, and to emphasize that neither the problems attacked nor the solutions suggested are restricted to a particular domain of application or performance program design. The dialog is a real example of TEIRESIAS in action with a few words substituted in a medical example: e.g. *E. coli* became *AT&T*, *infection* became *investment*, etc.*

An example of the performance program in action is shown in Section IVD. The program interviews the user, requesting various pieces of information that are relevant to selecting the most appropriate investment, then prints its recommendations.

B. The knowledge base

The knowledge base of the performance program contains a collection of decision rules of the sort shown in Fig. 3. (The rule is stored internally in the INTERLISP (Teitelman, 1975) form, the English version is generated from that with a simple template-directed mechanism.) Each rule is a single "chunk" of domain-specific information indicating an *action* (in this case a conclusion) which is justified if the conditions specified in the *premise* are fulfilled.

---

* See the article by Shortliffe (this volume) for examples of explanation in the medical domain.

RULE027

If   [1.1] the time-scale of the investment is long-term, and
     [1.2] the desired return on the investment is greater than 10%, and
     [1.3] the area of the investment is not known,
then AT&T is a likely (.4) choice for the investment.

PREMISE   ($AND (SAME OBJCT TIMESCALE LONG-TERM)
                 (GREATER OBJCT RETURNRATE 10)
                 (NOTKNOWN OBJCT INVESTMENT-AREA))

ACTION   (CONCLUDE OBJCT STOCK-NAME AT&T .4)

Fig. 3

The rules are judgmental, i.e. they make inexact inferences. In the case of the rule in Fig. 3, for instance, the evidence cited in the premise is enough to assert the conclusion shown with only a weak degree of confidence (0·4 out of 1·0). These numbers are referred to as *certainty factors*, and embody a model of confirmation described in detail in Shortliffe and Buchanan (1975). The details of that model need not concern us here; we need only note that a rule typically embodies an inexact inference rather than an exact rule.

Finally, a few points of terminology. The premise is a Boolean combination of one or more *clauses*, each of which is constructed from a *predicate function* with an *associative triple* (*attribute, object, value*) as its argument. For the first clause in Fig. 3, for example, the predicate function is SAME, and the triple is "*timescale* of *investment* is *long-term*". (The identifier OBJCT is used as a placeholder for the specific object to be referred to; the actual binding is established each time the rule is invoked.)

C. The inference engine

The rules are invoked in a simple backward-chaining fashion that produces an exhaustive depth-first search of an AND/OR goal-tree (Fig. 4). Assume that the program is attempting to determine which stock would make a good investment. It retrieves (the pre-computed list of) all rules which make a conclusion about that topic (i.e. they mention STOCK-NAME in their action), and invokes each one in turn, evaluating each premise to see if the conditions specified have been met. For the example shown in Fig. 4, this means first determining what the timescale of the investment ought to be. This is in turn set up as a subgoal, and the process recurs.

The search is thus depth-first (because each premise condition is thoroughly explored in turn); the tree that is sprouted is an AND/OR goal-tree (because rules may have OR conditions in their premise); and the

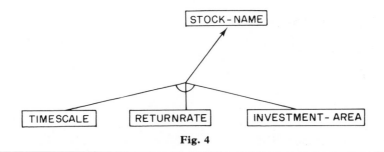

Fig. 4

search is exhaustive (because the rules are inexact, so that even if one succeeds, it was deemed to be a wisely conservative strategy to continue to collect all evidence about the subgoal.)

We have noted earlier that the expert must have at least a high-level understanding of the operation of the inference engine and the manner of knowledge representation to enable him to express new knowledge for the performance program. That level of understanding is well supplied by the information in Sections IVB, C, together with an equally brief summary of the model of confirmation described in Shortliffe and Buchanan (1975). This should make plausible the assumption in Section III that the expert might indeed be able to understand these things sufficiently without having to deal with details of implementation. Note too that TEIRESIAS's basic design and the notion of interactive transfer of expertise does not depend on this particular control structure, only on the (non-trivial) assumption that an equally comprehensible explanation can be found for whatever control structure is actually used in the inference engine.

D. Performance program: an example

An example of the performance program is shown in Fig. 5. The dialog is directed primarily by the program, whose questions are for the most part multiple-choice style. The program in effect "interviews" the user about his present situation, and then prints its conclusion (see the article by Shortliffe in this volume for a more detailed example of the interactive facilities available in a consultation).

V. Explanation

A. Introduction

The fundamental goal of an explanation facility is to enable a program to display a comprehensible account of the motivation for all of its actions.

Investment Advisory Program

1) Investor's name?
**FRED SMITH

2) Age?
**40

3) Present taxable income?
**40,000

4) Number of dependants?
**5

5) Occupation?
**LAWYER

6) Amount of previous investment experience? (slight = less than one year; moderate = 2 to 4 years; extensive = more than 4 years)
**MODERATE

7) Does the investor subscribe to the Wall Street Journal, or any securities market newsletters?
**Y

.

.

.

{*This question and answer process continues until the performance program has collected all the information it requires in order to reach a conclusion.*}

The following investments appear to be the most appropriate at this time:

Varian-Corporation
American-Telephone-and-Telegraph

Fig. 5

This section explores steps taken toward this goal, examining the extent to which "all" actions of a program can be explained. It considers what is required for a "comprehensible" account and offers a framework in which to understand "motivations" for one particular system.

The utility of an explanation facility should be clear. Even for an experienced programmer, the attempt to account for program behaviour by hand simulation is difficult for any sizeable program. It is often difficult enough to discover how a program got to where it is. Trying to account for past behaviour (e.g. function calls that have long since existed) is often impossible because critical variables have been overwritten.

For consultation programs, in particular, the problem of explanation is worse because they deal with an audience assumed to know nothing about programming. This requires a different standard of comprehensibility, one defined in terms of the application domain rather than the language of computation. A naive user (e.g. a student) should find the explanations educational; a more experienced user should find them reassuring, employing them to satisfy himself that the conclusions the system has reached are based on acceptable reasoning; an expert should find them useful in discovering gaps or errors in the knowledge base. We describe below how each of these objectives is accomplished.

This section begins by outlining and discussing the plausibility of the fundamental assumptions behind the techniques used in TEIRESIAS. This is followed by several examples of the capabilities that have been developed and a description of how they are achieved. Finally, as a prelude to knowledge acquisition, we end by exploring how TEIRESIAS may be used to discover the source of problems in the knowledge base of the performance program.

B. Basic assumptions

The techniques used in TEIRESIAS for generating explanations are based on a number of assumptions about the system being explained. These assumptions are reviewed here to help motivate what follows and to characterize their range of applicability.

1. Generalities: two assumptions

We assume, first, that a recap of program actions can be an effective explanation as long as the correct level of detail is chosen. This assumption simplifies the task considerably, because it means that the solution requires only the ability to record and play back a history of events. In particular, it rules out any need to simplify those events.

But this assumption is perhaps the source of greatest limitation as well. It is not obvious, for instance, that an appropriate level of detail can always be found. A large program with cooperating parallel processes might prove sufficiently complex that it required a sophisticated interpretation and simplification to be comprehensible. Neither is it obvious how this approach can be applied to programs that are primarily numeric. With a program that does symbolic reasoning, recapping offers an easily understood explanation. But simply recapping the arithmetic involved in determining parameters of a complex electrical network, for example, would explain little of the reasoning involved and would teach little physics. Understanding it requires a much higher level of sophistication: it assumes that the viewer can interpret each numeric step in symbolic terms. The lack of any mechanism for either simplifying or reinterpreting computations means our approach is basically a first order solution to the general problem of explaining program behaviour.

If a simple recap is going to be effective, there must be several constraints on the level of detail chosen. It must be *detailed enough* that the operations it cites are comprehensible. For example, if a chess program were to explain a move with the justification that it "picked the best choice", the explanation would explain very little because it would not reveal what was involved in the operation of choosing. Some explanation in terms of alpha/beta search and evaluation functions might provide the relevant information.

The level must also be *high enough* that the operations are meaningful to the observer and that unnecessary detail is suppressed. Describing the chess program in terms of register-transfer operations, for instance, would lose any sense of task specificity and introduce pointless detail.

Finally, the explanation must be *complete enough* that the operations cited are sufficient to account for all behaviour. Completeness is easiest to achieve if the operations are free of side-effects and the system design is reasonably "clean". If the alpha/beta search used in the chess program had numerous subtle side-effects, it would be difficult to find a level of detail that could account for the side-effects without introducing other irrelevant information.

The second major assumption is that there exists some framework for viewing the program's actions that will allow them to be comprehensible to the observer. The likely validity of this assumption depends on both the program's fundamental mechanisms and the level at which these are examined. Consider a program that does medical diagnosis using a statistical approach based on Bayes' Theorem. It is difficult to imagine what explanation of its actions the program could give if it were queried while computing probabilities. No matter what level of detail is chosen, the approach is not (nor is it intended to be) an accurate model of the reasoning process typically employed by physicians (see Tversky and Kahneman (1974) for some experimental verification). As effective as these actions may be, there is no easy way to interpret them in terms that will make them comprehensible to a physician unacquainted with the program.

With the current state of the art, then, the desire to have a program capable of explaining its actions strongly constrains the methodology chosen and the control structure that can be used. There do not yet appear to be general principles for generating explanations of arbitrary control structures in the way, for example, that an experienced programmer can read unfamiliar code and then explain it to someone else. As a result, the capability cannot easily be tacked on to an existing performance program. To make the problem tractable, the desired capabilities must be taken into account early in the program-design process.

2. Specifics: how the assumptions were applied

The fundamental organization of the performance program described earlier provides an environment in which both of these assumptions can be satisfied. The simple AND/OR goal-tree control structure and the domain-specific rules invoked in a *modus ponens* mode offer a basis for explanations that typically need little additional clarification. The invocation of a rule is taken as the fundamental action of the system. This, along with the goal-tree as a framework, accounts for enough of the system's operation to make a recap of such actions an acceptable explanation. In terms of the constraints noted earlier, it is sufficiently detailed—the actions performed by a rule in making a "conclusion", for instance, correspond closely enough to the normal connotation of this word that no greater detail is necessary. It is still at an abstract enough level that the operations are meaningful. Finally, it is generally complete enough—there are typically no other mechanisms or sources of information that the observer needs to know in order to understand how the program reaches its conclusions.

The success of this technique relies to some extent on the claim that the performance program's approach to its domain is sufficiently intuitive that a summary of those actions is a reasonable basis for explanation. While we have not yet attempted to prove the claim in any formal sense, there are several factors that suggest its plausibility.

First, the performance program is dealing with a domain in which deduction, and deduction in the face of uncertainty, is a primary task. The use of production rules seems therefore to be a natural way of expressing things about the domain and the display of such rules should be comprehensible. Secondly, the use of such rules in a backward-chaining mode seems to be a reasonably intuitive scheme. *Modus ponens* is a well-understood and widely (if not explicitly) used mode of inference. Thus, the general form of the representation and the way it is employed should not be unfamiliar to the average user. More specifically, however, consider the source of the rules. They are supplied by human experts who were attempting to formalize their own knowledge of the domain. As such, the rules embody accepted patterns of human reasoning, implying that they should be relatively easy to understand, especially for those familiar with the domain. As such, they also attack the problem at what has been judged an appropriate level of detail. That is, they embody the right size "chunks" of the problem to be comprehensible.

Many of the capabilities of the current explanation system also depend on the stylized encoding of rules described in Section IVB. This makes possible, in particular, dissection and interpretation of the rules, techniques which form the basis for many of TEIRESIAS's capabilities.

We have referred several times to explanations that are "comprehensible" and "complete", which raises the questions "Comprehensible to whom?" and "Complete enough for whom?" As indicated, our efforts have been directed at users from the application domain. It is with respect to this audience that "comprehensible" and "complete" are used, and it is with respect to their conceptual level that appropriate explanations must be produced. While a different level would have to be chosen for a different audience (e.g. experienced programmers), the criteria above remain valid if the explanations are to be based on a recap of program actions.

C. Design criteria

There were three criteria central to the design of the explanation facilities.

Accuracy
Above all else, the explanations generated had to provide an accurate picture of what was going on in the performance program. This meant overcoming several temptations; in particular, the desire to "dress things up just a bit", to cover over some of the less impressive (or less transparent) aspects of the performance program's behaviour. If the facilities were to be an effective debugging tool, they had to be accurate.

Comprehensibility
Since computer consultants are intended for use by a non-programming audience, the explanations generated by TEIRESIAS had to be tailored accordingly. This meant restrictions on content and vocabulary and an emphasis on brevity. This criterion was the main source of the temptation to gloss over parts of the performance program's behaviour, to avoid having to justify in layman's terms the decisions that were based on computational considerations.

Human engineering
Consideration was also given to a collection of user-oriented factors like ease of use, power, and speed.

D. Basic ideas

The basic ideas behind the design of the explanation facilities can be viewed in terms of the four steps discussed below.

Determine the program operation that is to be viewed as primitive
This gives the smallest unit of program behaviour that can be explained. Examples further on will demonstrate that it is possible to generate different degrees of abstraction, but the level chosen in this step determines

the level of maximum detail. In our case, the invocation of an individual rule was selected as the primitive operation.

Augment the performance program code to leave behind a record of behaviour at this level of detail
The result is a complete trace of program behaviour, a history of performance. The relevant sections of the performance program's control structure (i.e. the inference engine) were augmented in this way to write a history of rule invocation attempts.

Select a global framework in which that trace can be understood
This framework is important especially where computationally naive users are concerned. The trace provides a record of behaviour, but the framework supplies a way of understanding that behaviour. Its selection is thus a central task in the construction of the facilities.

The framework was readily supplied by the performance program's control structure—the AND/OR goal-tree offered a natural perspective in which to view program behaviour and its explanation. The tracing task is structured in terms of tree traversal, and the user is offered a set of commands designed around it. The goal-tree view is of course specific to this particular control structure, but analogous frameworks are possible for other system designs.

Design a program that can provide the user with an interpretation of the trace
The program should be capable of systematic examination of the trace and should use the framework chosen to provide an interpretation of events recorded there. A body of code to do this forms the explanation program in TEIRESIAS and enables the user 'to examine the behaviour of the performance program. It interprets the trace in terms of the AND/OR goal-tree framework and provides a set of commands that allows the user to examine previous, current, or future (potential) behaviour.

These ideas form the foundation for the basic set of explanation capabilities. They are illustrated below with a number of annotated examples.

E. Example: explanations for performance validation and transparency

> Modern-day computers are amazing pieces of equipment, but most amazing of all are the uncertain grounds on account of which we attach any validity to their output. (Dijkstra, 1972)

We explore first the use of explanation as a means of validating system performance and a means of increasing transparency. We want to provide the user with a carefully designed probe for exploring the behaviour of the performance program. It should allow him to uncover the rationale behind the program's behaviour, to satisfy himself that it is indeed appropriate, yet it should shield him from drowning in a wealth of (to him) meaningless programming details.

Since explanation is viewed in terms of traversal of the AND/OR goal-tree, the command set is designed accordingly. The two basic commands are "WHY" and "HOW", corresponding to ascent and descent of the tree. It is the performance program's invocation of rules in a goal-directed fashion that makes tree traversal operations plausible interpretations of the commands.

Several annotated examples are given below, in this and subsequent sections. In each case, a single question from the consultation has been extracted and the explanation facilities have been used to examine the reasoning behind it. Figure 6 shows the part of the reasoning tree being examined in the first example.

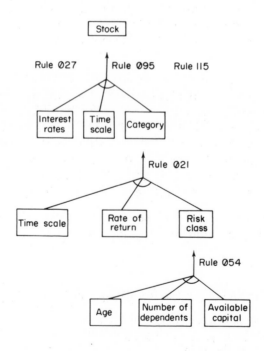

Fig. 6

In the trace below, computer output is in mixed upper and lower case in this font, user responses are in **BOLDFACE CAPITALS**, while annotations are indented in {*italics inside braces*}.

How much capital is available for investment?
★★ **WHY**
[i.e. Why is it important to determine the amount of capital available for investment?]

[1.∅] This will aid in determining what level of risk the investor can assume.
　　It has already been established that:
[1.1] the age of the client is between 35 and 4∅, and
[1.2] the number of dependants of the client is greater than 4, therefore, if:
[1.3] the amount of capital available for investment is less than $1∅,∅∅∅ then
there is suggestive evidence (.6) that the risk class of the investment should be
　　moderate.
[RULE∅54]

　　{*As Figure 6 shows, the issue of "amount of available capital" is one subgoal, "risk class of the investment" is another at the next level up, and rule 54 links them. The "reason" for asking the original question, then, is to invoke rule 54 to determine the higher subgoal, and the answer to "why" is simply a display of the goals and the rule linking them.*
　　　Considerable attention has been paid to making this as lucid a display as possible. First, since "why" has several other interpretations and no more extensive natural language capabilities are available, the question is expanded by TEIRESIAS *to indicate the sense in which it will be answered. The higher level goal is then presented, followed by the rule. The premises of the rule are divided into those already established and those yet to be determined using a partial evaluation of the rule (this mechanism is described in detail in Davis and Lenat (1981; Davis et al., 1977)).*}

★★ **WHY**
　　{*Further sections of the reasoning chain can be examined by repeating the command.*}

[i.e. Why is it important to find out what level of the risk the investor can assume?]

[2.∅] ... in order to find out the category of the stock to invest in.
　　It has already been established that:
[2.1] the time-scale of the investment is long-term, and
[2.2] the desired rate of return is greater than 1∅%,
　　therefore, if:
[2.3] the level of risk the investor can assume is moderate,
　　then
there is strong evidence (.8) that the category of the stock to invest in is income-stocks.
[RULE∅21]

** **WHY**
[i.e. Why is it important to determine the category of the stock to invest in?]
[3.0] ... in order to find out what stock to choose.
      It has already been established that:
[3.1] the current interest rates are high, and
[3.2] the time-scale of the investment is long-term,
      therefore, if:
[3.3] the category of the stock to invest in is income-stocks,
      then
there is suggestive evidence (.6) that Pacific Gas and Electric is a likely choice for
the investment.
[RULE095]

** **HOW [3.0]**
      {*How can be used to climb "down" the reasoning chain and gives a picture of all
      the ways any subgoal may be achieved. In the examples demonstrating its use,
      numbers following the command refer to the corresponding items above (e.g. the
      [3.0] above).*}
[i.e. How were you determining what stock to choose?]
[4.0] At that point RULE095 was being used. In addition,
[4.1] RULE027 was used to conclude that AT&T is a likely (.4) choice for the
      investment,
[4.2] RULE115 will be tried later, as well.
      {*Once again the question is underspecified and is expanded by* TEIRESIAS.
      *Note that the system can indicate reasoning chains previously followed, those
      currently being examined, and those yet to be tried. Each can be further
      explored.*}

** **HOW [4.1]**
[i.e. How was RULE027 used?]
[5.0] It has already been established that:
[5.1] the time-scale of the investment is long-term,
[5.2] the desired rate of return on the investment is greater than 10%, and
[5.3] the area of the investment is not known,
      Therefore,
it is likely (.4) that AT&T is a good choice for the investment.
[RULE027]

** **HOW [4.2]**
[i.e. How will RULE115 be used?]
If [6.0] the category of the stock is income-stocks, and
      [6.1] disposable personal income is keeping pace with inflation, then there is
evidence (.5) that GM is a likely choice for the investment. [RULE115]

F. The need for an information metric

[In an explanation] we must not carry reasoning too far back, or the length of
our argument will cause obscurity; neither must we put in all the steps that

lead to our conclusion, or we shall waste words in saying what is manifest. (Aristotle, 1926)

One problem anticipated in the use of the WHY command, and one that is common to explanations in general, is the issue of an appropriate level of sophistication and detail. It is generally of little use to discover that

If: 1) The price-earnings ratio (P/E) of the stock is low, and
    2) The category of the stock is growth-stocks
Then: Is it definite (1.∅) that the class of the stock is low P/E-growth.

Fig. 7. RULE14∅.

Depending on the individual user, it might be best to display all steps in a reasoning chain, to omit those that are definitional or trivial, or, for the most sophisticated user, to display only the highlights. This presumes that we have some idea of what constitutes "the details". In terms of the goal-tree, it means knowing how "far" it is conceptually from one node to another, which is difficult since this depends very much on the (constantly changing) state of the user's knowledge. It is also very important since the best explanations are those based on a clear understanding of the extent of the user's comprehension.

In a very rough analogy to information theory, we use the log of the certainty factor $-(\log CF)$ to provide this measure. Definitional rules (with $CF = 1 \cdot 0$) thus have no information, while those with smaller CFs have progressively more. This is clearly imperfect. It does not take into account the state of the user's knowledge, and since CFs are not probabilities there is no formal justification that $-(\log CF)$ is a meaningful number. It's primary utility, however, is as a "dial" with which the user can adjust the level of detail in the explanations. Absolute settings are less important than the ability to make relative adjustments.

The adjustment is made via an optional argument to the WHY command. The entire "distance" from the current node to the top of the goal-tree is normalized to 10, and the argument following the WHY is taken as some fraction of that distance. Thus, rather than the multiple WHYs seen above, the user might have asked "WHY 4":

How much capital is available for investment?
** **WHY 4**

We are trying to find out how much capital is available for investment in order to determine what stock to invest in.

Fig. 8. A "high-level" explanation.

Since the three steps in the chain shown in Fig. 5 constitute roughly two-fifths of the "distance" to the top, they are compressed into a single answer. This command may be repeated as often as necessary, allowing the user to follow the reasoning chain in step sizes of his own choosing.

The user may occasionally choose a step size that is too big, compressing too many steps into a single answer, leaving him with an incomprehensible explanation. In this case he can invoke the EXPLAIN command, which will cover the same starting and ending points in the reasoning, but in more detail. Thus, if the explanation in Fig. 8 above proved to be too obscure, the user might say EXPLAIN and have it expanded out in complete detail. He might also say EXPLAIN 2, to have it expanded out in steps roughly half as big (the argument has the same meaning for both the WHY and EXPLAIN commands).

G. Example: explanations for debugging

Early work on giving a program the ability to explain its actions (Shortliffe *et al.*, 1975) was originally motivated by concerns about acceptibility: consultation programs are unlikely to be accepted by users if they function as "black boxes" that simply print their final answers. Much of the work described above is similar in spirit.

But there is another, different, and very useful application of explanation: program debugging, in particular as a means of setting an appropriate context for knowledge acquisition. One of the options TEIRESIAS offers the expert is having the performance program stop after it has presented its conclusions, to give the expert a chance to comment on them. This pause provides a natural starting place for evaluation and debugging. Once the bug is found, the acquisition process then allows the expert to repair the problem by teaching the performance program the new rule.

In the interaction shown below, an expert is challenging the investment advisory program with a particular case, observing the program's performance, and then using TEIRESIAS's explanation facilities to track down the source of an error. (The bug encountered here was created by deleting an existing rule from the knowledge base and removing all references to it. While the deleted rule was chosen to make possible an example that displays a large number of TEIRESIAS's capabilities in a single example, it is special in no other sense, however, and offers a real trace of the system in action.)

This example will be continued in Section VIB, where we will see how the expert repairs the bug by teaching the system the "new" rule.

Investment Advisory Program

User?

** **RD**

Hello, Randy.

> {*The expert identifies himself to the program, and then, responding to the program's enquiries, describes a particular case as a test of performance. This is the beginning of the example we saw in Fig. 5 earlier.*}

1) Investor's name?

****FRED SMITH**

2) Age?

****40**

3) Present taxable income?

****40,000**

4) Number of dependants?

****5**

5) Occupation?

****LAWYER**

6) Amount of previous investment experience? (slight = less than one year; moderate = 2 to 4 years; extensive = more than 4 years)

****MODERATE**

.

.

.

> {*Most of the consultation with the performance program has been edited out for brevity (see Davis and Lenat (1981) for a complete example). The interaction continues with the program printing out its conclusions.*}

The following investments appear to be the most appropriate at this time:

Varian-Corporation

American-Telephone-and-Telegraph

> {*At this point* TEIRESIAS *steps in, and since the interaction is with an expert (rather than an ordinary user), it requests an evaluation of the performance program's results.*
>
> *From here on the dialog takes place between* TEIRESIAS *and the expert, with the performance program in the background being manipulated by* TEIRESIAS. *The expert indicates that the results are incorrect ...*}

Are all these correct?

++** **N**

> {*... and then specifies the problems.*}

Are there any missing?

++** **Y**

Which one(s)?

++⋆⋆ **DIGITAL-EQUIPMENT DATA-GENERAL**

Are there any that shouldn't have appeared?

++⋆⋆ **Y**

Which one(s)?

++⋆⋆ **AT&T**

Do you want to

    1] track down the problem yourself, or

    2] allow me to guide the debugging, or

    3] ignore it for now and fix it another time?

Type 1, 2 or 3

++⋆⋆ **2**

> {*The first option allows the expert to use the explanation facilities described earlier (Section VE) to track down the problem. The facility indicated by the second option is based on a model of the control structure of the performance program that allows a simple algorithmic search for the error, and will be demonstrated here. The third is for human engineering purposes, and allows the expert to sidestep this whole process if desired.*}

We'll start with the AT&T first.

> {*Heuristics derived from our experience in debugging rule-based systems are built into* TEIRESIAS. *One such heuristic suggests that the best approach is to (1) track down one problem at a time, and (2) start with a result that should not have appeared (if there is one). Experience indicates that this class of bug is often a manifestation of a deeper bug causing several problems, so curing it will often solve several problems at once.*}

The following rules were used in deducing that the investment should be AT&T:

RULE027

Since [1.1] the area of the investment is not known, and

       [1.2] the desired return on the investment is greater than 10%, and

       [1.3] the time-scale of the investment is long-term,

then AT&T is a likely (.4) choice for the investment.

Is this rule correct?

++⋆⋆ **Y**

Should its premise have failed for this case?

++⋆⋆ **Y**

Which clause of the premise should have been false? [give #]

++⋆⋆ **1**

> {*The expert indicates that this rule should have failed, so the debugging continues by looking further back in the chain. Had he indicated that rule 27 had been invoked properly, then* TEIRESIAS *would have indicated that the problem was probably a missing rule which tended to* rule out *AT&T.*}

No conclusions were reached concerning the area of the investment.

Should it have been possible to conclude an area?
++ Y

> {*The error might have been a failure to rule out an investment area.*}

Which one?
++ **HIGH TECHNOLOGY**

There were no rules successfully invoked in the attempt to deduce that the area of the investment should be high-technology.

The following (potentially applicable) rules were NOT executed because the starred [**] clause failed:

RULE116

If   1) the desired return on the investment is greater than 1∅%,
     2) the time-scale of the investment is long-term,
 ** 3) the number of dependants of the client is less than 3, **
     4) the age (in years) of the client is less than or equal to 35
then there is evidence (.4) that the area of the investment should be high-technology

RULE∅5∅

If   1) the time-scale of the investment is long-term,
     2) the desired return on the investment is greater than 1∅%,
 ** 3) the risk class of the investment is speculative **
then there is evidence (.6) that the area of the investment should be high-technology

Are all these rules correct?
++ Y

Should any of them have been successfully invoked?
++ N

> {*This would have been the case if one of the starred premise clauses were false because it was "stepped on" by yet another rule further back in the chain.*}

Is there a rule missing?
++ Y

Ok, then I need a rule that would allow me to deduce that the area of the investment should be high-technology.

Would you like to give me such a rule now?
++ Y

Good ...

> {*To review briefly: the expert is tracking down the reason why the system incorrectly concluded that the stock to invest in was AT&T. Shown below is the sequence of rules which were involved:*}

```
RETURN
TIME SCALE
★★DEPENDANTS★★
  AGE                ==== RULE116 ====>|
                                       |→AREA
  TIME SCALE         ==== RULE050 ====>|  RETURN === RULE027 ===> AT&T
  RETURN                                  TIME SCALE
★★RISK CLASS★★
```

AT&T appeared because the system executed rule 27 successfully.

This occurred in part because investment area was unknown.

Investment area was unknown because all rules to conclude it (rules 50 and 116) failed.

Since the expert believes all existing rules are correct, the knowledge base must be missing a rule that will conclude about investment area, in particular, that the area should be high-technology. Such a rule will cause area to be known, inhibiting rule 27, fixing at least this first problem.

Note how sharply focused the issue has become, for both the expert and TEIRESIAS, *as a result of the large amount of contextual information available. The expert is not being asked to "discuss the stock market"; instead the system can at this point say*

... I need a rule that would allow me to deduce that the area of the investment should be high-technology.

and it must be a rule which is invokable in the current situation. Thus it is easier for the expert to specify a rule that may never before have been explicitly stated or recognized as such. This can be an important advantage in any domain where the knowledge is not yet fully formalized.

The contextual information is useful for TEIRESIAS *as well. The information provides a number of expectations about the content of the rule which are used both in understanding what the expert types in, and in checking the new rule to make sure that it does indeed solve the problem at hand. Details of this process are explained in Section VIB, where the example is continued.}*

★★★

To provide the debugging facility shown, TEIRESIAS maintains a detailed record of the actions taken by the performance program during the consultation, and then interprets this record on the basis of an exhaustive analysis of the performance program's control structure. This presents the expert with a comprehensible task because (a) the backward-chaining technique used by the performance program is sufficiently straightforward and intuitive, even to a non-programmer; and (b) the rules are designed to encode knowledge at a reasonably high conceptual level. As a result, even though TEIRESIAS is running through an exhaustive case-by-case analysis of the preceding consultation, the expert is presented with a task of debugging *reasoning* rather than *code*.

The availability of an algorithmic debugging process is also an important factor in encouraging the expert to be as precise as possible in his responses. Note that at each point in tracking down the error the expert must either approve of the rules invoked and conclusions made, or indicate which one was in error and supply the correction.* This is extremely useful in domains where knowledge has not yet been formalized, and the traditional reductionist approach of dissecting reasoning down to observational primitives is not yet well established.

TEIRESIAS further encourages precise comments by keeping the debugging process sharply focused. For instance, when it became clear that there was a problem with the inability to deduce investment area, the system first asks which area it should have been. It then displays only those rules appropriate to that answer, rather than all of the rules on that topic which were tried.

Finally, consider the extensive amount of contextual information that is now available. The expert has been presented with a detailed example of the performance program in action, he has available all of the facts of the case, and has seen how the relevant knowledge has been applied. This makes it much easier for him to specify the particular chunk of knowledge which may be missing. This contextual information will prove very useful for TEIRESIAS as well. It is clear, for instance, what the *effect* of invocation of the new rule must be (as TEIRESIAS indicates, it must be a rule that will "deduce that the area of the investment should be high-technology"), and it is also clear what the *circumstances* of its invocation must be (the rule must be invokable for the case under consideration, or it will not repair the bug). Both of these will be seen to be quite useful (see Sections VIB, F).

VI. Knowledge acquisition

A. Overview of the main ideas

Having tracked down the shortcoming in the knowledge base, the expert's next step is to teach the system the appropriate rule to fix the problem. We will see how this works in Section VIB, which continues the example of the previous section.

Before continuing with that example, however, we describe briefly the

---

* The debugging process does allow the expert to indicate that while the performance program's results are incorrect, he cannot find an error in the reasoning. This choice is offered only as a last resort and is intended to deal with situations where there may be a bug in the underlying control structure of the performance program (contrary to our assumption in Section III).

ideas which make possible the capabilities to be displayed. The list below serves primarily to name and briefly sketch each in turn; the details are supplied in reviewing the example.

1. Knowledge acquisition in context

Performance programs of the sort TEIRESIAS helps create will typically find their greatest utility in domains where there are no unifying laws on which to base algorithmic methods. In such domains there is instead a collection of informal knowledge based on accumulated experience. This means an expert specifying a new rule may be codifying a piece of knowledge that has never previously been isolated and expressed as such. Since this is difficult, anything which can be done to ease the task will prove very useful.

In response, we have emphasized knowledge acquisition in the context of a shortcoming in the knowledge base. To illustrate its utility, consider the difference between asking the expert

What should I know about the stock market?

and saying to him

Here is an example in which you say the performance program made a mistake. Here is all the knowledge the program used, here are all the facts of the case, and here is how it reached its conclusions. Now, what is it that you know and the system doesn't that allows you to avoid making that same mistake?

Note how much more focused the second question is, and how much easier it is to answer.

2. Building expectations

The focusing provided by the context is also an important aid to TEIRESIAS. In particular, it permits the system to build up a set of expectations concerning the knowledge to be acquired, facilitating knowledge transfer and making possible several useful features illustrated in the trace and described below.

3. Model-based understanding

Model-based understanding suggests that some aspects of understanding can be viewed as a process of matching: the entity to be understood is matched against a collection of prototypes, or models, and the most appropriate model selected. This sets the framework in which further interpretation takes place, as that model can then be used as a guide to further processing.

While this view is not new, TEIRESIAS employs a novel application of it, since the system has a model of the knowledge it is likely to be acquiring from the expert.

4. The intersection of data-driven and goal-driven processing

The process of interpreting the expert's new rule proceeds in what has been called the "recognition" mode: it is the intersection of a bottom-up (data-directed) process (the interpretations suggested by the connotations of the text) with a top-down (goal-directed) process (the expectations set up by the choice of a model). Each process contributes to the end result, but it is the combination of them that is effective.

This intersection of two processing modes is important where the interpretation techniques are as simple as those employed here, but the idea is more generally applicable as well. Even with more powerful interpretation techniques, neither direction of processing is in general capable of eliminating all ambiguity and finding the correct answer. By moving both top-down and bottom-up, we make use of all available sources of information, resulting in a far more focused search for the answer. This technique is applicable across a range of different interpretation problems, including text, vision and speech.

5. Multiple knowledge sources

In either direction of processing, TEIRESIAS uses a number of different sources of knowledge. Any one of these sources alone will not perform very well, but acting in concert they are much more effective (a principle developed extensively in Reddy (1973)).

They are listed and described briefly below; their use is explored in more detail in the sections that follow. Since much of the interpretation process can be viewed in terms of forming hypotheses (interpretations) from a set of data (the text), each knowledge source is also labelled in these terms.

(a) Data-driven knowledge source

Connotations of individual words (data interpretation). As explained in more detail below, each English word may have associated with it a number of connotations. These indicate attributes, objects, values, or predicate functions to which the word may plausibly be referring.

Degree of ambiguity of individual words (ambiguity of the data). This is used to constrain the search for an interpretation of the text.

Function template (structure of the hypothesis). There is associated with each predicate function a template indicating the order and generic type of its arguments, much like a simplified procedure declaration. Generating code is essentially a process of filling in this template; it thus provides a primary source of direction for the interpretation process.

Degree of success of the template completion process (degree of success of hypothesis construction). The expert may be terse enough in his rule statement that the contents of certain slots in the template must be inferred rather than sought in the text. Such inferences are made with different degrees of confidence.

Consistency of meaning assignment (consistency of data interpretation). Where ambiguity exists, several plausible interpretations of a clause may arise; the appropriate book-keeping is done to assure that each word is understood in only one way for any given interpretation.

Accounting for all words in the text (accounting for all the data). Preference is given to those interpretations that leave fewer words unaccounted for in a line of text.

Consistency of attribute, object, and value interrelationships (internal consistency of hypothesis structure). This is used in several ways. For instance, in assembling an interpretation, ambiguity can sometimes be resolved simply by restricting interpretation to syntactically valid triples (e.g. there may be several attributes and values suggested by the text, but perhaps only one of the possible pairings is syntactically valid). Also, knowing one of the three may help guide the search for another (e.g. if the attribute is known or postulated, then TEIRESIAS can refer to it to determine the appropriate kinds of values to seek).

(b) Expectation-driven knowledge sources

The model. As noted above, a model chosen during debugging is used as a source of advice (or hints) about the possible content of the new rule.

B. Example: knowledge acquisition

We continue now with the example begun in the previous section, and take up again at the point where the expert was about to type in the new rule. The rest of the example is divided into four phases for later reference.

```
**********
{PHASE I: interpreting the rule}
**********
```
Would you like to give me such a rule now?
   ++** **Y**
Good ...

The new rule will be called RULE383

If: 1 — **THE CLIENT'S INCOME TAX BRACKET IS** 50%
   and 2 — **THE CLIENT IS FOLLOWING UP ON MARKET TRENDS CAREFULLY**
   and 3 —
Then: 1 — **THERE IS EVIDENCE (.8) THAT THE INVESTMENT AREA SHOULD BE HIGH TECHNOLOGY**
   and 2 —

This may take a few moments ...

{*Generally in the order of 10 to 30 seconds of cpu time.*}

This is my understanding of your rule:
RULE383

If   1) The client's income-tax bracket is 50%, and
     2) The market has followed an upward trend recently, and
     3) The client manages his assets carefully
Then   there is evidence (.8) that the area of the investment should be high-technology

{*TEIRESIAS's initial interpretation is not entirely correct (and the example was chosen in part for this reason). The first line of text and the conclusion have been interpreted correctly, but the second line has been turned into two clauses (numbers 2 and 3) in the system's initial attempt at understanding. (The expert occasionally types what should be two separate clauses as one line of text. The system is capable of handling this, but this same capability at times produces spurious clauses like #3).*

This results primarily from the system's simple word-by-word approach to meaning. While the result is in part incorrect, it will become clear below that the interpretations are both "reasonable" and "consistent" in light of the techniques used.}

****
{**PHASE II: modifying the interpretation**}
****
Okay? (Yes or No)
++** **N**

{*The expert indicates there is a problem with the interpretation, and uses TEIRESIAS's rule editor to specify the changes needed.*}

Change premise?
   ++** **Y**

What clause should be changed in premise? (type HELP for list of commands)
++** **CHANGE 2**

Suppose (2) were changed to read-
     2 — The client follows the market carefully
Would that be ok?
++** **Y**

{*Several simple heuristics are invoked to select the next most likely interpretation, based on the English source of this clause and the set of interpretations already rejected. In this case the second choice is correct.*}

Then you'll probably want to delete:
3) The client manages his assets carefully
Correct?
++★★ **Y**

{TEIRESIAS *enforces certain consistency constraints on its interpretation of the English text. One of these constraints indicates that if the new interpretation of clause # 2 is correct, then clause # 3 must have arisen spuriously (because, among other things, it requires a different interpretation for the word carefully).*}

Anything else?
++★★ **?**
1 — the client's income-tax bracket is 5∅%
and 2 — the client follows the market carefully
and 3 —   < deleted >

Anything else?
++★★ **N**

Change action?
++★★ **N**

This is my understanding of your rule:
RULE383

If: 1) the client's income-tax bracket is 5∅%, and
       2) the client follows the market carefully,
Then: there is evidence (.8) that the area of the investment should be high-
       technology.

Okay? (Yes or No)
++★★ **Y**

{*This is the standard test of comprehension : the original English text has been turned into a rule coded in* LISP, *and is then retranslated back into English for approval. Compare the results with the expert's original input. Now that the expert is satisfied that* TEIRESIAS *understands the rule that he entered,* TEIRESIAS *checks several things about the rule to see if* <u>it</u> *is satisfied with the rule content.*}

★★★★★★★★★★
{**PHASE III: "second guessing"**}
★★★★★★★★★★
I hate to criticize, Randy, but did you know that most rules about what the area of an investment might be, that mention—
       the income-tax bracket of the client, and
       how closely the client follows the market

ALSO mention—

    [A] — the amount of investment experience of the client

Shall I try to write a clause to account for [A] ?

++★★ **Y**

> {*The mechanism that makes possible this sort of "second guessing" by* TEIRESIAS *is explained in detail below. Briefly,* TEIRESIAS *maintains a model of the information in the knowledge base. In checking to see how this new piece of information "fits in" to that model, it discovers that its expectations have been only partially met. It indicates to the expert what expectations were left unfulfilled, and asks if it should attempt to fill in the missing parts.*}

How about—

    [A]   The amount of investment experience of the client is moderate

Ok?

++★★ **Y**

> {*The expert agreed to the inclusion of the new clause and* TEIRESIAS *is able to construct a plausible guess as to its content. Note that it must be possible to invoke the new rule in the current situation, in order to fix the known bug.* TEIRESIAS *used this fact to guide its construction of the new clause. Details of this process are explained below.*}

Also, most rules about what the area of an investment might be ALSO conclude about—

    [A] — the desired risk classification of the investment

Shall I try to write a clause to account for [A] ?

++★★ **N**

> {*The system noticed another unfulfilled expectation concerning the action part of the rule, but the expert always has the option of overriding the system's suggestions, and does so.*}

★★★★★★★★★★

{**PHASE IV: final checkout, bookkeeping, rerunning the consultation**}

★★★★★★★★★★

The rule now reads:

RULE383

    If: 1) the income-tax bracket of the client is 50%, and,

          2) the client follows the market carefully, and

          3) the amount of investment experience of the client is moderate

    Then: there is evidence (.8) that the area of the investment should be high-technology.

Please describe briefly why you added (or changed) this rule.

Type an empty line when done.

++★★**THE SYSTEM FAILED TO REALIZE IT COULD CONCLUDE INVESTMENT**

++**AREA, AND THIS ALLOWED RULE027 TO BE INVOKED INAPPROPRIATELY**
++**

{Experience suggests that in building any large knowledge base it is very useful to keep fairly detailed records about the source of various contributions. The new rule is automatically tagged with a range of such information (including author, date, and a record of the consultation which prompted its creation), along with any comments which the expert may care to make for his own future reference.}

RULE383 has now been added to the knowledge base.

I will now rerun the consultation to check the effectiveness of your new rule. Get comfortable, since this may take a bit.

Also, new questions may be asked as a result of this new rule. If a question is printed, please answer it with reference to this current client.

.
.
.

{The consultation is then rerun, but all the previous answers are saved, so the expert can in most cases just watch it proceed. This has been edited out here for brevity.}

The following investments appear to be the most appropriate at this time:

Varian-Corporation
Data-General
Digital-Equipment

Well, it appears that things are straightened out.

{The new conclusions are the ones the expert indicated earlier as the correct answers. This does not go unnoticed.}

Are all these values correct now?
++** **Y**

{As always, however, the expert gets the last word, and TEIRESIAS waits for approval before proceeding.}

Good, then the problem's been fixed.

{How is it that three errors disappeared with the addition of one rule? This is explained schematically below:

★ RULE116 ★
★ RULE050 ★
RULE383 ========> AREA ==== ★ RULE027 ★ ===> AT&T
                           ====   RULE084   ===> DATA-
                                                   GENERAL
                                                   DIGITAL-
                                                   EQUIPMENT

As before, rules 116 and 50 failed (hence the ★★'s), but now the new rule, 383, has succeeded, supplying a value for investment area. This in turn means that rule 27 now fails, as hoped.

*However, rule 84, which requires a value of area, failed last time because the
system was unable to deduce one. Now that rule 383 supplies one, rule 84 can fire,
and it turns out to yield the missing answers.*}

C. Phase I: interpreting the rule

As is traditional, "understanding" the expert's natural language version of
the rule is viewed in terms of converting it to an internal representation,
and then retranslating that into English for the expert's approval. In this
case the internal representation is the INTERLISP form of the rule, so the
process is also a simple type of code generation.

There were a number of reasons for rejecting a standard natural language
understanding approach to this problem. First, of course, understanding
natural language is well known to be a difficult problem, and was not a
central focus of this research. Secondly, our experience suggested that
experts frequently sacrifice precise grammar in favour of the compactness
available in the technical language of the domain. As a result, approaches
that were strongly grammar-based might not fare well. Finally, technical
language often contains a fairly high percentage of unambiguous words, so
a more simple approach that includes reliance on keyword analysis has a
good chance of performing adequately.

As will become clear, our approach to analysing the expert's new rule is
based on both simple keyword spotting and predictions TEIRESIAS is
able to make about the likely content of the rule. Code generation is
accomplished via a form of template completion that is similar in some
respects to template completion processes that have been used in generating natural language. Details of all these processes are given below.

1. Models and model-based understanding

To set the stage for reviewing the details of the interpretation process, we
digress for a moment to consider the idea of models and model-based
understanding, then explore their application in TEIRESIAS.

In the most general terms, a model can be seen as *a compact, high-level
description of structure, organization, or content* that may be used both to
provide a framework for lower-level processing, and *to express expectations
about the world.* One particularly graphic example of this idea can be found
in the work on computer vision by Falk in 1970. The task there was
the standard one of understanding blocks-world scenes: the goal was to
determine the identity, location, and orientation of each block in a scene
containing one or more blocks selected from a known set of possibilities.

The key element of his work of interest here is the use of a set of
prototypes for the blocks, prototypes that resembled wire frame models.
While it oversimplifies slightly, part of the operation of his system can be

described in terms of two phases. The system first performed a preliminary pass to detect possible edge points in the scene and attempted to fit a block model to each collection of edges. The model chosen was then used in the second phase as a guide to further processing. If, for instance, the model accounted for all but one of the lines in a region, this suggested that the extra line might be spurious. If the model fit well except for some line missing from the scene, that was a good indication that a line had been overlooked and indicated as well where to go looking for it.

While it was not a part of Falk's system, we can imagine one further refinement in the interpretation process and explain it in these same terms. Imagine that the system had available some *a priori* hints about what blocks might be found in the next scene. One way to express those hints would be to bias the matching process. That is, in the attempt to match a model against the data, the system might (depending on the strength of the hint) try the indicated models first, make a greater attempt to effect a match with one of them, or even restrict the set of possibilities to just those contained in the hint.

Note that in this system: (i) the models supply a compact, high-level description of structure (the structure of each block); (ii) the description is used to guide lower-level processing (processing of the array of digitized intensity values); (iii) expectations can be expressed by a biasing or restriction on the set of models used; and (iv) "understanding" is viewed in terms of a matching and selection process (matching models against the data and selecting one that fits).

2. Rule models

Now recall our original task of interpreting the expert's natural language version of the rule, and view it in the terms described above. As in the vision example, there is a signal to be processed (the text), it is noisy (words can be ambiguous), and there is context available (from the debugging process) that can supply some hints about the likely content of the signal. To complete the analogy, we need a model, one that could (a) capture the structure, organization, or content of the expert's reasoning, (b) be used to guide the interpretation process, and (c) be used to express expectations about the likely content of the new rule.

Where might we get such a thing? There are interesting regularities in the knowledge base that might supply what we need. Not surprisingly, rules about a single topic tend to have characteristics in common—there are "ways" of reasoning about a given topic. From these regularities we have constructed *rule models*. These are abstract descriptions of subsets of rules, built from empirical generalizations about those rules, and are used to characterize a "typical" member of the subset.

EXAMPLES	the subset of rules which this model describes
DESCRIPTION	characterization of a "typical" member of this subset
	characterization of the premise
	characterization of the action
	which attributes "typically" appear
	correlations of attributes
MORE GENERAL	pointers to models describing more general
MORE SPECIFIC	and more specific subsets of rules

Fig. 9

Rule models are composed of four parts (Fig. 9). They contain, first, a list of EXAMPLES, the subset of rules from which this model was constructed. Next, a DESCRIPTION characterizes a typical member of the subset. Since we are dealing in this case with rules composed of premise-action pairs, the DESCRIPTION currently implemented contains individual characterizations of a typical premise and a typical action. Then, because the current representation scheme used in those rules is based on associative triples, we have chosen to implement those characterizations by indicating (a) which attributes "typically" appear in the premise (action) of a rule in this subset, and (b) correlations of attributes appearing in the premise (action). (Both (a) and (b) are formed via simple statistical thresholding techniques, described in more detail in Davis and Lenat (1981).)

Note that the central idea is the concept of *characterizing a typical member of the subset*. Naturally, that characterization would look different for subsets of rules, procedures, theorems, or any other representation. But the main idea of characterization is widely applicable and not restricted to any particular representational formalism.

The two remaining parts of the rule model are pointers to models describing more general and more specific subsets of rules. The set of models is organized into a number of tree structures, each of the general form shown in Fig. 10. At the root of each tree is the model made from all

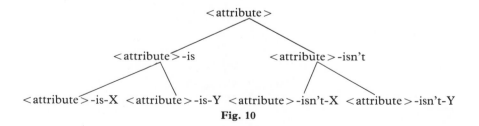

Fig. 10

the rules which conclude about <attribute> (e.g. the INVESTMENT-AREA model), below this are two models dealing with all affirmative and all negative rules (e.g. the INVESTMENT-AREA-IS model), and below this are models dealing with rules which affirm or deny specific values of the attribute.

These models are not hand-tooled by the expert. They are instead assembled by TEIRESIAS on the basis of the current contents of the knowledge base, in what amounts to a very simple (i.e. statistical) form of concept formation. The combination of TEIRESIAS and the performance program thus presents a system which has a model of its own knowledge, one which it forms itself.

Figure 11 shows a rule model; this is the one used by TEIRESIAS in the interaction shown earlier. (Since not all of the details of implementation are relevant here, this discussion will omit some. See Davis and Lenat (1981) for a full explanation.) As indicated above, there is a list of rules from which this model was constructed, descriptions characterizing the premise and the action, and pointers to more specific and more general models. Each

INVESTMENT-AREA-IS

EXAMPLES   (RULE116 .3)
              (RULE050 .7)
              (RULE037 .8)
              (RULE095 .9)
              (RULE152 1.0)
              (RULE140 1.0))

DESCRIPTION
  PREMISE   ((RETURNRATE SAME NOTSAME 3.8)
              (TIMESCALE SAME NOTSAME 3.8)
              (TREND SAME 2.8)

              ((RETURNRATE SAME) (TIMESCALE SAME) 3.8)
              ((TIMESCALE SAME) (RETURNRATE SAME) 3.8)
              ((BRACKET SAME) (FOLLOWS NOTSAME SAME)
                              (EXPERIENCE SAME) 1.5))

  ACTION   ((INVESTMENT-AREA CONCLUDE 4.7)
              (RISK CONCLUDE 4.0)

              ((INVESTMENT-AREA CONCLUDE)
              (RISK CONCLUDE) 4.7))

MORE-GENL   (INVESTMENT-AREA)
MORE-SPEC   (INVESTMENT-AREA-IS-UTILITIES)
                      Fig. 11

characterization in the description is shown split into its two parts, one concerning the presence of individual attributes and the other describing correlations. The first item in the premise description, for instance, indicates that "most" rules about what the area of an investment should be mention the attribute *rate of return* in their premise; when they do mention it they "typically" use the predicate functions SAME and NOTSAME; and the "strength" or reliability of this piece of advice is 3·8 (see Davis and Lenat (1981) for precise definitions of the quoted terms).

The fourth item in the premise description indicates that when the attribute *rate of return* appears in the premise of a rule in this subset, the attribute *timescale of the investment* "typically" appears as well. As before, the predicate functions are those typically associated with the attributes, and the number is an indication of reliability.

3. Choosing a model

It was noted earlier that tracking down the bug in the knowledge base provides useful context, and, among other things, serves to set up TEIRESIAS's expectations about the sort of rule it is about to receive. As suggested, these expectations are expressed by restricting the set of models which will be considered for use in guiding the interpretation. At this point TEIRESIAS chooses a model which expresses what it knows thus far about the kind of rule to expect, and in the current example it expects a rule that will "deduce that the area of the investment should be high-technology."

Since there is not necessarily a rule model for every characterization, the system chooses the closest one. This is done by starting at the top of the tree of models, and descending until either reaching a model of the desired type, or encountering a leaf of the tree. In this case, the process descends to the second level (the INVESTMENT-AREA-IS model), notices that there is no model for INVESTMENT-AREA-IS-HIGH-TECHNOLOGY at the next level, and settles for the former.

4. Deciphering the English text

Interpreting the natural language text of the rule can be viewed as a "recognition" process in which the data are allowed to suggest interpretations, but the system maintains certain biases about which interpretation is likely to be correct. TEIRESIAS does this by generating all consistent interpretations of each line of English text and then evaluating each interpretation in the light of the biases expressed by the choice of a specific rule model. The interpretations suggested by the text (data-driven, "bottom-up" mode) are thus intersected with the expectations (hypothesis-driven, "top-down" mode) provided by the debugging process.

The interpretation process works in a strictly line-by-line fashion, processing each line of text independently. This method is a source of some deficiencies, some of which are trivially fixed, while others are superficial manifestations of interesting and complex problems. Each of them is discussed in subsequent sections below.

Deciphering the text occurs in four stages:

(i) preprocessing the text,
(ii) checking the rule model,
(iii) generating the set of plausible LISP interpretations, and
(iv) scoring the interpretations by reference to the rule model.

As will become clear, our approach to natural language is very simple, yet powerful enough to support the performance required. The problem is made easier, of course, by the fact that we are dealing with a small amount of text written in a semi-formal technical language and dealing with a restricted subject, rather than with large amounts of text, using a wide vocabulary for unrestricted dialog. Even so, the problem of interpretation is substantial. The source of TEIRESIAS's power and performance lies in the ideas noted in Section VIA, illustrated in more detail in the sections that follow.

(a) Terminology and dictionary structure

The English version of a rule will be referred to as "text", while each of the components of the LISP version will be referred to as a "LISP clause". Thus *the area of the investment is high-technology* is text, and the corresponding LISP clause is (SAME OBJCT AREA HIGH-TECHNOLOGY). The terms "parse" or "interpretation" are used to mean creation of a single LISP premise or action clause.

The natural-language-understanding capabilities are primarily keyword based. The connotation of a single word is determined by a number of pointers associated with it. These are, in general, inverse pointers derived from the English phrases ("translations") associated with many of the data structures in the system. For instance, an attribute like INVESTMENT-AREA has a translation of *the area of the investment*. As a result, associated with the word *area* is a pointer to the attribute INVESTMENT-AREA. The creation and updating of these pointers are handled semi-automatically by routines that help to minimize the book-keeping task. The pointers are referred to collectively as "connotation pointers". (There are additional pointers to handle synonyms, but they are not relevant here.) The important point is that the appearance of any given word can be taken as evidence that the expert was talking about one of the attributes, objects, predicate functions, or values indicated by the pointers for that word.

(b) Pre-processing the text

The first step in processing the new rule is to take a single line of text and replace each word with its root word equivalent. (Root words provide a canonical form for plurals and other simple variations.) Common words like *a*, *and*, *the*, are explicitly marked in the dictionary as content free, and are ignored.

All the connotations of each word are then obtained by referring to the appropriate pointers. Figure 12 below shows the result of this process.

As should be clear, this technique is strictly word by word. A more sophisticated approach would have some grasp of grammar and would attempt to assign meanings to entire phrases.

(c) Checking the rule model

TEIRESIAS's next step is to verify the applicability of the rule model that was suggested by the debugging process (or supply a model, if it "came in cold", i.e. without going through the debugging phase). This is achieved by scanning each of the words in the action part of the rule and checking their connotation pointers to see which attributes or values are implicated.

If the debugging process has indicated which rule model to use, TEIRESIAS attempts to reconcile that model with the indications from the scan of the action text. If there is agreement, nothing unusual happens. If, however, it cannot reconcile any of the indications from the action text with the given model, the system indicates this problem and asks the expert for help.* A trace of this process is shown in Fig. 13. Assume the system entered as before, expecting a rule about investment area, but the expert suddenly thinks of another rule he has been meaning to enter (see Fig. 13). The important thing here is a fast and very simple checking process. The first (incorrect) guess is the result of other connotations of the word *investment*. There are rarely more than four or five connotations in any case, so even at worst, the expert sees only a few bad guesses.

If the system had "come in cold", the process would start at the point where it says "To aid in analyzing. ...." Even without the debugging process, then, all the benefits of the recognition-oriented approach are still available.

Once a model is selected, the interpretation process begins. As indicated, it proceeds line by line and is oriented primarily toward doing the best job

---

* While modelling human performance was not one of our motivations, it is interesting to note that both of these reactions are similar to human behaviour. Sudden changes in the topic of a conversation can violate expectations about what is to follow, resulting in an expression of surprise. Similarly, arriving in the middle of an ongoing conversation often requires a moment to become oriented and prompts a request for information. Elements of both of these are seen above.

TEXT	ROOT WORDS	CONNOTATIONS			
		predicate fn.	attribute	object	value
the	the	—	—	—	—
client	client	—	—	CLIENT	—
is	be	SAME	—	—	—
following	follow	—	FOLLOWS	—	—
up	up	—	—	—	UPWARD
on	on	—	—	—	—
market	market	—	—	MARKET	—
trends	trend	—	TREND	—	—
carefully	careful	—	CONSERVATIVE	—	CAREFULLY

Fig. 12

The new rule will be called RULE384
If　　1 — **THE RISK LEVEL FOR THE INVESTMENT IS HIGH,**
and　2 — **THE AREA FOR THE INVESTMENT IS CONSUMER-ELECTRONICS**
and　3 —
Then: 1 — **CRAIG CORP. IS A LIKELY (.6) CHOICE FOR THE INVESTMENT**
and　2 —

Hmm ... it seemed that this was going to be a rule to deduce the area for the investment.　But it doesn't appear to be ...

To aid in analyzing this rule, please answer yes or no (Y or N) to each of the following.

Is this a rule to deduce:
　the investment time-sclae
★★ **N**
　a likely stock to invest in
★★ **Y**
Thank you ...

Fig. 13

possible with the limited natural language techniques available. There are two important points to note. First, the system does what might be called "template-directed code generation", analogous to the way English is often generated by "filling in the blanks" of a template. Secondly, the system maintains several types of consistency in the parses that it generates.

(d) Generating a LISP clause
The next step is to generate the tree of possible parses. One example of the generation process will serve to illustrate the important ideas and explain what is meant by a tree of parses.

The process begins by determining which predicate function the expert might have had in mind, scanning the list of connotations, and choosing the predicate function that turns up most often. The template for this function is retrieved, and the rest of the process of creating a clause is guided by the attempt to fill in the template. For example, suppose the function is SAME and the template is

(SAME CNTXT ATTRIB VALUE)

Associated with each of the primitives in the high-level "language" is a routine that embodies much of the semantics of each primitive. The template is filled in by calling each routine as needed and allowing it to examine the list of connotations to find the kind of object it requires.

Consider the text from the first line in the trace: *the client is following up on market trends carefully*. The routine for VALUE would discover that one object of type VALUE suggested by the text was UPWARD (the direction of the market). The routine for ATTRIB would find several objects of type ATTRIBUTE (see Fig. 12). However, since the VALUE routine has already filled in UPWARD as a VALUE, this narrows the choice to those attributes for which UPWARD is a legal value, i.e. TREND. The routine for OBJCT notices that *market* can be interpreted as an object, one that is a valid object for the attribute TREND, and hence marks it as such. It returns the literal atom OBJCT, reflecting the fact that OBJCT plays the role of a free variable that is bound when the rule is invoked. This produces the clause

(SAME OBJCT TREND UPWARD)

But there is more work to be done. Not all the substantive words in the text have been accounted for, and additional interpretations are possible. There are also alternative interpretations for some words (e.g. *carefully*); hence alternative interpretations of the text are possible. The system uses a standard depth-first search with backtracking and, at this point, undoes its current set of meaning assignments and tries all the alternatives. Other clauses are generated as alternate interpretations.

As may be clear, the template parts are not necessarily filled in the order in which they appear in the template. The VALUE part (if there is one) is always tried first, for instance, since words indicating values are often totally unambiguous. (They are also sufficiently strong clues as to text content that the ATTRIB routines will supply the attribute which belongs with a given VALUE, even if no other indication of that attribute can be found.) This simple "first pass" strategy is built into the driver routines, but because one routine may invoke another, the order may soon become more complex.

The entire tree of parses is generated using the depth-first search with the back-up noted earlier. The result is a tree of clauses of the sort shown in Fig. 14 (part of the tree generated from the first line of text is shown). At each node of the tree is a potential premise clause, and any single path through the tree from the root to a leaf is a set of consistent interpretations.

Generation of the tree with alternative word meanings in different branches provides the notion of consistency between interpretations. Consistency is required in order to permit TEIRESIAS to get more than one LISP premise clause from a single line of text without making conflicting assumptions about that text. The current implementation takes care of the most obvious sources of such conflicts by insuring that only one meaning is chosen for each word.

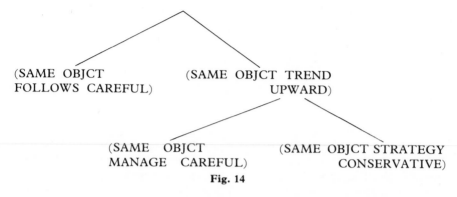

(SAME OBJCT
FOLLOWS CAREFUL)

(SAME OBJCT TREND
UPWARD)

(SAME OBJCT
MANAGE CAREFUL)

(SAME OBJCT STRATEGY
CONSERVATIVE)

Fig. 14

As each clause is completed, it is given a preliminary score that reflects how it was assembled. For instance, the highest score is given to those clauses for which independent evidence was found for both the value and attribute. If the attribute must be implied by the presence of a value, the score is somewhat lower. There are a number of other criteria that are also used in composing the score. The main idea is simply to provide some measure of how strongly the data (the text) suggested the interpretations (the LISP clauses) that were made.

(e) Scoring the parses

The next step is to select a single interpretation for the text by choosing a path through the tree of clauses. This is done with reference to the rule model chosen during the debugging phase. Each path is scored according to how well it fulfils the expectations expressed by the model. Recall that part of the model predicts the appearance of clauses containing specific attributes and predicate functions, while the rest predicts the appearance of associations of clauses containing certain attributes. The score for each path is the sum of the strengths of the predictions that it fulfils.

There are thus two scores. The individual score for a given LISP clause indicates how strongly the clause was suggested by the English text. The score for an entire path indicates how well the set of clauses meets expectations. These two are combined in a way that emphasizes the expectations and candidates are ranked according to the outcome. The system will thus "hear what it expects to hear" if that is at all possible; otherwise, it will choose the best alternative interpretation.

D. Phase II: modifying the interpretation

TEIRESIAS has a simple rule editor that allows the expert to modify existing rules or (as in this example) indicate changes to the system's

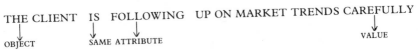

(SAME OBJCT FOLLOWS CAREFULLY)
The client follows the market carefully
Fig. 15

attempts to understand a new rule. The editor has a number of simple heuristics built into it to make the rule modification process as effective as possible. In dealing with requests to change a particular clause of a new rule, for instance, the system re-evaluates the alternative interpretations, taking into account the rejected interpretation (trying to learn from its mistakes), and making the smallest change possible (using the heuristic that the original clause was probably close to correct). In this case this succeeds in choosing the correct clause next (Fig. 15 shows the correct connotations and resulting code).

E. Phase III: "second guessing", another use of the rule models

After the expert indicates that TEIRESIAS has correctly understood what he said, the system checks to see if *it* is satisfied with the content of the rule. The idea is to use the rule model to see how well this new rule "fits in" to the system's model of its knowledge—i.e. does it "look like" a typical rule of the sort expected?

In the current implementation, an incomplete match between the new rule and the rule model triggers a response from TEIRESIAS. Recall the last line of the premise description in the rule model of Fig. 11:

((BRACKET SAME) (FOLLOWS NOTSAME SAME)
(EXPERIENCE SAME) 1.5))

This indicates that when the tax BRACKET of the client appears in the premise of a rule of this sort, then how closely he FOLLOWS the market, and how much investment EXPERIENCE he has typically appear as well. Note that the new rule has the first two of these, but is missing the last, and the system points this out.

If the expert agrees to the inclusion of a new clause, TEIRESIAS attempts to create it. Because in this case the agreed upon topic for the clause was the amount of investment EXPERIENCE of the client, this must be the attribute to use. The rule model suggests which predicate function to use (SAME, since that is the one paired with EXPERIENCE in the relevant line of the rule model), and the template for this function is retrieved. It is filled out in the usual way, except that TEIRESIAS checks the record of the consultation when seeking items to fill in the template blanks. In this case only a VALUE is still missing. Note that, as the answer to question 6 of the consultation, the expert indicated that the amount of experience was **MODERATE**, so TEIRESIAS uses this as the value. The result is a plausible guess, since it ensures that the rule will in fact work for the current case (note the further use of the "debugging in context" idea). It is not necessarily correct, of course, since the desired clause may be more general, but it is at least a plausible attempt.

It should be noted that there is nothing in this concept of "second guessing" which is specific to the rule models as they are currently designed, or indeed to associative triples or rules as a knowledge representation. The fundamental point was that mentioned above of testing to see how the new knowledge "fits in" to the system's current model of its knowledge. At this point the system might perform any kind of check, for violations of any established prejudices about what the new chunk of knowledge should look like. Additional kinds of checks for rules might concern the strength of the inference, number of clauses in the premise, etc. Checks used with, say, a procedural encoding might involve the number and type of arguments passed to the procedure, use of global variables, presence of side effects, etc. In that case, for example, we can imagine adding a new procedure to a system which then responds by remarking that "... *most procedures that do hash-table insertion also have the side effect of incrementing the variable* NUMBRELEMENTS. *Shall I add the code to do this?*" In general, this "second guessing" process can involve any characteristic which the system may have "noticed" about the particular knowledge representation in use.

Note also that this second use of the rule model is quite different than the first. Where earlier we were concerned about interpreting text and determining what the expert actually said, here the task is to see what he plausibly *should have* said. Since, in assembling the rule models, TEIRESIAS may have noticed regularities in the reasoning about the domain that may not yet have occurred to the expert himself, the system's suggestions may conceivably be substantive and useful.

F. Phase IV: final checkout, book-keeping, re-running the consultation

Now that both the expert and TEIRESIAS are satisfied, there is one final sequence of tests to be performed, reflecting once again the benefit of knowledge acquisition in context.

At this point, TEIRESIAS examines several things about the rule, attempting to make sure that it will in fact fix the problem uncovered. In this case, for instance, the action of the new rule should be a conclusion about investment area, the area mentioned should be high-technology, and the conclusion should be affirmative. The premise should not contain any clauses which are sure to fail in the context in which the rule will be invoked. All these are potential sources of error which would make it obvious that the rule will not fix the bug.

The rule in the current example passes all the tests, but note what would have happened if the user had (perhaps accidentally) typed *the client's income tax bracket is 20%*:

The rule now reads:
RULE383

If   1) the client's income tax bracket is 2∅%, and
        2) the client follows the market carefully, and
        3) the amount of investment experience is moderate.
Then: there is evidence (.8) that the area of the investment should be high-technology.

Sorry, but this won't work. For FRED SMITH, clause #1 ("the client's income tax bracket is 2∅%") is sure to fail.
Would you like to change the rule?
++★★

(Since the answer to question 3 of the consultation indicated that the client had a taxable income of $40,000, TEIRESIAS is able to determine (by referring to the appropriate tables) that his tax bracket would not be 20%, hence the rule cannot succeed). The expert then has the option of either editing the current rule or writing a new one (because the one he wrote may be correct, only inapplicable to the current problem). If he edits it, the tests are run again, until TEIRESIAS is satisfied that there is nothing obviously wrong with the rule.

There are also a number of straightforward book-keeping tasks to be performed, including hooking the new rule into the knowledge base so that it is retrieved and invoked appropriately (e.g. in this case it gets added to the list of rules that conclude about INVESTMENT-AREA), and tagging it with information which will make it easier to maintain the large and constantly changing body of rules (e.g. the name of the rule author, date of creation, author's justification for adding the rule, a pointer to the consultation which prompted its creation, etc.).

At this point, the system also performs any necessary recomputation of rule models. The operation is very fast, because it is clear from the action part of the rule which models may need to be recomputed, and the

EXAMPLES part of the model then supplies the names of the other relevant rules.

TEIRESIAS then reruns the performance program as a sub-process, and checks the results to see if all the problems have been repaired.

VII. Overview

A. Limitations of the mechanisms supplied

There are of course a number of limitations to the mechanisms we have supplied for explanation and knowledge acquisition.

1. Explanation

For example, TEIRESIAS's explanation facilities are based on viewing explanation in terms of replay. That is, it is assumed that replaying the steps taken by the performance program will constitute a clear coherent explanation of the program's behaviour. This view is not, of course, a particularly sophisticated model of explanation. This becomes evident in several ways. It was noted earlier, for instance, that "why" and "how" are underspecified and must necessarily be expanded by TEIRESIAS to avoid misinterpretation by the user (e.g. "Why" might mean "Why did you ask about that instead of ...," or "Why did you ask about that now," etc.). These other interpretations are valid questions about the system, yet there is no way in the current framework to answer them.

The lack of a user model in the information metric has been mentioned, and this too is an important element. In our current model, two rules with the same certainty factor have the same information content, yet a user who is familiar with only the first of them will find much more information in the second.

Next, while our approach generates high-level explanations by leaving out detail, there is another sort of abstraction that would be very useful. The system should be able to describe its actions at different conceptual levels, perhaps at levels ranging from rule invocation to LISP interpretation, to function calls, etc. A limited form of this kind of ability is described in Sacerdoti (1977), but there it arises from code that has been intentionally structured in this multilevel form. More interesting would be an ability to generate such explanations from an understanding of the process at each level. Some of the work on models of disease processes described in Weiss *et al.* (1978) may be relevant here.

There is also the possibility of decoupling explanation from control flow. We noted above a fundamental assumption of our approach: that a recap of program actions can be a plausible explanation. This assumption need not be made and explanations could be considered separately, distinct from execution (as in Brown (1975)). This is common human behaviour—the account someone gives of how he solved a complex problem may be quite different from a simple review of his actions. The difference is often more than just leaving out the dead ends or omitting the details of the solution. Solving the problem often produces new insights and shows results in a totally different view, one which often admits a much more compact explanation. There is greater flexibility from an approach of this kind because it can be used to supply a wider variety of explanations; but it also requires a new and separate basis for generating explanations and, hence, is more difficult.

Another limitation is the lack of a substantive ability to represent control structures. In the current system, the closest approximation comes from the use of the goal-tree framework as a model of the control structure. But this "model" exists only implicitly, expressed by the organization of code in the explanation facility rather than as a separate entity. Shortcomings are evidenced by the fact that almost any alteration of the control structure of the performance program requires an analogous recoding of TEIRESIAS's explanation routines. If there were instead some representation of the control structure that the explanation routines could examine, the system would be much more flexible.

Given some representation of the control structure and a body of knowledge about what an explanation is, TEIRESIAS would generate a comprehensible account of performance program behaviour. Supplying either of these seems to be a formidable but interesting prospect. The fact that a programmer can scan a strange piece of code and then explain the behaviour of a program executing it, suggests that the task is at least plausible. Formalizing the knowledge of what it means to "explain" does not seem to have received extensive attention. Some of the work on affects and intensions by Faught *et al.* (1974) may be relevant, as may be the conceptual dependency work in Reiger (1974) and the work on computer-aided instruction in Brown (1975).

Some small steps toward representing the control structure in an accessible form are described in Davis and Buchanan (1977). There we explore the use of meta-rules to express certain aspects of the performance program's control structure, and hence render them accessible to the current explanation mechanism.

A more sophisticated form of representation is needed, however. The source code of a program is not a particularly good choice for two reasons. First, it carries too much implementation detail. It may be useful to know only that a piece of code is, for instance, an iterative loop, and the detail of how it is implemented often only confuses the issue. Secondly, it carries too little intentional information. LISP's CAR operation, for example, can usually be read as *first element* of a list; but inside a loop, it might be more appropriately viewed as *next element*.

The task requires some way of suppressing implementation detail and emphasizing intentions. There is a common style of programming that accomplishes some of this. It emphasizes the use of extended data types (e.g. record structures) and macros (or functions) designed for the task at hand. It may include two functions called FIRST and NEXT, for instance, even though both perform the same CAR operation. Something along this line has been suggested in Hewitt (1971), but the emphasis there is on program correctness and automatic programming. The point here is simply to give the programmer a way of expressing his (perhaps informal) intentions for each section of code so that the program can later be explained. Note that these intentions might include not only descriptions of control structure but might go on to specify many other things about the code: design considerations, algorithm choices, and perhaps other kinds of information of the sort found in well-written documentation. Thus, where the efforts in program correctness have concentrated on describing precisely "what" a program should do, intentional information might include descriptions of the "how" of program design. The work in Goldstein (1974) suggests the multiple uses that might be made of such annotations: that system based its debugging of simple programs on an understanding of common error types plus remarks in the code that indicated the programmer's "plan" for solving the problem.

Flow charts are a second possibility; some text-oriented representation of them might prove useful. In an analogy to some of the work on program correctness, they might be annotated with "motivation conditions", providing, thereby, both a representation of the control structure and the information necessary to explain it. Both of these are clearly very speculative; there is much room for additional work.

All of these examples point the way to useful extensions to TEIRESIAS that would give it a far more general and powerful explanation capability.

2. Knowledge acquisition

The knowledge acquisition facilities present several limitations as well. As noted, our approach involves knowledge transfer that is interactive, that is set in the context of a shortcoming in the knowledge base, and that transfers a single rule at a time. Each of these has implications about TEIRESIAS's range of applicability.

Interactive knowledge transfer seems best suited to task domains involving problem solving that is entirely or primarily a high-level cognitive task, with a number of distinct, specifiable principles. Consultations in medicine or investments seem to be appropriate domains, but the approach would not seem well suited to those parts of, for example, speech understanding or scene recognition in which low-level process play a significant role.

The transfer of expertise approach presents a useful technique for task domains that do not permit the use of programs which autonomously induce new knowledge from test data. The autonomous mode may most commonly be inapplicable because the data for a domain simply do not exist yet. In quantitative domains (like mass spectrum analysis (Buchanan and Mitchell, 1978)) or synthesized ("toy") domains (like the blocks world in Winston (1970)) a large body of data points is easily assembled. This is not currently true for many domains, consequently induction techniques cannot be used. In such cases interactive transfer of expertise offers a useful alternative.*

Knowledge acquisition in context appears to offer useful guidance wherever knowledge of the domain is as yet ill-specified, but the context need not be a shortcoming in the knowledge base uncovered during a consultation, as is done here. Our recent experience suggests that an effective context is also provided by examining certain subsets of rules in the knowledge base and using them as a framework for specifying additional rules. The overall concept is limited, however, to systems that already have at least some minimal amount of information in their knowledge base. Earlier than this, there may be insufficient information to provide any context for the acquisition process.

The rule-at-a-time approach is also a limiting factor. The example given earlier works well, of course, because the bug was manufactured by removing a single rule. In general, acquiring a single rule at a time seems well suited to the later stages of knowledge base construction, in which bugs may indeed be caused by the absence of one or a few rules. We need not be as lucky as the present example, in which one rule repairs three bugs; the approach will also work if three independent bugs arise in a consultation. But early in knowledge base construction, where large sub-areas of a domain are not yet specified, it appears more useful to deal with groups of rules, or, more generally, with larger segments of the basic task (as in Waterman (1978)).

In general then, the interactive transfer of expertise approach seems well

---

* Where the autonomous induction technique can be used, it offers the interesting advantage that the knowledge we expect the system to acquire need not be specified ahead of time, nor indeed even known. Induction programs are in theory capable of inducing "new" information (i.e. information unknown to their author) from their set of examples. Clearly the interactive transfer of expertise approach requires that the expert know and be able to specify precisely what it is the program is to learn.

suited to the later stages of knowledge base construction for systems performing high-level tasks, and offers a useful technique for domains where extensive sets of data points are not available.

Several more detailed issues arise as well. There is, for instance, a potential problem in the way the rule models are used. Their effectiveness in both guiding the parsing of the new rule and in "second guessing" its content is dependent on the assumption that the present knowledge base is both correct and a good basis for predicting the content of future rules. Either of these can at times be false and the system may then tend to continue stubbornly down the wrong path.

The weakness of the natural language understanding technique presents a substantial barrier to better performance. Once again there are several improvements that could be made to the existing approach (see Davis and Lenat (1981)), but more sophisticated techniques should also be considered (this work is currently underway; see Bonnett (1978)).

There is also the difficult problem of determining the impact of any new or changed rule on the rest of the knowledge base, which we have considered only briefly (see Davis and Lenat (1981)). The difficulty lies in establishing a formal definition of inconsistency for inexact logics, because, except for obvious cases (e.g. two identical rules with different strengths), it is not clear what constitutes an inconsistency. Once the definition is established, we would also require routines capable of uncovering them in a large knowledge base. This can be attacked by using an incremental approach (i.e. by checking every rule as it is added, the knowledge base is kept consistent and each consistency check is a smaller task), but the problem is still substantial.

B. Strengths

Despite these limitations, TEIRESIAS has proven to be a useful first step in the attempt to develop effective lines of communication between the user and a performance program.

Its explanations are in general comprehensible to a user-community of non-programmers. It provides a tool that allows the user to examine the inner workings of the performance program, making that program more transparent, and offering as well the possibility of educational benefit. The facilities described have also given evidence of their utility in one interesting and unexpected way: often even the programmers associated with this research effort find it easier to "ask the program what it did" than to try to trace through the body of code.

The knowledge acquisition facilities offer an existence proof of sorts: they have demonstrated that it is possible to establish high-level communication between an application domain expert and a performance program. The expert does not have to learn how to program, but can instead engage the system in a dialog, which, while restricted in vocabulary and style, is still natural enough to be useful. TEIRESIAS also offers the user a significant amount of assistance, as it tries to make "educated guesses" about the rule the expert is trying to formulate.

In summary, consider the difference in the nature of the task facing the expert if TEIRESIAS did not exist. He would be faced with a problem requiring keeping track of a very large amount of detail, a problem requiring the ability to trace back through the behaviour of a large program to find out where it went wrong, and a problem of encoding his ideas in a format and language (INTERLISP) that was foreign to him. TEIRESIAS's central contribution in these terms, then, has been to insulate the expert from the detail and the programming aspects of the task, bringing the interaction up to a level where he might find the task feasible and the style of interaction comfortable.

VIII. Acknowledgements

This chapter describes work done while the author was in the Computer Science Department, Stanford University, Stanford, California. The work was supported in part by the Bureau of Health Sciences Research and Evaluation, under HEW Grant HS-01544, and by the National Science Foundation under contract MCS 77-02712. Support for some of the basic research underlying this work was provided by ARPA, under ARPA Order 2494. The work was done on the SUMEX-AIM Computer System at Stanford; the system is supported by the NIH under grant RR-00785.

IX. References

Aristotle (Translated 1926). *Rhetoric*, translated by J. H. Freese, G. P. Putnam, New York.

Bonnett, A. (1978). BAOBAB, a parser for a rule-based system using a semantic grammar. Stanford University HPP Memo 78-10, Stanford, California.

Brown, J. S. (1975). Uses of AI and advanced computer technology in education. Bold, Beranek and Newman, Technical report, Cambridge, Massachusetts.

Buchanan, B. G. and Mitchell, T. (1978). Model-directed learning of production rules. *In* D. Waterman and F. Hayes-Roth (Eds), *Pattern-Directed Inference Systems*, pp. 297–312. Academic Press, London and New York.

Davis, R. (1977a). Generalized procedure calling and content-directed invocation. *Proceedings of the Symposium on Artificial Intelligence and Programming Languages, SIGART/SIGPLAN* combined issue, August, pp. 45–54.

Davis, R. (1977b). Interactive transfer of expertise: acquisition of new inference rules. *Proc. 5th IJCAI*, August, pp. 321–328.

Davis, R. and Buchanan, B. G. (1977). Meta-level knowledge: overview and applications. *Proc. 5th IJCAI*, August, pp. 920–928.

Davis, R. and Lenat, D. B. (1981). *Knowledge-based Systems in Artificial Intelligence*. McGraw-Hill, New York.

Davis, R., Buchanan, B. and Shortliffe, E. H. (1977). Production rules as a representation for a knowledge-based consultation system. *Artificial Intelligence* **8**, 15–45.

Dijkstra, E. O., Dahl, J. and Hoare, C. (1972). *Structured Programming*. Academic Press, New York and London.

Falk, G. (1970). Computer interpretation of imperfect line data. Stanford University AI Memo 132, August, Stanford, California.

Faught, W., Colby, K. and Parkison, R. (1974). The interaction of affects, intentions and desires. Stanford University AI Memo 253, December, Stanford, California.

Goldstein, I. (1974). Understanding simple picture programs. MIT AI Memo 294, September.

Hayes-Roth, F. and McDermott, J. (1977). Knowledge acquisition from structural descriptions. *Proc. 5th International Joint Conference on AI*, Cambridge, Massachusetts, pp. 356–362.

Hewitt, C. (1971). Procedural semantics—models of procedures and the teaching of procedures. *Natural Language Processing* **8**, 331–350.

Reddy, D. R. *et al.* (1973). The HEARSAY speech-understanding system: an example of the recognition process. *Proc. 3rd IJCAI*, Stanford, California, pp. 185–193.

Reiger, C. J. (1974). Conceptual memory: a theory and computer program. Stanford University AI Memo 233, July, Stanford, California.

Sacerdoti, E. (1977). *A Structure for Plans and Behavior*. Elsevier, New York.

Shortliffe, E. H. and Buchanan, B. G. (1975). A model of inexact reasoning in medicine. *Mathematical Biosciences* **23**, 351–379.

Shortliffe, E. H., Davis, R., Buchanan, B. G., Axline, S. and Cohen, S. (1975). Computer-based consultations in clinical therapeutics. *Computers and Biomedical Research* **23**, 351–379.

Teitelman, W. (1975). *The* INTERSLIP *Reference Manual*. Xerox Corp.

Tversky, A. and Kahneman, D. (1974). Judgment under uncertainty: heuristics and biases. *Science* **185**, 1129–1131.

Waterman, D. (1978). Exemplary programming. *In* D. Waterman and F. Hayes-Roth (Eds), *Pattern-Directed Inference Systems*, pp. 261–280. Academic Press, London and New York.

Weiss, S. *et al.* (1978). A model-based method for computer-aided medical decision making. *Artificial Intelligence* **11**, 145–172.

Winston, P. H. (1970). Learning structural descriptions from examples. Project MAC TR-76, MIT, September, Cambridge, Massachusetts.

5. A human–computer interface encouraging user growth

J. PALME

Swedish National Defence Research Institute, Stockholm, Sweden

I. The human–computer environment

A. Computer effects on user conditions

In human society, a major problem-solving approach has always been that of making rules. A body of well-informed people analyse the problem and put to paper their knowledge of how best to handle forthcoming cases. The product of their effort is called by names such as "rule", "law", "code", "regulation" or "checklist". This problem-solving approach can be called the legal way of handling problems.

Today, a new variant of the legal approach is becoming more and more common. The new approach is called "system development" and the ruling text produced is called a computer program. The users are bound by the rules laid down in the computer program in the same way as people are bound by other kinds of rules in society.

The legal approach has always had advantages and disadvantages. The advantages have been to ensure uniformity, to avoid mistakes and to disseminate knowledge and moral values. The disadvantage has been that the reality of life is always much more diversified and complex than can be understood by rules, so that the rules often do not fit the circumstances of the actual real cases met in practice. This means that in actual practice, rules and laws are always bent to accommodate reality. This bending of rules is often unconscious, but strict adherence to given rules will often have disastrous effects on the functionality of an organization, as is shown for example by the effects of certain "go slow" strikes.

In an organization using computers, the rules built into the computer

DESIGNING FOR HUMAN–COMPUTER COMMUNICATION
ISBN 0 12 643820 X

programs will in similar ways govern the people using the computer. The difference, however, is that a computer requires a program which is much more complete than most other rules in society. Every case must be covered, and the computer will not do anything not put into its program. The system developers are thus forced to prepare much more detailed rules when these rules are to be executed by computers than when the rules are to be executed by human beings.

When the software is ready, the computer will act as a tool for enforcing the rules built into its programs, and this tool is much more powerful in enforcing exact adherence to its rules than ordinary written rules. But because the world-view built into the software must always by necessity be simplified and idealized, it will not fully fit the many-facetedness of reality.

The effects of this will be that an organization using computers will often have difficulties in adjusting its behaviour to special cases or a changing environment. The people working with the computers will find themselves restricted and hindered by the "stupidity" with which the computer adheres to its program. This will make people feel frustrated and dissatisfied and make them perform less efficiently, because the ability to influence one's working conditions is very important to comfort and good performance.

Because a computer is such a powerful tool for enforcing rules, people with a yearning for power often use a computer to enforce their will upon others. It is therefore easy to understand why organizations involved in a struggle for power, like the trade unions fighting to increase the power of the employees and their organizations against the employers, or big organizations with a wish to increase centralized power, are well aware of the importance of computers to hinder or aid them in achieving their goals.

But even when there is no conscious intention to use the computer as a tool for enforcing rules, the effect will often be the same. Even the most well-meaning group of people, representing all interested parties and only wishing to produce the best computer software, will often produce software which, when put into practical use, is found to be too restricting. There are several causes for this. One is that reality is so complex that it is not possible to put into a program all the special cases which will be encountered in real practice. The developers often have a false impression of their program being more complete than it really is. Another cause is that it is natural for well-meaning people to try to put their knowledge of what to do and what to avoid into the computer programs. It is natural to say things like:

This is not good practice, do not put it into the program

or

This person does not need that information, so the computer should not allow him/her to get the information

In non-computer usage, technical means are sometimes used to enforce rules, like for example locks on doors. But in most cases, rules are not enforced by such technical means. And if we tried to use technical means to enforce all rules in society, we would encounter large problems. This is not only because the rules have to be bent to allow society to work, but also because a rule to stop certain unwanted practices will often also be simplified in a way which causes it to make allowed practices much more difficult.

When computers are to be used, there is a tendency to wish to put all rules into the computer software—making the software allow only permitted practices and forbid all unwanted practices. This tendency will create software which is restrictive and hinders development. And it is not necessary to put all restrictive rules into the actual computer programs; it is often sufficient and much better to only put the most important rules into the program, and enforce other rules by ordinary human ways like, for example, talking to people who are breaking a rule when necessary.

It is very important not to confuse user influence during the development of a system with user influence when they are actually using the system. Both kinds of influence are important, and one cannot replace the other. Even with user influence during system development, there is still a large risk that a system is created which is found too restrictive in actual practice.

Computer users who are inexperienced and insecure also like software which is fairly restrictive and guides them along predetermined paths. But as their experience grows, they will instead be frustrated by the restrictiveness of the same software. The ideal software must therefore accommodate users in different stages of experience and development.

The ideal software for the experienced user is flexible and lets the user decide how to use the computer. The computer can in this case be regarded as a collection of tools. The user decides what to do by choosing which tools to apply and in which order.

Computer software often goes through several stages of development. When the software is new, its users are inexperienced and prefer software which is simple and fairly restrictive. But as the users learn more and more, they require more and more flexibility and sophisticated functions. The software maintenance group tries to keep up with this by adding more and more additional functions and commands to the original software. After several years of this kind of development, the software is very complex, with a command structure which can only be mastered after long training. This is not, however, a difficulty for the original users, because they have acquired each addition, one at a time over a long time period, and people have an astonishing ability to learn how to master complex systems if learnt in this way. However, to the outsider or the beginner, such complex systems can be rather frightening. C. A. R. Hoare has described the people who master these complex systems as a new kind of priesthood understanding the magic rites (Hoare, 1975).

The same flexibility and functionality can often be achieved with a much simpler system, if rewritten from the beginning. To avoid this problem, a computer system can be designed in such a way that it is basically very flexible, and avoids restrictive rules. But there should be a top-level for inexperienced users, which is more restrictive and guides them in their use of the computer. As a user learns more, that user can step from the top-level to the more flexible base-level, but not as one big step but rather in many small steps as the user learns more and more about the system.

This chapter presents one approach of designing such a system with levels adjusted to users with different degrees of experience.

B. Human–computer interfaces

Assume a computer software package which is going to be used by many people. Many of them are inexperienced with computers. They need an interface, in which the computer guides them along with carefully worded questions, where they only have to answer the questions from the computer. Such an interface is simple for beginners to use, because the computer tells them what to type (Palme, 1975).

Other users are experienced. Perhaps they have used the package for a long time and have other computer experience. Those users are often dissatisfied with a computer-guided interface. They feel that it takes too much time to get things done, and that their freedom is restricted. They want an interface in which they can get the computer to do what they want with short simple commands. They want the freedom to decide what to do with as few arbitrary restrictions as possible (Palme, 1975).

Another requirement put forward by experienced users is to be able to add new facilities to the package. For example, if they need to do similar actions many times, they do not want to have to repeat the same sequence of inputs to the computer again and again. They want to add this sequence of inputs as a new facility to the package. This could be discussed on the basis of Fig. 1. Point c in the figure represents users, who are taxed by a too-advanced system. Point a represents users who find the work dull and tedious because of a too simple and restricted system. But this may be the same system for two different users, or even the same system and the same user at different times. Thus the ideal system should adjust itself to the user so that all users can be as close as possible to point b in the diagram.

There are many software packages of the computer-guided kind for

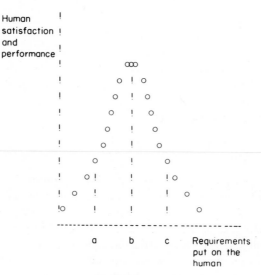

Fig. 1

inexperienced users. There are also many packages of the kind which gives much power to the experienced users. But the ideal package should perhaps be both at the same time, be able to adjust to the experience of the user, and encourage the user to grow with the package.

II. The idea of gradual growth

Rather than two different systems, one for the novice and one for the experienced user, the system should allow for gradual growth. Gradual growth has many advantages:

(1) The user can move towards the advanced level in small steps, all the time feeling secure with the system before taking the next step.

(2) Depending on the needs of one user, the system can be advanced where this user needs it, and simple in those areas in which this user does not feel that is worth learning advanced ways of usage.

(3) The novice and the advanced system use the same basic routines, which saves programming effort, ensures consistency after updates, and means that as much as possible will work and look alike to the novice and the advanced user.

III. Our application

This chapter presents this idea using a real example. The Swedish defence needed a new system for budgeting. The system was to be used by hundreds of people all over Sweden. The system described in this chapter exists as a prototype system. The final system did not contain all the facilities of the prototype system.

A. Database organization

The users input their budget data into the computer. This is stored in a database. The budgets from each local government can be combined into a total budget for a region or for the whole country. One solution is to have just one big database, with one slot for each budgetary entry. All the users access the same database when they use the system.

Another solution is to have essentially one database for each local budget. This allows greater freedom to the local users. They can add their own local data, which need not be seen by the regional and central authorities, because all the data in the local budgets need not be reported to higher authorities. Also, each local user can have several databases with different parts or versions of the budget, and combine and compare them at will. However, the use of one total database makes it easier to access centrally and review all items in the whole budget at any time. We chose local databases, because one of our goals was to increase the power of the individual user.

B. Level A: conversation led by questions and menus

When new users first enter the system, they will be led along by questions and menus from the computer. Menus have the advantage compared with yes–no questions in that the user has more alternatives to choose from, which gives more user power and fewer steps toward a desired user goal. A typical interaction at this level may be:

(C: means computer, U: means user.)

C: Do you want to?
C: 1 Modify records in the budget
C: 2 Add records to the budget
C: 3 Delete records from the budget
C: 4 Do something else
U: 1
C:
C: Give name of record to be modified:

C. Level B: help facility

When users do not understand what the computer program is expecting, they are ripe to learn of the existence of the help facility. In our system, this can be invoked by typing a question mark (?) in response to any question from the computer. A single question mark causes a short help text to be printed which explains what the computer is expecting when the ordinary execution was interrupted by the help command.

The user has now learned two important new concepts: you can give commands to the computer instead of being led by it, and you can interrupt one sequence of operations and do something else instead.

The next command to be learned is perhaps two question marks (??), which can also be given at any time. Instead of giving a text suited to the interrupted interaction, two question marks invoke the general help facility, in which the user can get answers to all kinds of questions through a special set of menus asking what the user wants to know. After using the help facility, the user gets back to the original interaction where it was interrupted. Thus they have encountered the idea of a sub-routine call.

D. Level C: other user commands for interruption

Often, users will feel a need to temporarily interrupt the normal sequence of instructions for other reasons than to use the help facility. They may, for example, feel that the value being entered into the database needs a special explanation, a footnote, added to it. Instead of entering the value, they can then use the "footnote" command. To distinguish commands from normal answers to questions from the computer, commands are preceded by the percent character (%). Example:

C: Input the cost for this item:
U: %footnote
C: Input footnote text:
U: This cost is extraordinarily high because of exchange
U: of the main engine.
U:
C: — END OF %FOOTNOTE COMMAND —
C:
C: Input the cost for this item:
U: 34000

Note that when the footnote was ready, the user returned to the question which was interrupted by the %footnote command.

The availability of footnotes is a general-purpose way of increasing the power of the user by allowing the user to add, when needed, other facts than those which fit into the specified slots in the database.

A second example:

```
C:   Which budget do you want to work with?
U:   ?
C:   You must enter the name of an existing budget, or
C:   type "NEW" if you want to start a new budget.
C:   Type "%LIST BUDGETS" if you want to know which existing
C:   budgets are available.
C:   — END OF HELP TEXT —
C:
C:   Which budget do you want to work with?
U:   %LIST BUDGETS
C:   Available budgets: REPORT BUDGET, CHARLIES BUDGET,
C:   JULY BUDGET.
C:   — END OF %LIST BUDGETS COMMAND —
C:
C:   Which budget do you want to work with?
U:   Report budget
```

In this example, the user interrupted the main question twice with interruption commands before answering the question. First the user applied the help facility, which told the user of the %LIST BUDGETS command. The user applied this command next, to learn what budgets were available as answers to the main question from the computer, and then chose one of them as an answer to the main question.

E. Level D: parameters to commands

At the previous level, users learnt that there was a set of commands which could be given instead of the normal answer to a question from the computer. This increased the power and flexibility of the users, but they had to learn or look up the commands to use the new facility. This was thus a typical level of getting more power for users learning more about the system.

Commands can be made more flexible by adding parameters to them. Assume, for example, that a large number of different budgets were available to a user. Users might want to know which budgets of other people were available. The %LIST BUDGETS command in the previous example might be extended with parameters, so that the user could tell the computer which budget names to list:

```
C:   Which budget do you want to work with?
U:   %LIST BUDGETS for me and Charlie
```

In our system, parameters are preceded by keys such as "for" in the example above, and can be expressions with combining operators such as "and" in the example. For some commands, there is no key on the first parameter.

The advantage of keys on parameters is that all parameters need not be given. If a parameter is omitted, the computer can, for example, assume a default answer. For example, the level c user who only typed "%LIST BUDGETS" did not need to know that this command actually took parameters, and that the default value "me" was assumed for the omitted "for" parameter.

F. Level E: a command-driven user interface

Users going through the previous levels have gradually been introduced to the idea of giving commands to the computer. Until now, commands have only been used as a way of specifying interruptions from the normal flow of execution.

Whenever desired, users can move to the command level by writing the command "%BUDGOL" as the answer to a question from the computer. They will then stay at the command level until they give a command to re-enter the computer-led mode, such as the command "%CONTINUE", which continues in the computer-led mode where it was interrupted by the command "%BUDGOL".

The system can thus be used as a command-driven system. Instead of telling the computer what to do through answers to a series of questions and menus from the computer, the user can apply commands from the beginning. The commands should as much as possible represent the same real activities which were previously achieved in a computer-led way. Often, the same words which were previously items in menus, are now used as commands. To achieve this, it is important that the commands be defined at the same time and together with the computer-led dialog. How this can be done will be presented later in this chapter. Example:

Computer-led dialog: Command-driven dialog:
C: Do you want?   U: %MAKE BUDGET: test budget;
C: 1 Make a new budget
C: 2 Change a budget
C: 3 Stop
U: 1
C:
C: Give budget name
U: Test budget

The users are never forced to give parameters to commands. If parameters are omitted, the computer is programmed to either:

(1) Use default values, which may depend on what the individual users have done or required previously.
(2) Ask the users conversationally.

Example:

```
U:  %MAKE BUDGET
C:  Give budget name
U:  Test budget
```

This is the same conversation as before, but the user did not give any value to the parameter, and thus got a conversation which was a mixture between a command driven and computer-led dialog.

G. Level F: saving series of commands

When the users have begun to use commands, they will soon find that they often have to repeat the same series of commands. This is the natural time to introduce the idea of saving a series of commands under the name of a new command. Example:

```
---------- Charlies tasks ----------
—  %Look at budget: Charlies budget;   —
—  %line:  &header;                    —
—  %list tasks;                        —
------------------------------------
```

The three commands above are stored under the new command name "Charlies tasks", so that when the user gives the command "%Charlies tasks", this series of commands are performed.

H. Level G: parameters to user-defined commands

The users already know that parameters can be given to commands. The next level is thus natural: adding parameters to user-defined commands. Example:

```
---------Write tasks---------
—  %Parameters: for &person;   —
—  %Look at budget: &person;   —
—  %line: &header;             —
—  %list tasks;                —
-------------------------
```

If the user gives the command "%WRITE TASKS for Charlie", then this series of commands is executed with "Charlie" substituted for "&person". If the user gives the command "%WRITE TASKS" without parameters, the interpreter will automatically ask for the value of the missing parameter.

J. Level H: model language

Those users who wish to step even further can move to level H, learning to write simple computer programs in the model language. The series of stored commands learnt in level F and G are in fact very simple cases of sub-routines.

How should this model language work? We can immediately make certain conjectures:

(1) "Command" and "sub-routine" are two words for the same thing. The user can invoke a sub-routine by giving its name as a command.

(2) The statement for invoking a sub-routine should have the same or similar syntax whether the command is given by the user directly or executed in a sub-routine.

(3) All but one of the parameters to a command must be preceded by a key, since this allows users to omit parameters, and the computer still knows which parameters have been given and which have been omitted.

(4) The syntax should be the same or similar for commands which invoke model language sub-routines and for commands which are part of the basic system.

(5) The model language should also be simple and easy to learn, it is probably interpreted rather than compiled.

When commands are typed at the terminal, users dislike having to type long commands. We are therefore planning to let the system accept commands typed with only enough letters to make the command distinct from other available commands. This is not implemented in the prototype system.

The system will include a simple text editor for the writing of model language routines. This editor will include an editor, which makes routines "prettier" by (a) block indentation, (b) upper case for commands and keys, lower case for values, and (c) conversion of short forms of commands to the full length.

K. Parameter definition in the model language

A natural way for users to define commands is to list the command as it is to be used, but with parameter names where parameter values are to be substituted. The following example shows how this is done in our system:

```
%Command: seek;
%Parameters: task &task in budget &budget;
%end of parameters;
   ...
```

This command may be invoked by writing:

   U: %SEEK task 54321 in budget Charlies budget

The command may also be used without parameters:

   U: %SEEK
   C: Task?
   U: 54321
   C: In budget?
   U: Charlies budget

Or the command may be given with just one parameter:

   U: %SEEK in budget Charlies budget
   C: Task?
   U: 54321

Look again at how the command was defined in the model language:

```
%Command: seek;
%Parameters: task &task in budget &budget;
%end of parameters;
   ...
```

The statement "%end of parameters;" will cause the interpreter to check which parameters have been defined and which are undefined, so that the questions in the dialog above can be generated.

If the programmer wants to assume default values for omitted parameters, this is also possible:

```
%Command: seek;
%Parameters: task &task in budget &budget;
%set: &budget := &previous.budget;
%end of parameters;
   ...
```

If the variable "&previous.budget" has previously been given a value then this is used, so that "%end of parameters" does not have to ask for a value for this parameter. If, however, &previous.budget is undefined, then a question to the terminal is generated.

In the case where a value for the parameter "&budget" is given in the invoking command, then the "%set" statements are never executed, because there is a rule in the language which says that "%set" statements are not executed if they precede "%end of parameters" and if the variable already has a defined value.

L. Further features of the model language

Further features of the model language are similar to other programming language. Thus there are IF ... THEN ... ELSE clauses, BEGIN ... END brackets, output and input statements etc. Also, all commands of the system can be given in model language programs.

The basic data type of the model language is a text string of varying length. In addition to computational expressions, the language also allows text expressions like concatenation. For example, "%line 'The cost will be ' &cost * &inflation;" is a statement where the text string "The cost will be " is concatenated to the value of the subexpression "&cost * &inflation".

The data types in the model language will vary with the application. In our application we have references to budgetary entries as an additional data type.

We are also considering the idea of allowing users to augment the data structure definitions in the system using the model language. For example, one user may wish to add the field "priority" to the budgetary records created by that user.

M. Writing interactive programs in the model language

To simplify the writing of interactive programs in the model language, there are two special functions in the model language for questions and menus. Here is an example of use of the question function:

```
%SET &task := %QUESTION:
    query text: Which task?
    check:   %Legal task
    help:   %Task help;
```

Note that the syntax of functions is very similar to the syntax of commands (= sub-routine calls). Just as with commands, there are defaults when a parameter is omitted.

The parameter "legal task" is the name of a function which will take the user answer to the question as parameter and return "yes" or "no". If "legal task" returns "no", then an error message is given and the user is asked to repeat the answer to the question.

There are several such built-in check functions; for example, ""%yes or no" which only accepts the two parameters "yes" and "no" and ""%number" which only accepts numbers. The users may of course also write their own check functions.

If no parameter "legal task" is given to the function ""%question" in the model language routine, then all user answers to the question are considered legal.

The parameter "task help" is a user-defined sub-routine which prints a help message to the user. This may consist of only text, but the model language programmer is free to add questions to the user to select appropriate explanations.

N. Model language and base system

If the software package is going to be used by many users in different places, then the integrity of the system will also become a problem. One user cannot be allowed to write model language sub-routines which interfere with other normal users. One way to achieve this, which we have chosen, is to divide the system into the two main parts: the base system and the top-level consisting of model language routines defined by the user.

The interpreter for the model language is part of the base system, and full integrity control is done at the interface between the base system and the top system, for example when base system commands are given by users directly or in model language sub-routines.

P. User communication

All users will probably not advance through all the levels to model language programmers. This depends on their interests, ability and use of the system. However, users need not learn to use the model language themselves to benefit from it.

Very often, one of a group of users becomes more interested and more advanced in the technical aspects of the system than the other users. They turn to this user for help when they have problems. Such an advanced user is called a "local expert" and is considered very important for the success of a computer applications system (Damodaran, 1976). If the "local expert" learns to write routines in the model language, then he/she can do this for the other users in the group. In this way, the model language is a vehicle for the local expert to communicate his/her knowledge to the other users.

Model language routines may also be written by a central maintenance group for individual users. One reason why central maintenance groups are so reluctant to do what people ask them to do is that a change in the system needed by one user may be detrimental to other users or even threaten the security of the system.

Because model language routines can be local to just one user, and because the integrity of the system is checked at the interface between model language routines and the base system, no one except one user is affected by the new command. This will make it easier for the central development group to create additional facilities for local users.

If one user has written a model language routine which is really useful, then other users may begin to use that routine too (this can be automatically traced by the system). Finally, the routine may be adopted for general use and included in the base system. In this way, the model language can act as a vehicle for communication between users.

On the other hand, some parts of the general system can be written in the model language. This is a good way in which the general system can be adjusted to the needs of special user groups. In our case, for example, we may have separate sets of model language routines for the army, the navy and the air force.

A further way of generating model language routines which we are considering is to write conversational programs, which put questions to the user and then generates appropriate model language routines.

IV. Experience with the model proposed

A. The system development process

The system model described above was developed in 1976 as part of the work of designing a new budgeting system to be used in the Swedish defence. A computer program was written in two months by myself in the early stages of the design effort. That program incorporated all of the features described in this chapter. The program was never intended for actual use—it was written very quickly using methods producing a working program, sacrificing efficiency.

By producing a working computer model of the system in this way, at an early stage in the development, had the advantage that the model could be tested and shown to users to get their reactions at a stage where it was easy to take their requirements into consideration, because the programming of the final system had not begun.

In our case, this working model was very useful in gaining experience on how to design the system, but the model was used and tested mostly by the system developers and not by the future users. The final system was then developed and tested on a small group of users in 1977. After further development, the system is now fully used by about 200 users all over Sweden.

The final system is based on the principles described in this chapter but does not incorporate the model language (Levels F to H in this chapter). I would personally have liked to give the users a system including a model language, but this was not done because of the cost of development and because the interpreter for the model language might have made the system too complex and inefficient. (A partial cause of this may be that the model of the system developed in the beginning was very inefficient.)

B. System development problems

The structure of the system is such that the user has great freedom in deciding in which order to make certain actions. This has caused some programming difficulties. Suppose, for example, that a user circumvents the normal order of doing things and tries to make an action which requires data which were to be input at the circumvented stage. To avoid this problem, the code of every action has to be written in such a way that it checks that the necessary preconditions are fulfilled.

This way of coding the system has caused other problems. If, for example, a user tries to do action B, which requires action A to be ready, the system will first take the user into action A. The user may then again try to go to action B, and the system goes back recursively to action A again. In such cases, the users often do not understand what is happening.

Another problem occurs when users interrupt one action to do something else, then interrupts that action again and so on, adding more and more unfinished actions to an internal stack in the program. When each action is ready, the program will then go down in the stack, but the user has often forgotten what happened and does not understand what the program is trying to do.

This problem can be avoided by limiting the recursiveness of the program. If a user interrupts one action to do a small supplementary action, then the user is returned to the interrupted action again, and a full explanation is given as to where the program is returning. If the user interrupts to do something big, the user is not returned to the interrupted action again, but is returned to the top level of the program instead. These programming problems were no great hindrance, and the program is successfully in use.

The system development method has been different from the development of other systems. The conventional way of writing this kind of system is to have a rather large group of COBOL programmers supervised by system designers producing detailed descriptions of the program. In our case, the whole program was produced by three programmers using the high-level language SIMULA. SIMULA, which is an extension of ALGOL, is well suited to structured programming. The system was developed and tested on a DECsystem-10 computer, which has good facilities for program development and testing. Production execution is then done on a Univac 1100 computer. This way of developing on one computer and using the system on another computer has worked very well and forced us to produce a well-defined and machine-independent program.

C. User experience with the system

Our experience is that users do use the system in the way intended. New users begin with the computer-guided menu-driven interface, but turn to the user-guided command-driven interface after a few weeks of experience.

In the first production version now in use, there is a rather sharp limit between the menu-driven and command-driven interfaces. In the next version, this limit will be less sharp, making it easier for users to move between the levels.

One problem is that as the program grows larger, all escape commands cannot be made available with similar function throughout the program. The users will then complain when an escape command which worked in one part of the program does not work in another part. The total experience is however good. The system works in the intended way, the users are satisfied and the effort is used as a model for developing new systems.

V. Acknowledgements

Staffan Lööf made a number of important suggestions during the design of this system. The basic idea on the handling of command parameters not given by the user is partly his. Ideas came also from Erik Sandewall and Sture Hägglund. The system was tested by Lars-Åke Larsson, who provided a number of suggestions for improvements. The design of the QUESTION and MENU commands are based on ideas in SAFEIO, developed by Mats Ohlin. Mats Ohlin and Lars Enderin have helped me check the report.

The model system was developed by me, but the final system was developed by a group of three programmers, in which Lars-Åke Larsson was responsible for the human–machine interface part of the program. He developed a general-purpose package in SIMULA for writing this kind of interaction, which means that he can set up a new interaction of the same kind (with a menu-driven level with defined menus and a command-driven level) in just a couple of days.

VI. References

Aaro, I. (1977). *Design and Implementation of a Software System for Interactive Scientific Computing*. Department of Information Processing, Royal Institute of Technology, Stockholm.

Damodaran, L. (1976). *The Role of User Support—Actual and Potential*. Department of Human Sciences, University of Loughborough.

Grip, A. (1974). *ADB-system och kommunikation*. Hermods-Student-litteratur. Lund, Sweden.

Hoare, C. A. R. (1975). Software design, a parable. *Software World* 5, Nos 9 and 10.

Marguiles, F. (1976). *Evaluating Man–Computer Systems*. Austrian Federation of Trade Unions, Vienna.

Ohlin, M. (1976). SAFE Conversational SIMULA Programs Using Class SAFEIO. *FOA 1 Report C 10044*.

Palme, J. (1975). Interactive Software for Humans. *FOA 1 Report C 10029*, July. (Also available in Swedish.) (A shortened version was published in *Management Datamatics*) 5, 4, 139–154.

Palme, J. (1976). Internationall kurs om interaktion mellan människa och dator. *FOA 1 Rapport C 10056*.

Palme, J. (1977). BUDGOL-DAPU, ett system för människa-dator-interaktion vid budgetering. *FOA 1 Rapport C 10076*, October.

Palme, J. (1979a). A Human–Computer Interface for Non-Computer Specialists. *FOA 1 Report C 10128*, April.

Palme, J. (1979b). Datorers betydelse för samhällets och människorans sårbarhet. *FOA 1 Rapport C 10122*, March.

Stewart, T. F. M. (1976). *The Specialist User*. Department of Human Sciences, University of Loughborough.

6. A translator to encourage user modifiable man–machine dialog

R. F. BATEMAN

Royal Signals and Radar Establishment, Great Malvern, England

I. Introduction

An on-line, real-time, computer-based system is often judged by its immediate impact upon the user or users of that system. Most of the operators have little, if any, knowledge of what the computer is doing "behind the scenes", but are much more aware of their own interface to the machine in the form of the dialog between them. A poorly designed dialog will cause user resistance to, or even rejection of, a system that in all other respects may be adequate or even excellent.

Dialogs have been offered for use in which the required responses from the operator is uncertain or unlikely and the error messages unintelligible without reference to a programming manual and/or the system designer. In response to the machine generated question:

"SOURCE?"

the user response could be "YES", "NO", "Y", "N", a file name or a number and he is unlikely to know the correct response unless he has the reference manual by his side. Only a few vague questions of this sort are required to instil a feeling of incompetence or rebellion in the user. Similarly, error messages of the form:

"ERROR 32"

which the user must check against a list in the manual, or

"R 32 19372 43 – 1 2491"

representing machine register contents, are unlikely to fill the user with enthusiasm.

DESIGNING FOR HUMAN–COMPUTER COMMUNICATION
ISBN 0 12 643820 X

It is possible to design dialogs in such a way that the answer to any machine-generated question is inherent in the question. For example, the position of one label from a set of labelled touch-wires forming a menu is inherently the answer. Similarly, in teleprocessing, the machine question:

"DO YOU WISH TO CONTINUE? Y OR N"

indicates the range of possible answers, "Y", or "N". Error messages of the form:

"ERROR 32"

should be avoided at all costs and replaced with a sensible and informative description of the error which should also indicate the corrective action required from the operator.

"THIS FILE DOES NOT EXIST. PLEASE TYPE THE CORRECT FILE NAME IN THE FORM ABC/XYZ;"

Because every individual tends to interpret both questions and statements in slightly different ways it would be useful if, following initial familiarization with a given system, the user could change the formats of both into a form more readily acceptable to him. This is not an overwhelming problem and should be seriously considered by system designers because it would help to convert *"the computer system"* into *"my computer system"* for each user. There would be a consequent improvement in morale, work-rate, pride and job satisfaction.

The provision of a well-designed dialog is particularly critical for Air Traffic Control (ATC) Systems where the users (the controllers) form an intelligent, well educated, group who work under considerable pressure and cannot, for safety reasons, tolerate a "slow" or unintelligible response from the system. ATC systems tend to evolve fairly rapidly due to the changes in aircraft types (Concordes, 747s), airport layout, international agreements and user pressure. Because the system must remain live at all times any modifications to it must be correct and must also take place rapidly and in a well-controlled manner.

Most of these systems have dialogs based upon menu-selection techniques using a display, or displays, and a suitable input device such as a keyboard, touch-wires, rolling ball, light pen, etc. The menu-selection technique consists of displaying a number of legends, followed by selection of one of them, this in turn causing a new set of options to appear on the display. This allows the man to follow a preset, but complex, set of routes through the program. Typically, the man will select one aircraft from a list of callsigns, causing information concerning this aircraft to be displayed, along with selector fields such as heading, height, SSR code etc. Selection of, say, heading, will in turn activate a numeric keyboard to allow the man to input a new heading for the aircraft. Eventually, the display will revert to the callsigns picture to enable the process to be repeated with another aircraft. In this way a very subtle and complex dialog may be followed without the need for the man to remember every little detail of each step in the transaction.

The technique is also very valuable for leading the operator through little-used procedures. A good example of this would be the alerting process in the event of an accident or disruption on the airfield or in the air. The controller is required to activate the emergency procedures; inform the police, fire-brigade, ambulance, etc., possibly clear the runways and taxiways, re-schedule or re-route other aircraft, notify the airline, and so on. It would be easy to forget one of these procedures, so that by making the computer remember them in the form of a dialog to ensure that each procedure is initiated and "ticked-off" in the right order, would seem a very reasonable thing to do.

Occasionally, a task may be so large that, despite computer assistance, it must be split between a number of operators. Almost invariably these operators, because they are performing similar tasks, are given the same input and output devices and the same dialog. It is a truism to say that "no two people are alike", which automatically condemns this approach, but unfortunately it is often forgotten that no one person is alike over an extended period. People change as they learn a particular task, get bored, frustrated and so on. A dialog for a completely untrained man, the sort usually implemented, is completely unsuitable for him within a matter of hours, or even minutes, of initial use. The dialog is usually self-explanatory and therefore lengthy and restrictive and the user begins to feel that the "machine's" verbosity is preventing him from performing his job in the best possible way, i.e. His way. Occasionally, two or three levels of dialog, or at least, levels of abbreviation, have been implemented in an attempt to overcome this problem, but this is seldom an adequate solution.

Another problem exists—that of presenting the right data to the right man. Most Command and Control systems are manned in a hierarchical fashion and the requirement for, and level of, information presented and handled is entirely different at each command level. The commander wishes to give simple, compound commands of the form "investigate and (if necessary) attack those bombers", and eventually receive confirmation of the attack and whether it was successful. His subordinates must progressively expand this compound command into a large number of subgoals or tasks each requiring a different level of help and response from the machine. For example, the commander's immediate subordinate would probably split the original command into orders to track the bombers, to establish which airfields have interceptors within range, whether the interceptors are fuelled and armed. If in-flight refuelling is required then the tanker airfields must be notified, etc. It is unlikely that the system, when first delivered, will have all the levels of presentation correctly established. Such systems are far too complex for rational analysis. It would be helpful if the customer could change his mind and alter the system.

Currently, most large, real-time software systems are produced by a team which includes a project manager, system analyst, designers and programmers. It may be several years before the manager, analysts and designers see the results of their early decisions which makes it very difficult to correct any deficiency in the design. It would be useful if early experimentation could be performed to define the dialog, especially if the experiments can be carried out rapidly and easily by people untrained in programming, but who know a great deal about the system requirements. Furthermore, if these experiments result in a well-defined, working program, then a very real advantage is gained.

A Dialog Generator has been produced which allows a man sitting in front of a display console to compose a dialog. He will be led through a series of "drawing" operations to enable him to produce the pictures very rapidly and these pictures may be changed at will. Finally, a high-level language (CORAL 66) program will be generated automatically to implement the dialog he has specified. This system has been implemented on a Modular One Computer and is written in CORAL 66.

II. The dialog generator

The Dialog Generator allows the user to define, implement and modify his dialog very rapidly and easily.

A conversation between a man and machine implies a sequential process in which, for example, the machine outputs information and selectable items on to a display, the man responds by selecting one of the items and this causes the machine to output another picture. Therefore, the Dialog Generator must be capable of handling both parts of the interchange.

The sequencing aspects and also the basic symbology, be they words typed in from a keyboard, touch-wires representing the current legend on the display or even X, Y co-ordinates obtained from a rolling ball, can be handled very effectively using Syntax Analysis techniques.

Syntax Analysis has been applied very successfully to the production of High-Level Language Compilers for computers. Most notably, it was used to define the language ALGOL 60 with a precision previously unknown in the compiler writing field. At its most rudimentary level it is simply a description of a range of sequences of events by exposing the structure of the language and decomposing it to its atomic elements. At best it will enable a description (now a definition) of a language to be analysed by a computer and cause an automaton to be automatically produced, which in turn will analyse sentences written in the defined language.

A Syntax Analyser Generator (STAG) has been produced having many specialized features to enable it to be used for analysing man–machine dialogs. Thus, it will handle a display and input devices of various types. Its output consists of a CORAL 66 module, generated automatically from the Syntax Rules.

The second tool required is a Picture Generator which will allow the user to "draw" the display formats that he requires. This is based on fairly conventional Computed Aided Design principles, but it too produces CORAL 66 text which can be compiled and then linked with the output from STAG to form a complete program capable of producing the required dialog at the console position. Other CORAL segments may be linked in at will to form the remainder of the system. The main components of the Dialog Generator are shown in Fig. 1.

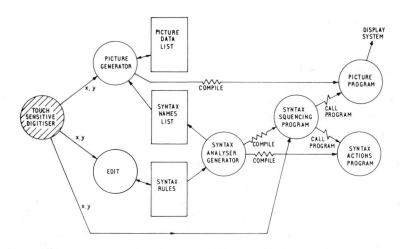

Fig. 1. The Dialog Generator.

III. Syntax analysis

The Syntax Analyser Generator (STAG) is used to convert a set of Syntax Rules into a CORAL 66 segment. These rules specify the sequence of events and the names which will be meaningful to the machine during the dialog. Only names declared at the head of the rules will be acceptable when forming the required pictures during the Picture Generator phase. The Syntax Rules, therefore, act as the formal specification of the dialog and, except for trivial changes to the associated pictures, must be modified if the dialog is changed. The Rules are the Master document.

The short example below represents a fictitious Air Traffic Control situation where the controller has selected an aircraft from a list and wishes to modify a chosen data field. The possible fields are aircraft-type, -height, -speed and -heading. The rule names following the selections will be activated whenever the particular selection is made.

```
Select option = (PICT option,
                          (INPUT type, type rule)
                          (INPUT height, height rule)
                          (INPUT speed, speed rule)
                          (INPUT heading, heading rule),
                                    select option);
   type rule = (PICT aircraft type, select type,
                OBEY store type);
```

In these rules:

   = means "the rule is defined as"
   () surround rule alternates and inner alternates
   , separates sequential items
   ; terminates the rule
   PICT means "output the named picture"
   INPUT means "input the following symbol"
      (probably a legend on the display)
   OBEY precedes a language insert, e.g. CORAL 66

The sequence of events through these rules would be:

   (a) Enter rule "select option" having selected an aircraft.
   (b) Output the picture "option" which will consist of a menu of "type", "height", "speed" and "heading". One of these will be selected, say "type", and this will cause "typerule" to be entered.
   (c) When "typerule" is entered the picture "aircraft type" is output which will presumably display a menu of types.

(d) An aircraft type is selected by entering and leaving the, here undefined, rule "select type".
(e) On exit from "select type", the action "OBEY store type" is performed.
(f) Finally, the rule "typerule" is exited and control returns to the rule "select option" following the point at which "typerule" was called. The recursive call of "select option" is then obeyed. Control will therefore return to (a) and re-enter "select option".

STAG will analyse the text of the formal syntax rules in order to check them for consistency and will then form an association tree for the functional display name, the picture names and the input names. A declaration at the head of the rules contains a list of pictures associated with the display name, and the analyser can trace which input names follow a given picture name in the rules. Thus, the input names "type", "height", "speed" and "heading" will be associated with picture "option". This list will be used later on by the Picture Generator so that only valid names may be chosen when drawing a picture.

The analysis of the rules consists of checking the names for consistency, ensuring that the rules layout is consistent with the inner syntax governing them, that no rule clashes occur and that unbreakable cycles do not occur. These checks are performed in a series of processes which gradually build up data tables representing the rules. The tables may be thought of as a special-purpose machine code which will be "run" or emulated with the aid of a small run-time analyser program. Indeed, it is possible to convert directly the tables into real machine code for a given machine and remove the need for an analyser. This will result in very fast analysis, but tends to require excessive amounts of storage.

On completion of the analysis phase, STAG will output a CORAL 66 segment consisting of a preset table, containing the sequencing control data, a procedure which will operate on the data and will act as a run-time analyser and an action procedure. This segment will be incorporated in the system program.

STAG also outputs the list of associated names which the Picture Generator will use.

IV. The picture generator

When the Syntax Rules have been analysed and found to be correct it only remains to produce the picture called for in the rules. This can be achieved using the Picture Generator. The Picture Generator is basically a

Computer Aided Design facility. It uses a display and a touch sensitive digitizer (TSD) or rolling-ball input device. Both of these input devices allow the co-ordinates of a position on the display to be injected into the computer and therefore permit both menu-selection and positioning to be carried out.

The user of the Picture Generator operates via a dialog which is defined by a set of syntax rules. The Mk II version has been produced by bootstrapping, i.e. the pictures required for the Picture Generator's dialog are produced with the aid of a hand-written Picture Generator. This has acted as a large-scale test of the system and will also allow rapid changes to be made to it in the future.

The dialog starts by requesting the user to select whether he wishes to generate or amend a picture or macro. A macro is a sub-picture which may be used to build up other pictures or macros. If the macro is a new one it must be assigned a name and a "move" state (i.e. it is fixed in position or positioned by the user when called?).

Having selected a picture or macro name the user may choose from a set of "drawing" and display control functions. On completion of the function the control returns to allow the next function to be selected. For example, he may draw a line, insert a message, draw a box, select a macro, etc. Some of the macros are likely to be squares or rectangles to be used as input areas or "touch-boxes". These represent an area on the TSD which the machine will recognize as corresponding to a legend inside the touch-box.

Such touch-boxes will be represented in the picture list by a complete specification consisting of the picture name, the legend, the box width and height, and the position assigned to it on the display. This specification will eventually be used to form preset tables which a procedure called "FINDBOX" will operate on. FINDBOX forms part of the CORAL 66 text produced by the Picture Generator and is used to associate a touch position in the running system with a legend in order to feed the legend name into the on-line syntax analyser for validity checking and sequence definition.

The touch-box acts in the same way as a touch-wire. Therefore, when a macro is called and positioned, the dialog continues by asking whether a legend is required for this macro and, if so, presents a list of the remaining legends for this picture. The selected legend will be placed inside the box and removed from the list to prevent accidental selection of it in the future. Any entity, be it a line or a complete picture, can be deleted, usually by simply pointing at it. This can lead to some interesting problems. Supposing it is required to delete a line forming part of a box. If the box is part of the main picture then the line can be deleted; if it is part of a macro it cannot, the macro may have been called elsewhere and it is unlikely that the user wants the line to disappear in an uncontrolled manner from several pictures. The method implemented is to delete the single call of the macro from this picture so that the whole shape is removed. This, of course, also removes any nested macros as well. Should the user want to change the basic shape, however, he can do so by electing to modify the basic macro by re-entering the generator at the "select picture or macro" point.

It is unlikely that the user will want to generate all the pictures in one session. Accordingly, when he terminates the program, the data list specifying all the pictures generated to date will be preserved on a named disk file for future use. At this point he can elect to output CORAL text to another file.

The CORAL text, a complete LIBRARY segment, consists of a number of procedures representing the macros and pictures and having the same names. It also includes the procedure called "FINDBOX", together with an associated data structure to enable TSD touches to be assigned to the appropriate legends, which will feed back the legend value to the on-line syntax analyser.

A complete list of the Picture Generator facilities are given in Section V.

V. The picture generator facilities

The Picture Generator facilities (Fig. 2) show the main selection format for the generator. The large box (top-centre) represents the picture being generated, shown half-size. (Unfortunately, the display hardware only offers single-sized characters and overlap can occur.) The boxes surrounding it are touch-boxes and selection of one of them leads on to an appropriate touch-box sequence to enable the required function to be performed. Only a brief description of the options available will be given below. Two methods can be used, at any point in the sequence, to inject X, Y co-ordinates and either can be used at will. They are:

(a) A point may be defined by touch using the TSD or rolling ball. This is fast, but inaccurate.
(b) By "typing" in co-ordinates from a display keyboard. This is slow, but accurate.

The facilities are:

LOOK   This expands the generated picture to full size to enable the user to check it. Touching the screen anywhere returns control to the main function picture. (This will be abbreviated to "return".)

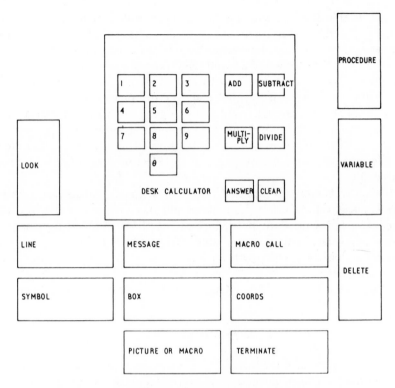

Fig. 2. Desk calculator.

LINE   This allows the user to generate a line. He
                          selects one of four brightness controls, one of
                          five modulations and whether the line is flash-
                          ing and then injects the co-ordinates defining
                          the ends of the line, which then appears. He
                          can also connect either or both ends of the new
                          line to an existing line or lines by touching the
                          existing line in the centre. The ends of the two
                          lines that are nearest each other are connected
                          by adjusting the co-ordinates of the new line.
                          This process may be repeated, followed by a
                          return.

MESSAGE   This allows the user to generate a string of
                          characters and position them on the screen. He

selects a brightness control and flash-state and is then presented with an alpha keyboard. He may shift to a numeric and symbol keyboard, back erase continuously and terminate the string. The message will appear in the correct position following a return.

MACRO CALL

A shape may be selected from a list of pre-viously generated macros. If, and only if, it was designated as "moveable" when it was gene-rated, the user is allowed to inject the co-ordinates of the starting position for the macro. The shape will then appear. The user will be asked whether a legend is required and if so a list of valid legends will be played out. The selected legend is placed inside the macro before returning.

SYMBOL

This facility allows a user to associate special symbols to a particular function. It is based upon the assumption that the programmer has been sufficiently general and written state-ments like "display (symbol (17))" to rep-resent, for example, aircraft above 30,000 ft. The user can now allocate any symbol to number 17 by selecting from a list and typing in the number before returning.

BOX

This is simply an extension of the line facility, but is so frequently used that it has been implemented as a special case. The user selects brightness control, flash and modulation before typing in the width and height of the box. The reference point for positioning is in the top left-hand corner of the box. Return.

COORDS

The co-ordinates of any line may be found by touching the line. Return by touching the screen.

PICTURE OR
MACRO

Allows the user to generate either a picture selected from the list handed over by STAG or an old or new macro. If he elects to generate a new macro then he is presented with an alpha-numeric keyboard to enable him to type in the name. He also selects the "moveable state". He can also select whether the macro is to be a common "keyboard" and, if so, from which picture the legends are to be selected.

PROCEDURE   This facility allows the user to allocate a name to an, as yet unwritten, procedure that will perform some special task. The procedure call will be part of the picture procedure.

VARIABLE   Not yet implemented. This facility will allow the user to set up a data structure to hold variable information like aircraft callsigns, speeds, etc. The table will consist of a user-defined number of entries, each entry being defined by a set of fairly basic display calls.

                          e.g. L1 := AT(X,Y)
                                    PRINT(HEIGHT);
                               L2 := VECTOR(X2,Y2);
                                              etc

                          Each of the labelled entries may be changed at will by a user-defined module by using the table entry number and the label, which gives an offset within an entry.

DELETE   This allows any of the entries described above to be deleted at will. The type of entity, line, message, etc., must be selected and then the user either touches it (lines, messages, boxes) or selects from a list (pictures, etc.) and the item will be removed on return.

TERMINATE   Causes the picture to disappear, the data list defining the pictures to be safely stored on disk and, optionally, the CORAL 66 segment derived from this list to be dumped. All un-fulfilled (i.e. not used) legends will be listed on a monitor file. The program then terminates.

The following section shows how the system is used.

VI. A dialog generator example

The problem chosen to illustrate the use of the Dialog Generator is that of producing a "Desk Calculator" program using a display and TSD. The calculator will operate upon integers and a calculation can consist of any number of terms, e.g.:

$$32 + 17 \star 3 + 4/6 = 25$$

The expression will be evaluated from left to right as each term is selected.

For clarity, no attempt has been made to detect or prevent arithmetic overflow and it is assumed that all calculations continue to the end.

The process starts by defining the syntax rules. Some difficulty may be experienced with the various separators used in the example below because they have been selected to avoid clashes with CORAL symbology. These are listed in the rule heads as shown. The main ones of interest are:

= =	"rule (etc) is defined as"
(= and =)	alternate brackets
. .	separator
%%	terminator
IP	input symbol
OBEY	introduces a CORAL insert
C	surrounds comment

The rules are:

```
desk calculator
start
sep is . .
term is %%
```

descodes are DEVICE. .TCODE. .RULENAMES. .DISPLAY. .SYNTAX. .
             (:. .:). .= =. .(= =). .(@. .@). .OBEY. .IP. .ANY. .
             C. .PICT. .FINISH. .CHECK. .FAIL. .((:. .:). .
             IPVAL. .CHECK FAIL%%
C this preceding block introduces all the symbols required by STAG C
DISPLAY(:1:)dc= = dcpict%%
C a display named dc has one picture, dcpict, associated with it C
DEVICE(:1:)DISPLAY= =0. .1. .2. .3. .4. .5. .6. .7. .8. .9. .
             add. .subtract. .multiply. .divide. .answer. .clear%%
C a device of type display has these legends associated with it C
RULENAMES= = desk calculator. .dcalc. .opterm. .operator. .
             integer. .tail. .digit%%
C list of the rule names required C
SYNTAX   C introduces the syntax rules C

C these rules define the simple desk calculator C
desk calculator = = (OBEY initialise display channel. .dcalc =)%%
C the display channel is opened and rule 'dcalc' is called C
dcalc = = (= PICT dcpict. .OBEY at (− 350,320). .integer. .OBEY
      number: = int. .opterm. .dcalc =)%%
C the picture 'dcpict' is output to the display 'dc' and the starting point for the
   scratch line (x = − 350,y = 320) is output, the first integer is read in C
opterm = = (operator. .opterm =)%%
operator = = (= IP add. .OBEY output 'lit'(+)). .integer. .
              OBEY number: = number + int =)
      (= IP subtract. .OBEY output('lit'(−)). .integer. .
              OBEY number: = number − int =)
      (= IP multiply. .OBEY output('lit'(*)). .integer. .
              OBEY number: = number*int =)
      (= IP divide. .OBEY output('lit'(/)). .integer. .
              OBEY number: = number/int =)
      (= IP answer. .OBEY output('lit'(=));print(number,5). .
              IP clear. .dcalc =)
      (= IP clear. .dcalc =)%%
C the appropriate operator is output to the display and the operation is
   performed C
integer = = (= digit. .OBEY int: = dig;punch(dig). .tail =)%%
C read in first digit of integer C
tail = = (= digit. .OBEY int: = int*10 + dig;punch(dig). .tail =)
              (= =)%%
C reads in subsequent digits and form integer C
digit = = (= IP 0. .OBEY dig: = 0 =)(= IP 1. .OBEY dig: = 1 =)
      (= IP   2. .OBEY (dig: = 2 =) (= IP   3. .OBEY   dig: = 3 =)(= IP
      4. .OBEY dig: = 4 =)
      (= IP 5. .OBEY dig: = 5 =) (= IP 6. .OBEY dig: = 6 =)(= IP 7. .OBEY
      dig: = 7 =)
      (= IP 8. .OBEY dig: = 8 =) (= IP 9. .OBEY dig: = 9 =)%%
C read one digit and set 'dig' to correct value C
FINISH%%

These rules will be read and analysed by the Syntax Analyser Generator (STAG) and, if valid, will produce two files, the first containing the names association list and the second a CORAL 66 module consisting of the run-time analyser, a set of tables for the analyser to work on and the actions. The analyser can now be compiled.

Following a successful run of STAG, the user may run the Picture Generator in order to produce the display pictures required (Fig. 3). (In this case one picture.) As a result, a second CORAL 66 module will be produced automatically which will be compiled in turn.

The code produced by the two CORAL modules may now be linked,

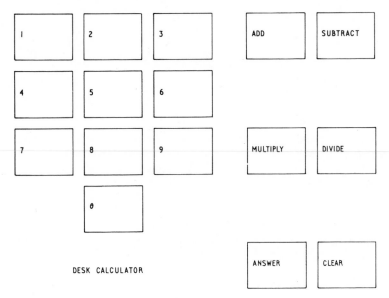

Fig. 3. Desk calculator.

along with any other user-defined modules, to produce a complete program capable of producing the required dialog.

VII. Conclusions

The Dialog Generator has reached a relatively stable, although incomplete, state of development. Many display manipulation facilities could be readily added without changing the basic concepts. Hopefully, the Dialog Generator and allied systems will be increasingly used in the development and maintenance of large, real-time projects and will at last give the users and designers the very real advantage of changing their minds at the final moment.

The concept of individual users performing the same task, but able to log-on and run their "own" system, i.e. their own dialog, appears to cause horror in the breasts of many designers. Technological advances (e.g. the intelligent graphical visual display units at very low prices) will shortly force such ideas to be met and accepted. The users revolution is upon us, the tools already exist, and we should welcome the freedom from unnecessary constraint that it offers.

7. Psychological issues in the design of database query languages

J. C. THOMAS

IBM, T. J. Watson Research Center, Yorktown Heights, New York, USA

I. Introduction

Computers are getting cheaper, faster, and more common. Largely initiated by hardware developments, this computer revolution has profound implications for other aspects of the computer industry and for society as a whole. The proportion of total data processing budget required for software is probably near 80% and rising (Boehm, 1973). The total speed of a human–computer system is becoming more critically limited by the speed of the human component and the quality of the interaction between the human and the computer. Computer *systems* must be increasingly designed for people who do not have an unusual capacity to memorize and use arbitrary codes. The import of all these trends is that it is becoming more and more important for computer systems to be designed with the use and the user in mind.

Unfortunately, a completely adequate unified theory of human performance in learning and using query languages is not available. Perhaps the most encompassing quantitative relevant theory is Halstead's (1977) software science which deals with first-order effects in programming. While Halstead's treatment ignores many of the second- and third-order effects that psychologists have found to be important, it does offer a framework for organizing some of the findings in this chapter. Space does not permit an extensive treatment here; the interested reader is referred to Halstead (1977). Briefly, Halstead claims that both errors and speed of writing software depend upon the number of tokens and the log (base 2) of the number of distinct types. He defines the notion of program volume (V) (= number of tokens X log (2) number of types) and of potential volume

(V⋆) (volume if an algorithm were expressed in the most succinct possible way in *any* language). The ratio of minimum volume to actual volume expresses the "program level", symbolized by 'L'. Errors are proportional to volume and the time taken to program an algorithm is estimated by V/SL where S is the "Stroud number", a constant somewhere between 4 and 20 that is purportedly the number of elementary mental discriminations that can be made in one second.

Even in theory, it is clear that several important variables are ignored. For example, research has conclusively demonstrated that people, according to payoffs, can trade off speed and accuracy. Weinberg (1971) has made the point that programmers can also modify their programming behaviour depending upon what they are trying to accomplish (finish quickly, produce efficient code, produce error-free code, etc.). A person can increase speed by allowing more errors or can make fewer errors by slowing down. This "speed-accuracy trade-off" suggests that rather than predict speed and accuracy independently, their combination could be more accurately predicted. Separate predictions would also be possible if some information about the relative payoffs for speed and accuracy were available. In addition, Halstead treats both internal symbols (or chunks, p. 85) and the speed of mental discriminations (Stroud number, p. 48) as constants for a given situation. Yet both probably vary according to experience and intelligence. Another important determiner of difficulty, particularly for beginners, is the ease of translation from English into the query language. Translating from English "salary" into "SALARY" must surely be easier than translating into the arbitrary symbol: "xyzzy" (cf. Reisner, 1977). Despite (or perhaps because of) these simplifications, Halstead provides an elegant and accurate fit to basic performance data in a number of diverse human symbol processing situations. In preparing this chapter, some attempt was made to apply this theory to query writing. It should also be noted that independent investigators have generally found Halstead's formulations to predict difficulty better than lines of code for programming (Woodfield, 1979; Curtis *et al.*, 1979).

Lest the reader be disappointed however, it should be admitted now that most of the information in this chapter consists of reporting results and giving separate recommendations and not in providing a simple, elegant, yet all-encompassing theory that predicts all results and dictates query language design. More specifically, this chapter reviews three kinds of information especially relevant to the designer of a query system. (For a more general review of behavioural issues in interactive systems, see Miller and Thomas (1977) or Thomas and Carroll (1981)). First reviewed are studies which have been directed at examining and comparing human performance with various specific query languages. Such studies, reviewed in Section II below, form the major focus of this chapter. Also important are a number of psychological findings which are relevant to database query language design. Generally, such findings do not *strictly imply* a particular design choice. Rather, they should serve as general background knowledge which the systems designer(s) must integrate with other technical information. Some data of this kind are presented in Section III. Finally, some issues for the designer to address are presented in Section IV. Other references which specify and treat these issues include Miller (1968), Martin (1973), and Miller and Thomas (1977). Shneiderman (1978, 1979) is particularly recommended.

II. Studies of database query languages

In this section, studies which examine the behaviour of people attempting to learn and write in query languages are presented. In each study, people learned to use a slightly modified version of a real query language. In each case, subjects used paper and pencil rather than an existing on-line system and translated questions presented in English into the query language.

The following chain of variables should provide the reader with a framework for thinking about these studies. What we are really interested in primarily is the difficulty of learning and using a query language or a particular query language feature. These variables cannot be directly observed, however. The teaching method, the teacher's ability, the time spent, and the learner's motivation and ability are groups of variables that in conjunction with the language produce a level of knowledge in the learner's head. This knowledge, in turn, again interacts with the variables of time since learning, task difficulty, prompts, and the learner's ability and motivation. Together, these variables determine the query writer's *performance* typically *measured* in terms of time and accuracy. From these dependent variables of time and accuracy, we attempt to infer something about the query language or task difficulty. Comparisons across studies are therefore only valid to the extent that teacher method and competence, subject motivation and ability, and learning time are roughly comparable.

A. Interactive Query Facility (IQF)

Gould and Ascher (1975) performed one of the first studies of a query language and examined the performance of non-programmers learning a language similar to IBM's Interactive Query Facility (IBM, 1972). The purpose of the study was to determine the general features that make query languages difficult. An example of a question written in the version of IQF used in the study is shown below.

For illustrative purposes, commands are all in upper case letters, attributes are capitalized, and values are all lower case. The query illustrated (from Gould and Ascher, 1975), is: "List the average salary of employees who were in Chicago, have at least a Bachelor's degree, and are married; and the average salary of engineers over 50 years of age working in St. Louis."

1. FROM Personnel FILE
2. FOR chicago Location
3. AND FOR Highest Degree bs, ms, phd
4. AND FOR married Marital Status
5. COUNT
6. LET Count BE CALLED Count 1
7. TOTAL Salary
8. LET THIS BE CALLED Total 1
9. ALSO
10. FOR Age 51 or more
11. AND FOR engineer Jobtype
12. AND FOR st. louis Location
13. COUNT
14. LET THIS BE CALLED Count 2
15. TOTAL Salary
16. LET THIS BE CALLED Total 2
17. LET Total1/Count1 BE CALLED Avg. 1
18. LET Total2/Count2 BE CALLED Avg. 2
19. LIST Avg1, Avg2

1. Method

Seven college students and ten middle-aged file clerks were individually taught a modified IQF. Each subject had to pass a criterion during training before receiving the final test. On the final test, each subject translated 15 questions in English into the query language. These questions varied in having one, two, or three segments (major OR's) and orthogonally in having one, three, or five conjunctive restrictive modifiers per segment. In addition, several of the questions required computations on returned records and two were poorly formulated in the original English.

The subjects read each question and rewrote it in their own words in English. The time taken to do this was referred to as formulation time. The subjects were then required to write in their own words a plan for the query. The time required for this was referred to as planning time. Finally, subjects were required to code the query and the time required was called coding time.

2. Results

The training took from 4·0 to 13·5 h for the college students and from 7·5 to 24·5 h for the clerks. Difficult concepts for the subjects to learn included the general notion of attribute and value, how to express these notions, and the necessity for attention to detail.

About 35% of the queries were written completely correctly. Of 195 queries written, ten were syntactically correct but would only return a subset of the required data. These and 18 other queries were judged to be incorrect because the subject did not really understand the original question in English. In 64 cases, the subject did not seem to understand how to use a feature of the language and in 35 cases, it was judged that the subject had merely made a clerical error. Overall then, only about half the erroneous queries reflected a fundamental misuse of some query language feature.

In a different breakdown of errors, 65 of a total of 342 errors were due to the inaccurate specification of an attribute (e.g. "YEAR" instead of "YEARS"). The prevalence of these kinds of minor clerical errors suggests that one should allow the user to select rather than spell out the attribute.

The time taken to write queries varied from about 5 min total for the easiest queries to about 12 min for the hardest queries. The attempt to break total query-writing time down into formulation time, planning time, and coding time was at least partly successful in that making the English question poorly formulated increased the formulation time but not the planning or coding time. Conversely, requiring computation on returned records increased planning and coding but not formulation time. For problems which were well-formulated and required no computation, formulation, planning, and coding times were highly correlated as would be expected on the basis of Halstead's theory.

Problem difficulty as measured by time or errors increased linearly with problem complexity. Formulation, planning, and coding time increased with increasing segments and with an increasing number of modifiers per segment. The results of this experiment, taken as a whole, suggest that the performance of naive users with a query language is regular and can be systematically studied. Not surprisingly, overall performance was quite a bit worse than one would expect from Halstead's (1977) results with experienced programmers. For example, consider the query "Print the names of employees whose salary is less than $12,000, are over 28 years old, and are managed by White." This requires seven operators (and all are unique) and seven operands (all unique) in IQF. The estimated proportion of errors per query is 0·021 while the actual proportion of errors was 1·08. Similarly, the estimated amount of time was 64 s (using 4 as the Stroud number). Yet, the actual time taken was about 100 s even after the subject had formulated and planned out the query. Given that these results were with naive subjects who had barely learned a new language, these results are not terribly surprising; clearly, the 'Stroud number', as pointed out in the introduction must be related to the experience and ability of the subjects. Perhaps Love's (1977) work could be useful as a basis for relating the Stroud number to individual differences. The separable effects of formulation and coding suggest that at least two phases are involved in translating from English to a query language; first, translating from English into some internal logical code; secondly, producing an external representation in the query language.

B. Query-by-example

1. Background

In a further attempt to understand the psychological processes involved in writing queries, a program of psychological study was begun (Thomas and Gould, 1975) to evaluate Query-by-Example (Zloof, 1977). In this query language, the query is written directly in the proper columns of the proper table(s). It is designed to operate on a relational database. Query-by-Example appears to be a very "high-level" language in Halstead's (1977) sense. If we calculate "program level" for various simple queries, the values are about an order of magnitude higher than for more traditional programming languages.

The queries "Print the names of employees whose salary is less than $12,000 are over 28 years old, and are managed by White;" and "Who else works in the same department as Riley?" are respectively shown below.

EMPLOYEE	NAME	SALARY	AGE	MANAGER	DEPARTMENT
	p.	< 12,000	> 28	White	
	p.				X
	Riley				X

Note that 'X' in the second query serves as a linking variable.

Because choosing the correct column is easier than producing an attribute, it is not clear whether to consider the column names as operands or not. If we ignore column choice, we get the same value for program level for both the above queries. Level = (2/(number of unique operators)) X (number of unique operands)/(total number of operands). Substituting, in the first case, for the three operators 'p.', ' < ', and ' > ' and the three operands '12,000', '28', and 'White' gives: Level = (2/3) X (3/3) = 0·667. Regardless of the details of how one might apply Halstead's metric to this query language, it should be intuitively clear that it is close to an absolute minimum of what MUST be said for the query to unambiguously specify the needed records.

2. Methods of study

Subjects were trained and tested in groups of 4–12. All subjects were high school or college students or recent graduates. Four of the college students had had some minor programming experience. The other 35 subjects had not had any experience with computers.

Subjects received about 1 h 45 min training on the main features of Query-by-Example. This training consisted of having the two instructors write queries on overhead projectors, and having students do examples at their seats. After the instructions, subjects were given the first test which consisted of translating 20 questions from English into Query-by-Example. After a short break, subjects received another 70 min of instructions dealing primarily with the use of universal quantifiers. After this, the subjects were given another test in which they translated each of 20 English questions into Query-by-Example. For each question, subjects wrote down the time when they began reading the question, read the question, wrote the Query-by-Example equivalent, gave a confidence rating (1 = very sure correct, 2 = fairly sure correct, 3 = 50–50 chance, 4 = fairly sure incorrect, 5 = very sure incorrect), and then wrote the time. Subjects received no feedback about the correctness of their queries during the testing. The answer booklets for subjects did contain reminders of the meanings of some special symbols such as ' < ', ' ¬ ', and 'p.'.

After this second test, the last 31 of the subjects were given five additional complex "problem situations" concerning a database for a school. For each problem (e.g. "The younger faculty feel that they are not being paid as much as they should be"), the subject was first to write a question in English whose answer: 1. would be relevant to the problem and 2. could be translated into Query-by-Example. Then the subjects translated their own English questions into Query-by-Example.

A memory test was also included in the study. Two weeks after initial testing, the 11 original subjects who had been hired from a temporary office help agency were asked to come back. Six of these were able to return; they were immediately given a surprise test on Query-by-Example which again required the translation of 20 questions from English into Query-by-Example. After an hour's "refresher" training, the subjects were given another test in which they had to translate 20 questions.

3. Results

Perhaps the most important result was simply that it was possible to train people with minimal or no computer experience so easily. No potential subject dropped out. Exclusive of the universal quantification, the system was learned in 2 h. Overall, two-thirds of the queries were written correctly. This percentage varied between subjects from 33–93%. There were no differences in speed or accuracy between high school students and college students nor between males and females. Otis IQ scores were available for the high school students and there was a correlation between IQ and accuracy on both the first test (0·6) and the second test (0·5). Subjects who were confident also tended to be accurate ($r = 0·63$, $p < 0·001$). However, there was no correlation between mean speed of query writing and accuracy.

Questions were translated from English into Query-by-Example very quickly on the average (1·6 min/query; S.D. = 1·09). The mean time varied from 0·83 min for the fastest problem to 3·64 min for the slowest one. Although there was no overall significant relationship between the speed and accuracy of *subjects*, queries that were written more quickly on average were also written more accurately on average (as predicted by Halstead).

A finding of major interest in this study was the degree to which errors could be accounted for. Fifty four per cent of the variance in query accuracy could be accounted for on the basis of four parameters of query complexity: the number of different operators, the number of rows, the number of attributes, and the number of linking variables. As in the IQF study, there was a linear change in measures of difficulty (accuracy, speed, confidence ratings) with a linear change in objective complexity. Both the intercept and the slope of the line relating difficulty to complexity were smaller for Query-by-Example than IQF.

Combining the above variables with mean confidence rating and mean time increased the percentage of variance accounted for to 75%. In order to increase accounted-for variance to 90%, it was necessary to look at the nature of the English question that the experimental subjects were translating *from*. Longer English questions, and questions which were worded to require operators or values different in Query-by-Example from the original English, were more difficult even when the effects of the factors previously mentioned were held constant. When these two factors concerning the English wording were also used, 90% of the total variance in accuracy was accounted for.

The fact that English wording had an effect in addition to query complexity again suggests that a two-stage process is involved: comprehending the English—i.e. translating into some "deep structure" and then choosing a way of expressing that structure in the query language.

Seven of the questions used in the IQF study were also used in the study of Query-by-Example. The mean proportion correct for these seven queries was 0·30 in the IQF study and 0·54 for Query-by-Example. The times taken to write queries in the two systems were highly correlated ($r = 0·98$, $p < 0·001$) although subjects wrote the queries much faster in

Query-by-Example. Although the results were broadly consistent with Halstead's predictions in that Query-by-Example showed faster times, fewer errors, and a higher program level, performance data were again poorer for Query-by-Example than would have been predicted on the basis of expert results. The actual error rate, for example, on the question "Print the names of people who make less than $12,000, are over 28 years old and work for White" was $10\cdot3\%$ while the predicted error rate was only $0\cdot52\%$. The estimated time for this query was $4\cdot7$ s while the actual time was $1\cdot2$ min. (This latter time includes reading time and the time to make a confidence judgement.) Counting the choice of columns as additional operands does not substantially alter these predictions. This is not a criticism of the theory; it just again points out the need to extend it to novices.

A look at the difficulty subjects had with particular concepts illustrates another needed extension of Halstead's framework; viz., all concepts are not created equal. Some are more difficult than others and the *relationship between* the expression of a concept in English and in the query language is an important determiner of performance for novices. One source of difficulty for subjects was cases in which the English question had been intentionally phrased differently from the labels of the attributes. For example, the tables had an attribute labelled 'Year of Hire'. An English question which used the phrase "the people who have worked for us for more than five years" caused difficulty. People had a tendency to directly translate the phrase "more than" into the '>' operator. In fact, what was required was for the subjects to ask for people whose year of hire was LESS THAN the current year minus five. Similar difficulties were found in the IQF study.

There were several features of Query-by-Example that were particularly easy to use. For instance, the concepts of AND and OR were not expressed by keywords but were implicit in the structure of the query. This technique avoided confusions between the words "and" and "or" in English surface structure and the logical concepts AND and OR. For example, in the question "List all the people in department 440 and all the people in 470", what is really desired is a major OR and not the intersection of the set of people in 440 with those in 470. In Query-by-Example, people made few errors with AND versus OR concepts (error probability = $0\cdot003$).

In the IQF experiment, subjects made many errors in specifying the proper attribute; e.g. "years" rather than "year" or "highest degree" instead of "degree". These sorts of clerical errors were largely avoided in Query-by-Example since the person merely *selected* attributes by placing portions of the query in the proper column of the proper table.

Free variables in Query-by-Example were shown to be such by

underlining. Variable names could therefore be examples of the values that one wished to find. This method of differentiating constants from variables seemed to work quite well. Subjects made errors in underlining only about 1% of the time. Pilot subjects who had been taught the system individually seemed to like this feature, particularly those who were "afraid of math". For those subjects, anything with a traditional variable name (e.g. 'X', 'Y', 'Z') seemed to induce anxiety while underlined examples did not. This preliminary observation needs to be followed up with more systematic study.

Six subjects were able to be retested on Query-by-Example after two weeks. Without further training, these subjects wrote 53% correct queries on this retest. One subject forgot to underline and a second subject consistently confused ' < ' with ' > '. The other four subjects did not forget. The syntax of the language seemed easy to remember as well as easy to learn initially; this is particularly important for the casual user.

Recall that 35 of the subjects were given problem situations for which they were to generate their own English questions. The answers to these questions were to help solve the problem and be translatable into Query-by-Example. After writing the question in English, each subject was to translate it into the query language. Though subjects had been able to translate from English into Query-by-Example with facility, they were not at all skilled at generating reasonable questions. In fact, a few subjects did not ask questions at all but attempted to provide solutions to the problems. Many of the questions subjects generated were irrelevant. The largest proportion of questions were questions that could not be answered by any database query system; e.g. "Are the older faculty paid too much?"

In retrospect, these findings are not particularly surprising because the subjects had no familiarity with query systems and we had given them no training at all in how to use a database to solve a problem. In estimating training time for learning a query system it is vital to differentiate between users who already understand how to use a database to answer questions and those who are not only to learn a query language but who must also learn how to use a database to solve problems. It should also be stressed that these subjects used pencil and paper; additional training for using a display screen is likely (Clark, 1981).

C. SQUARE and SEQUEL

1. Background
SEQUEL and SQUARE are two research languages developed at IBM's San Jose Research Laboratories to enable non-programmers to query

relational databases. SQUARE is a fairly formal-looking language with, for example, an explicit composition operator (Boyce *et al.*, 1975). SEQUEL, in contrast, is intended to be logically equivalent, but easier to use. It employs English keywords like 'SELECT', 'FROM', 'WHERE', etc. (Chamberlin and Boyce, 1974). The example queries shown above in Query-by-Example are shown below; first in SEQUEL, then in SQUARE.

```
SELECT NAME
FROM EMP
WHERE SAL < '12000'
AND WHERE AGE > '28'
AND WHERE MGR = 'WHITE'

SELECT NAME
FROM EMPLOYEE
WHERE DEPT =
        SELECT DEPT
        FROM EMP
        WHERE NAME = 'RILEY'

              EMP     (<'12000', >'28', 'WHITE')
NAME          SAL,AGE,MGR

              EMP    o    EMP    ('RILEY')
NAME          DEPT        DEPT    NAME
```

The purpose of the study described below (Reisner *et al.*, 1974; Reisner, 1977) was to determine the relative ease of use of the two languages and to determine features that were good or might need change before implementation.

2. Method

Sixty-one undergraduates and three graduate students participated in the study. Subjects were paid for their participation. There were four experimental conditions: programmers learning SQUARE, programmers learning SEQUEL, non-programmers learning SQUARE, and non-programmers learning SEQUEL. The languages were taught in four separate classes which met 12 (for programmers) or 14 (for non-programmers) times over a two-week period. Each class session lasted about 50 min. Frequent quizzes were given and each subject was given an open book final exam. Most of the tests consisted of having subjects translate questions from English into the query language.

3. Results

SEQUEL was easier for non-programmers to learn than SQUARE. This was NOT the case for the programmers (defined as having completed one or more previous programming classes). The percentage of queries written completely correctly on the final exam was 51% for non-programmers who learned SEQUEL but only 34% for those who learned SQUARE. The programmers got about two-thirds of the queries correct with either language. About one-half of the errors were judged to be essentially clerical in nature.

An important suggestion to arise from this study was Reisner's (1977) idea that the language be learned in "layers"; that is, those features of the language that had proved easy to learn and use (e.g. mapping, selection, projection) should be learned first. Other features (e.g. free variables), if needed, could be learned later.

4. Theory

Again in this study, as in the IQF and the Query-by-Example study, some of the errors apparently arose when people attempted to translate too directly; i.e. too much on a word-by-word or phrase-by-phrase basis. The theoretical framework for analysing the translation process put forth by Reisner (1977) could provide the basis for a quantitative model of query writing. In her model, the query writer engages in three basic processes: template generation, lexical transformation, and insertion of the lexical items into the template. In template generation, a template for the overall form of the query is selected from a list or generated from components. Lexical transformation is the translation—largely word-by-word—from elements of an English question (e.g. "salary") into the appropriate attribute or value in the query language (e.g. SAL). Insertion puts the proper items into the proper spots in the template.

Perhaps this theory can be further refined, quantified, and provide a more precise framework of the type suggested by Halstead's (1977) work.

D. SQL and TABLET

1. Background

The four languages mentioned above (Interactive Query Facility, Query-by-Example, SEQUEL and SQUARE) differ from one another in a number of ways. To the extent that it is even possible to make comparisons among the various studies, it is still difficult to know what features or properties of the languages or training are responsible for people being able to write queries more accurately, more quickly or more confidently. Welty and Stemple (1978) wished to study two query languages that differed only in one well-defined way. SQL (essentially like SEQUEL) and TABLET are basically the same except that TABLET is procedural while SQL is not. Both languages use the same data model (Codd, 1970), are relationally complete (Codd, 1971), have similar language levels as measured by Halstead (1977), and could run on the same terminal equipment. In addition, those elements of the languages that are independent of the procedurality are identical. For example, both languages use the concept and syntax: GROUP BY. It should also be pointed out that while TABLET is more procedural than SQL, it is only procedural at a very high level. One need not specify, for instance, *how* GROUP BY is done.

2. Method

College students served as subjects. There were 18 "experienced" (one 3 credit FORTRAN or BASIC course) students who learned SQL, and 17 experienced students who learned TABLET. There were also 17 "inexperienced" (no previous programming) students who learned SQL and 20 inexperienced students who learned TABLET.

Each of the four groups was taught the appropriate language in a classroom setting. The manuals and quizzes were identical, *mutatis mutandis*. The classes met twice weekly for a total of 15 sessions. The final exam consisted of translating 30 questions from English into the respective query language. In addition, a retention test was given after three weeks. The students were motivated to do well by course credit and a grade.

3. Results

There was no overall difference between the two languages in the percentage of correctly written queries. For SQL, this percentage was 61·05 and for TABLET 61·71. Students writing in TABLET were more accurate on 2-table and group functions, particularly on the retest. SQL subjects were better on the set function. The same pattern of results was evidenced for the experienced subjects (who wrote 66·9% correctly averaged over the two languages) and for inexperienced subjects (who wrote 56·4% correctly averaged over the two languages). The pattern was somewhat *clearer* however, for the experienced subjects.

Subjects who wrote queries in SQL, while not more accurate, were somewhat faster and significantly so on the retention test. In addition, by self-report, students learning TABLET studied about 20% longer. As in the SEQUEL/SQUARE study and the Query-by-Example study, those *concepts* that were more difficult produced a higher error rate for both languages. The results of this study illustrate again both the general correctness of Halstead—two languages at the same level gave about the same overall performance regardless of the difference in procedurality— and, at the same time, the need for refinement—particular features were easier in one language or another depending upon the "naturalness" of the mapping from the concepts in English to the concepts as expressed in the Query Language.

E. Greenblatt and Waxman (1978)

1. Background
Greenblatt and Waxman (1978) wished to compare three languages all based on Codd's (1970) relational database model in an experiment where the trainers, method, tests, and scoring procedures were identical. The three languages chosen were Query-by-Example, SEQUEL, and an algebraic language.

2. Method
All subjects were high school or college students. Students were assigned to groups randomly. The students were above average, with slight but non-significant differences between groups. The students varied in their computer background with the Query-by-Example subjects having had an average of 1·0 computer courses; the SEQUEL group, an average of 1·9 previous courses; and the students who learned the algebraic language, 3·5 previous computer courses.

Students were taught in groups by using the same set of 25 examples. Students attempted to write queries on their own and then checked their answers with the instructors. Training time was left free to vary so that the same set of examples could be used in all three groups. After the initial training period of about 1 h 30 min, students were given a test in which they were required to translate English questions into the query language. As in Thomas and Gould (1975), subjects were required to write the time, read the question, write the answer, give a confidence rating and again write the time.

3. Results
The training time required for Query-by-Example was shortest (1 h 35 min) followed by SEQUEL (1 h 40 min) and the algebraic language (2 h 5 min).

Query-by-Example exhibited a slightly (non-significantly) higher percentage correct (75·2) than SEQUEL (72·8) or the algebraic language (67·7). Students were also significantly more confident of their queries in Query-by-Example. The average confidence rating was 1·6 for Query-by-Example and 1·9 for the other two languages. In addition, students wrote the queries significantly faster using Query-by-Example averaging only

0·9 min/query while taking 2·5 min/query in SEQUEL and 3·0 min/query in the algebraic language.

Confidence rating was a fairly good predictor of correctness in all three languages. The confidence that people feel about their queries is more important than may be obvious at first glance. In many cases, it may be extremely laborious or impossible for the user to check answers manually. An answer that the user lacks confidence in, will not be portrayed convincingly to others and the user will tend to value the system less.

F. Conclusions from query language studies

1. Feasibility of non-programmers learning a query language

One overall result from the studies is that college and high school students with little or no previous experience with computers can learn the basic functions of query languages fairly rapidly either in a single concentrated session of 2–3 h or in a class extended over a 10–15 week period. They will tend to translate about 0·75 of the queries correctly for simple queries. Individuals, even with the same background, will differ in the accuracy with which they tend to write these queries from about 1/3 to 9/10 correct.

Results are suggestive that middle-aged file clerks with no previous computer background can also learn a query language, but it may take somewhat longer. With any kind of population, however, it should be noted that learning a query language is not equivalent to learning to use a query language to solve problems. In a particular real-world application, it may be necessary to familiarize people with the database, to train their problem solving skills, and to teach them the features of whatever I/O devices are used, besides teaching the syntax of a particular query language.

2. Comparisons between different languages

Taken together, the results suggest that Query-by-Example is somewhat easier to learn than the other query languages studied, and that people are somewhat more accurate with it once learned. Even stronger was the finding that queries could be written much more quickly in Query-by-Example. This may not seem particularly surprising given that one simply has to write less. A number of queries written in each of several languages were examined in detail by the author. Program level (Halstead, 1977) was consistently higher in Query-by-Example, which would predict the faster writing times that were found.

There is also some suggestion that SEQUEL, which contains English keywords, is easier for non-programmers to learn and use than the logically equivalent SQUARE. In addition, there is some evidence that two languages that differ only in procedurality (SQL and TABLET) are relatively comparable in difficulty except for certain features. In particular, a SET operation which *is* essentially non-procedural is better in the non-procedural SQL, while GROUP BY is more easily learned in TABLET where the order as written in the query corresponds to the order of operations that need to be performed (in contrast to SQL).

3. Suggestions for improved design

One of the unexpected findings of the Query-by-Example study was the degree to which erroneous queries could be accounted for. Partial confirmation was obtained in Greenblatt and Waxman (1978). One could imagine a query system that would monitor the total time taken to formulate a query, and look at the objective complexity of the query, perhaps measured in terms of Halstead's formulae. If a complex query were entered, the system might also ask the user for a confidence rating that the query were correct. If the query would take tremendous resources and was likely to be incorrect, the system may want to feedback the query to the user prior to searching the entire database a few times. General guidelines for software design can be found in Thomas and Carroll (1981). The most important single suggestion is that users and uses should be considered from the beginning of the design process (Thomas and Carroll, 1979).

4. Suggestions for improved implementation

A framework for thinking about the variables operating in an experiment was presented at the beginning of Section II. It should now be pointed out that performance in a real-world setting will also depend upon a number of variables in addition to the query language difficulty. Performance will depend upon training and help facilities, for instance, as well as the capabilities and motivation of the users.

A number of social factors will also have great influence. For instance, a number of studies indicate that an organizational change will tend to be accepted to the extent that those impacted by the change feel that they have participated in the decision-making and problem solving that led to the change (Bass and Barrett, 1972). In addition to the investment that a firm may make in capital equipment which may lead to an increase in productivity, the users of the equipment may also perceive an increased effort on their part and may expect some portion of the gain in productivity to be returned to them. If users perceive that a new system is simply forced upon them and that they have taken the effort to learn something which increases only the profit of others, increased turnover, absenteeism, and sabotage may cancel potential productivity benefits. The way to minimize such dangers is to make the end-user feel that he or she is a participant in the choice and implementation of a system and a beneficiary of the productivity increase.

As suggested by Reisner (1977), it is probably wise to implement a query system in layers with the users initial introduction to the system consisting of the easier, more commonly used functions. There is, however, a certain amount of difficulty in getting users to then move on to the more complex set. Users are likely to stay with a small, sufficient, but relatively inefficient set of commands (cf. Boies, 1974).

5. Summary of recommendations based on query language studies

(1) Have the user select rather than produce whenever feasible.
(2) Allow examples as variables.
(3) Be sure the user knows how to solve problems, is familiar with the database, knows how to use the I/O, and knows how to get help when needed.
(4) Have potential users participate as fully as possible in the design and implementation of the system.
(5) Have the user write the query directly into a format that reflects the instrinsic data organization.
(6) Predict the probability that a query is erroneous and when that probability is high and the retrieval looks costly, feed this information back to the user.
(7) Have users introduced to the system in layers, with the easiest functions introduced first.

III. Related psychological studies

The objective of a user of a database query language is to receive output information in response to an input query. Thus, the psychological studies can be conveniently grouped into those most relevant to: (A) the way user's perceive and understand computer output; (B) the way users produce inputs to the computer; and (C) interactions.

A. The user's perceptions and understanding

1. Understanding quantified expressions

Universal quantification is fundamental to many database ideas. Yet people seem to have difficulty with quantifiers, at least as logicians use them (e.g. Roberge, 1970; Ceraso and Provitera, 1971; Revlis, 1975). A number of studies were therefore performed in our laboratory in order to understand the difficulties people have with quantified statements (Thomas, 1976a,b, 1978). In these studies, several methods of judging people's understanding of quantifiers were used. Subjects in various experiments translated English questions into a query language, generated their own English questions, translated Venn diagrams into English, translated English into Venn diagrams, gave judgements about the consistency of two English statements, manually looked up answers in a database in response to English questions, participated in a simulated human–computer natural language dialog or communicated with each other via teletype about simple set relations.

In these various situations, subjects consistently showed difficulty in dealing with simple set relations. Set identity and set disjunction were dealt with relatively well; however, situations wherein A was a subset of B were handled less well. Partially overlapping sets caused even more difficulty. Most difficult of all were situations in which more than one set relation was possible. It is not that people used quantified expressions in some consistent way that was merely different from the way that logicians use these terms; people did not spontaneously agree completely among themselves about what is or might be meant by such statements as "Some A are B".

When people generated their own questions in attempting to solve a complex problem, they used several strategies that avoided having to formulate questions with complex explicit quantification, particularly universal quantification. These strategies included using negation and existential quantifiers rather than a universal quantifier (e.g. "Is anyone outside physics dissatisified?" rather than "Is everyone in every department except physics satisfied?"). Another strategy was to rely on feedback as in the game of 20 questions to help specify the relation. Thus, "Are the physicists satisfied?" with possible answers "yes", "no", and "partly" was preferred to "Is every physicist satisfied?" Another strategy was to use a series of simple questions rather than attempting to state one complexly quantified question.

In fact, in both the problem-solving situations and in the simulated human–computer dialogs, subjects seldom used any explicit universal quantification. There *were* implicit universal quantifiers and there were also occasions when subjects used the English word "all" but not in a sense equivalent to a logician's notion of universal quantification. The futility of trying to map the word "all" into universal quantification is illustrated in the following exchange between someone trying to understand an order-handling and billing system and the person trying to explain the system (Thomas, 1976a).

USER: Help.
SYSTEM: Which notion is causing difficulty?
USER: All notions.
SYSTEM: Like what?
USER: Like everything you've sent me.

The experiments summarized above as well as those of Roberge (1970), Ceraso and Provitera (1971), and Revlis (1975) indicate that certain kinds of set relations are easier for people than others. In addition, some people tend to exhibit certain common biases of interpretation. For example, the statement "Some X and Y" is most often taken to mean that Y is a proper subset of X or that X and Y are partially overlapping sets. People very seldom imagine that X is a proper subset of Y or that X and Y are identical. Yet these are logical possibilities.

Why do such biases exist? Can they be modified by the situation? According to Thomas (1978), people generally communicate in order to change what is in the head of another person (rather than simply *transmit* what is in their own head). It was hypothesized that under cooperative conditions subjects would follow Grice's (1975) conversational postulates. According to these postulates people will tend, for example, to be informative, relevant, and clear. Subjects describing a situation where X was a proper subset of Y, then, would not use the expression "SOME X are Y" (since saying that ALL X are Y was more informative and no more costly). Furthermore, if both subjects knew that they were in a cooperative situation, the person interpreting the message would seldom interpret "some X are Y" to mean that X was a proper subset of Y. These and similar predictions were upheld confirming the biases observed in earlier studies (e.g. Roberge, 1970).

In another condition of the study though, the designer and the interpreter of a message both knew that they were in a *competitive* situation. The person sending the message was constrained to send a true and relevant message. Nevertheless, they could send a message that was incomplete, ambiguous, or misleading. It was hypothesized in such a case that the person sending a message *would*, for instance, often use the expression "Some X are Y" to refer to a situation wherein actually *all* X's were Y's. It was further hypothesized that the interpreter of such messages, realizing the competitive nature of the situation, would often interpret "Some X and Y" as referring to situations where all X's were Y's. In other words, it was hypothesized that Grice's conversational postulates and the derived biases of production and interpretation would *not* hold for the competitive case. This prediction was also upheld.

The implication for computer query systems is this: quantified statements are constructed and interpreted by people depending upon their goals. The new user of a computer system will often erroneously tend to assume that the computer is engaged with them in a cooperative enterprise. Suppose the user asks "are some generators overloaded?" and receives the answer "yes". The user will tend to assume that this answer implies that ONLY SOME generators are overloaded. The data in the computer, however, may well imply that not only are some generators overloaded; ALL are. The user will tend to assume Grice's postulates are at work and thus be misled. The designer of a query system should either incorporate Grice's conversational postulates into the system or warn the new user *not* to think of the computer query system as being cooperative.

The following further recommendations are based on studies of quantifiers.

(1) Study the users, tasks, and goals for particular situations.
(2) Make it possible for users to use their natural strategies for querying unless you can specify and train better ones.
(3) If you use logical quantifiers, expect and prepare for errors.
(4) Limit wherever possible the user's task to producing or choosing descriptions that are consistent with their intentions rather than exactly specifying their intentions.
(5) Whenever possible have the system and the user communicate in terms of set identity and disjunction.
(6) In a natural language query system, rather than attempting to interpret, disambiguate, and answer exactly the user's exact question, provide data sufficient for the user's purpose.

This last point requires some clarification by example. If the user, for instance, asks for "Ford and GM earnings for 1967 and 1968", simply provide a two-by-two table with the marginal totals rather than trying to determine which of the possible "logical" questions the user meant.

Meister (1976) states that "in general, personnel gather too little information prior to making a decision. However, when more information is available, subjects are more efficient in selecting data items." This generalization again suggests that it may be wiser as a general rule to provide the user with slightly MORE data (properly labelled of course) than is asked for. Too much information will be ignored fairly easily and cost the system little in most cases. Providing such additional information to the user partially addresses the issue of the conversational postulate of informativeness raised above. Too little information, on the other hand, may result in confusion, additional queries, and often, in wrong decisions.

2. How people organize data

Psychological studies of how people can and do organize data are also relevant to the design of databases. If certain kinds of organizations are much easier for people to understand and use, then, *ceteris paribus*, it would be preferable to use those kinds of organizations.

Durding *et al.* (1977) examined the ways in which college students were able to organize word lists. In each of three experiments, the subjects were given several lists of 15–20 words. Each of these lists were pre-defined by the experimenters to exhibit a particular kind of organization. These pre-defined organizations included lists (with or without labels), networks, tables (with or without labels), hierarchies, or random. Short illustrative examples of words that could most naturally be organized in these ways are: Lists (Ford, Plymouth, Carnation, Rose, Daisy), Networks (Penny, Nickel, Metal, Wood, Paper), Hierarchies (Transportation, Cars, Planes, Ford, Concorde), and Tables (Input, Output, Digital, Analog, Keyboard, Joystick). The task of the subject, for each set of words, was simply to organize the words.

Overall, subjects used the organization presumed more natural by the experimenters about two-thirds of the time. There was a tendency on the part of some subjects to organize everything as a list. (Organizing in this way has fewer constraints for a correct answer typically than organizing into hierarchies or tables.) Some of the subjects were given specific examples of the various kinds of organizations, but this had no effect on the frequency with which they chose the appropriate organization. The facts that people usually chose the appropriate organization and that giving examples did not increase the probability of so choosing provides evidence that all of these ways of organizing data were familiar.

In a second experiment, subjects were given sets of words and, in addition, each page of words also contained a skeleton which showed the organization appropriate to that particular list of words. Subjects generally filled in these frames quite well. There was a tendency for lists to be the easiest organizations for people to fill in. Hierarchies were somewhat harder, followed by tables, and finally networks. If one looks at the ratio of correct arrangements to the total number of possible arrangements for these organizations, one obtains exactly the same ordering. Thus, the differences in accuracy may have been more a reflection of chance than differences in conceptual difficulty.

In the third experiment, subjects had difficulty when required to organize words into formats that were antithetical to the inherent semantic relationships. The three experiments together illustrate that most college students can understand and use most of the common database organizational schemes (at least for words) provided that these words are to be organized in an intuitively reasonable way.

3. Further characteristics of output

A number of studies have dealt with how data and how control information should be presented to people to enhance understanding. These issues are discussed at greater length in Engel and Granda (1975) and Miller and Thomas (1977). Briefly, information will be more comprehensible if it is tabular or graphic. Large output tables should have columns marked by vertical lines or spaces and also have horizontal lines or spaces every five items (see Wright and Fox, 1970; Wright and Reid, 1973; Kamman, 1975). In addition, a greater number of different alternatives can be discriminated when the alternatives are coded on a greater number of dimensions (Miller, 1956). A final point is that providing the user with contextual stimuli, even when those stimuli do not logically enter into the user's decision, *may improve* comprehensibility. Studies in cognitive psychology have shown, for example, that two words (e.g. CORD and WORD) are under some conditions easier to discriminate than two letters (e.g. C and W) (Wheeler, 1970). Adding a picture, title, or single sentence to a story can make it easier to comprehend and remember the story (Bransford and Franks, 1973). Brevity may be the soul of wit, but deleting locally redundant inf frm a prntout or disp may NOT alwys aid the usr or max tot human–machine sys perf (as the preceding clause illustrates). The messages a system outputs to the user can also impact productivity and attitude (Shneiderman, 1982).

B. The user's productions

1. Patterns of question-asking

Successive user queries are very seldom independent. Yet, query system designers often overlook the dependency. Different users and different tasks produce different patterns of questions (Bruner *et al.*, 1956; Malhotra, 1975; Thomas, 1976a). To capitalize maximally then on the relations within a sequence of queries, it would be necessary to study particular applications. Minimally though, query systems should make it easy for the user to retrieve and modify the immediately preceding query and to define, store, and retrieve commonly used query formats. A query system designer may also wish to consider storage management algorithms that utilize the user's view of how data items are related.

2. Problem solving strategies and aids

In designing a database system, it is probably wise for the designer to remind herself or himself occasionally that the purpose of having data available is to help people achieve their goals which may include: (1) finding data relevant to solving a particular problem, (2) finding background data to give them an intuitive feel for a problem, (3) finding data that will support a pre-existing answer they have already decided on ("don't confuse me with facts; my mind is made up"). If, in a particular case, the data will be honestly used to help *solve* a problem, then it is important that the problem solver be effective. Often, however, people do not spontaneously adopt optimal problem solving strategies. We can imagine that as computer systems become cheaper and used by a larger number of people it will become more and more necessary (and feasible) for a database system to do more than simply allow one to access data. A future system will be useful to the extent that it also encourages or helps the user to be an effective problem solver. In many cases, this will require more than simply passively waiting for the user to specify what data is needed. Rather, the system can help remind the user of various potentially relevant strategies, tactics, and problem characteristics. In this section, *very briefly*, some of the important findings in the psychology of problem solving are presented.

When people solve problems, their strategy is a primary determinant of their ability to solve (Meister, 1976); however, people often do not spontaneously adopt the best strategies (Bruner, 1959; Newell and Simon, 1972). In fact, what has often been attributed to other factors (e.g. ageing), is at least partly due to strategy differences (Welford, 1958; Hulicka and Grossman, 1967; Fozard and Thomas, 1975). People can learn to solve problems better (Stein, 1976). On the other hand, many people do not want to admit to any sort of imperfection, and will "yeah but" any suggestion that they could use the data in a database in a more effective manner. Rather than explicit training in problem solving skill, a more effective method of improving the user's problem solving performance is probably to embed good strategies in the query system. For instance, the initial menu for a query system could ask the user to select what phase of problem solving they were in, thus providing a subtle reminder that problem formulation (e.g.) should be a separate stage that precedes any attempt at problem solving. Similar comments apply to the choice of representation (Carroll *et al.*, 1981).

3. Naming and specifying

One of the fundamental types of actions that a user wants to do in any computer system is name things. For example, a database user may ask much the same questions every day. Regardless of the particular database language used, it would be useful for the user to be able to name and retrieve these common types of questions and then simply modify them for the particular questions of that particular day.

Some psychological research now exists on how people name things and how they *should* name things for maximum memorability. It is not true that just because a user chooses the names, that he or she will later be able to remember the names of desired query frames. For a review of naming research, see Carroll (1978). More recent studies include Carroll (1980), Baggett and Ehrenfeucht (1981), Black (1981) and Barnard (1982).

O'Dierno (1976) provides one real-world example of how studying the natural naming of end-users can enhance a computer system. He found that in cost-accounting and inventory applications at New York University, a great many errors were made with the numeric codes used for inventory items. Numbers are typically used to provide a unique key. If names are consistent and distinguishable enough, they can also theoretically provide a key. However, some mechanism is needed to insure a one-to-one mapping between names and things. In an effort to determine the feasibility of replacing numeric codes with English words, O'Dierno looked at the way users described 50,000 item types. On the basis of that study, he decided that 40 characters would suffice to provide unique natural language descriptors (adjectives and nouns) for each item. The system was implemented and resulted in far fewer operator errors than had been the case with numeric codes. The number of new descriptors that had to be added to the system fell over a two-year period from 37 per month to five per month. This study illustrates three important points: (1) even without changing the fundamental nature of a computer system, merely changing labels can improve performance; (2) unique natural language names are possible keys even with a large set of items; (3) to be usable, such a system needs to be extensible.

C. Man–machine interaction

1. Dialog characteristics

As already pointed out, successive questions are typically related. Cognitive scientists attempting to design query systems that operate completely in natural language realize that such a system must not only have an extensive semantic network relevant to the area of questioning but must also have a model of dialog in the system. A model of dialog characteristics, however, can be useful not only to a natural language system (which remains a program for the future) but also for any other question-answering system.

In an attempt to determine more about the characteristics of natural language dialog, several dialogs were recorded in which order-handling and billing systems were discussed via communicating display scopes (Thomas, 1976). Subjects were variously attempting to understand, describe, or diagnose a complex order-handling and billing system.

One finding of interest concerns vocabulary. There was considerable overlap in the vocabulary that different experimental subjects used when discussing business. For example, 461 types accounted for 91·3% of the tokens (as opposed to only 61·8% of the tokens in the American Heritage word count of Carroll *et al.* (1971)). In addition to generally common words like "I", "the" and "and", a fairly small core (52) of business/programming words were used. It is unlikely that a greater number of subjects would have substantially added to the number of business terms. Furthermore, while, *in general*, some of these words (file, active, charge, order) have a number of distinctly different meanings, within the dialogs their meaning was generally restricted to one meaning.

On the other hand, there was considerable diversity of vocabulary used to describe communication itself. A fair amount of the dialog material was in the form of explicit or implicit metacomments. An explicit metacomment makes explicit mention of some aspect of communication; e.g. "I think I am confused." An implicit metacomment is embedded within a content sentence but is intended to affect the *way* the other person processes the rest of the message. For example, "Now, ..." generally implies that the topic of discussion is about to change. One use of the word "however" is apparently to prevent the listener from concluding something which they might otherwise conclude and to signal that what follows is different from or even opposite to a natural inference or generalization. It would be important for a natural language question-answering system to understand the meaning of such signal words as "Now, ..." and "...; however, ...".

When asked to confine natural language to a fairly small set of words (predetermined by situation-specific usage statistics), dyads solving problems interactively were just about as effective as when using unconstrained natural language (Chapanis, 1976). This suggests that it is not too vital for a natural language query system to handle a large number of *words* provided it handles the requisite *concepts* (including both those relevant to content and those relevant to communication itself) in a sophisticated fashion.

2. Response time

Other things being equal, users would probably prefer to have fast rather than slow response time. There are several points that should be kept in mind, however. First, the user may be willing to tolerate a longer system response following a "large" transaction (Miller, 1968). Secondly, the user's performance and satisfaction with a system may depend more importantly on the *variability* of response rate than response rate *per se* (Miller, 1976). Thirdly, system response time correlates with user's response rate (Boies, 1974). Fourthly, it is possible that for complex tasks it may improve the user's performance to lock them out for a while to prevent them from responding too impulsively (Boehm *et al.*, 1971).

3. Richness of the interface

Reviews of traditional displays include Gould (1968), Martin (1973), McLaughlin (1973) and Rouse (1975). Recommendations exist for the maximum set size for rapid, error-free performance for coding by various separate visual dimensions like size (2-4), colour (6), flashing (2), line angle (8), brightness (2) and shape (10). What is often ignored, however, is that people are generally capable of discriminating and remembering more information if the information is encoded on more rather than fewer dimensions. (Though the total amount discriminable is somewhat less than the sum of the amounts discriminable in the separate dimensions.)

Largely for practical reasons, writing developed so that only the shapes of characters and their arrangement on the page encoded much information. With modern computer displays it is possible (but not common) to encode information by using combinations of motion, shape, size, colour, position, and flashing. Few existing commercial systems encode information as richly as would probably maximize human performance (and interest).

Perhaps the most dramatic existing example of what could be done in a database retrieval system that uses multidimensional encoding is the audio-visual "fly-through" database described by Fields and Negroponte (1977). In this system, which uses a wall-sized colour screen and octophonic sound, a user "flys" via joystick controls through a very iconic representation of the data. For example, the user may fly to "mapland" whereupon the user may zoom into a map of Cambridge, Massachusetts and zoom into the MIT campus and then zoom into a floor plan for a particular building and then zoom into a particular office.

Such interfaces have intrinsic reinforcing properties. Unless a system will be used in a setting in which the user's extrinsic rewards are closely tied to use of and performance on the system, it may be very important to have an interface with this kind of intrinsic interest. Otherwise, the reinforcements of social interaction, daydreaming, or even doing the job by hand may greatly reduce overall human–computer system performance. An additional positive aspect of such an interface is that it provides a coherent model to the user thus making learning and using easier (see Carroll and Thomas (1982) for issues relating to the use of metaphors in computer systems).

4. Summary of recommendations from related psychological studies

(1) Realize that users have difficulty with quantifiers and plan accordingly. (See specific recommendations above.)
(2) Have the organization of the database reflect the inherent semantic relationships in the data.
(3) Encode information richly.
(4) Provide some context information for the user.
(5) Provide structure for the user. Initially, it may be useful to explain the system metaphorically.
(6) Error on the side of giving too much, rather than too little, information in response to a query.
(7) If feasible, study the user's current strategies for problem solving—what kinds of questions are asked and why.
(8) Make system response time predictable to the user.
(9) Give the user feedback during long delays about what is happening.
(10) Use labels that are meaningful, particularly for naive or casual users.

IV. Issues to address in design

The first section above reviewed experiments specifically designed to find out more about the way people use query languages. The second section provides some important data and theory which the systems designer should "keep in mind" when designing a system. In the following section, a series of issues to address in database query systems are listed in a suggested sequence of consideration. These issues are largely illustrated by example questions that the designer should ask himself or herself. These sections concentrate on those issues that a designer is less likely to consider spontaneously.

A. The goals of the database system

Before attempting to design a system to satisfy some goals, the designer should know what the goals are. The first thing to be aware of is that different individuals, groups, or departments within an organization will all have somewhat different goals. The designer is often put in a bind. The end-users are not typically the people who have the decision-making power to commission a system. A system which completely satisfies the end-users but not management will never be sold. On the other hand, a system which, in principle, management supports but which later turns out to be unused by the end-users is also undesirable. This problem is further complicated by the fact that organizations sometimes "pretend" that all subgroups within the organization have identical goals. Provided an organization is open to discussing the diversity of goals within itself, Land's (1971) method of combining goals for computer systems may prove quite valuable.

B. The user (payoffs, capabilities, experience)

Who is going to use the system? What are their *actual* payoffs? Capabilities? Experience? Some attempt should be made to determine what motivates users. It is also important to know what management *thinks* motivates them, but the two will overlap to different degrees in different situations. Can the system be designed to make use of these payoffs? For example, if you would like people to use the system all day rather than bunching all requests at 9 am and 4 pm, is it likely to be sufficient merely to tell people that system response will improve? Probably not. Instead, determine what rewards can be used to modify behaviour.

Do people currently get social satisfaction from interacting with others to solve a problem? Will this kind of interaction be facilitated or diminished by the installation of the system? What are the rewards for users if they learn your system? If they use it well?

What are the capabilities of the users? Can they learn and use a complex language? Are they willing to learn arbitrary codes?

What are the previous experiences of the users? Are they familiar with the database? With the language? The equipment? The strategies of asking questions? Are they formulating their own questions or simply translating questions received from others into a computer-readable form?

Although the answers to these questions cannot yet be plugged into a formula, the very act of seriously considering them will enhance the designer's understanding of the situation.

C. The tasks as now performed

What are the tasks as now performed? What are the strategies that people use? Can these strategies be supported by the system? These questions are worth asking before going to the issue of Section D below.

D. The tasks as ideally performed

Can you think of a better way to get the same job accomplished? Here is where the traditional systems analysis often completely concentrates.

E. Layered, progressive system implementation approach

Ideally, the simplest parts of the system, which should also be the fastest and cover most of the applications, should be learned first. Leave the more complex, harder-to-learn functions for later. The problem then becomes: How can you motivate people to learn the more complex parts of the system if they can already get most of their job done with the simple parts? One possibility is to have career paths tied to increases in what the person knows how to use. As the person learns more function, they can take on greater responsibility and receive commensurate increases in pay and status. These matters are typically outside the jurisdiction of the systems designer. From the standpoint of industrial psychology, however, the ultimate success of a database query system will depend crucially on many non-computer factors such as how management internally markets the system and how they select, train, motivate, appraise, and perform the end-users. For this reason, the computer system designer might best be part of an inter-disciplinary team whose responsibility and authority encompass all these factors (cf. Papanek, 1971). For a discussion of and practical guide to addressing industrial psychology issues relevant to the implementation of a computer system, see London (1976).

F. Measure and modify

Today's system will not meet tomorrow's needs. The system will have to be modified. But in what ways? What features of a language give the users trouble and should be modified? One method to gather information is by questionnaire. Another is to wait for complaints. A third and more effective alternative is to include in the system the capability for automatically monitoring and summarizing statistics on usage patterns (see Boies (1974) for an example analysis of user behaviour). If this monitoring is an *integral part of the system design*, updating and modifying the system can be based on fact—not fancy—and the query language designer can profit from the insights provided by his previous efforts. The design cycle should not end with the delivery of a product (Sommer, 1972).

V. Conclusions

Here is where we stand. Though based on science and technology, design is an art. No-one can specify how to design a query system for a particular situation. There is a fairly good overall theory (Halstead, 1977) of programming effort which appears to generalize to writing queries, though it ignores many details that might be important in particular cases.

Several experiments have been done wherein novices learned particular query languages. These studies suggested the recommendations in Section IIE. A number of further psychological experiments provide additional guidelines for output to the user, input from the user, and dialog with the user. These guidelines are summarized in Section IIID. In addition, it is important for the designer of a query system to ask the questions posed in Section IV, particularly the questions concerning the goals, the users, and how to implement and modify the system. (Task questions are also important, but the designer is most likely to deal with those issues in any case.)

Additional research is required on at least three fronts: (1) theoretical work to attempt to integrate what is known by psychologists about problem solving, perception, learning, and human performance into a usable, quantified, more integrated framework; (2) research on the use of real-world complex systems—but this research must do more than ask users for opinions—it also requires theory and control; (3) basic research on the fundamental aspects of human performance—e.g. do sophisticated users of a query system continue to formulate questions in English and translate them into a query language or do they begin to formulate the questions in the query language? Prior to getting the answers to all these questions, database applications will continue to grow. Using the guidelines above will hopefully increase the chances that the user of a query language will be as effective as possible in helping people solve the problems that belong to us all.

VI. Acknowledgements

Thanks are due to John Gould, Jack Carroll, and Steve Boies who each made excellent suggestions concerning earlier drafts of this chapter.

VII. References

Baggett, P. and Ehrenfeucht, A. (1981). How an unfamiliar thing should be called. ONR Technical Report Number 111.

Barnard, P. J. (1982). Learning and remembering interactive commands. Presented at the Human Factors in Computer Systems conference.

Bass, B. M. and Barrett, G. V. (1972). *Man, Work, and Organizations*. Allyn Bacon, Boston.

Black, J. B. (1982). Learning and remembering command names. Presented at the Human Factors in Computer Systems conference.

Boehm, B. W. (1973). Software and its impact: A quantitative assessment. *Datamation* May, 48–59.

Boehm, B. W., Seven, M. J. and Watson, R. A. (1971). Interactive problem-solving—An experimental study of "lockout" effects. *Proceedings of the Spring Joint Computer Conference*, pp. 205–210.

Boies, S. J. (1974). User behavior in an interactive computer system. *IBM Systems Journal* 13, 1–18.

Boyce, R. F., Chamberlin, D. D., Kind, W. and Hammer, M. (1975). Specifying Queries as Relational Expressions: SQUARE. *Communications of the ACM*, November.

Bransford, J. D. and Franks, J. J. (1971). The abstraction of linguistic ideas. *Cognitive Psychology* 2, 331–350.

Bruner, J. S., Goodnow, J. J. and Austin, G. A. (1956). *A Study of Thinking*. Wiley, New York.

Carroll, J. B., Davies, P. and Richman, B. (1971). *The American Heritage Word Frequency Book*. Houghton Mifflin, Boston.

Carroll, J. M. (1978). Naming: an interdisciplinary review. *IBM Research Report*, RC-7370.

Carroll, J. M. (1980). Naming personal files in an interactive computing environment. *IBM Research Report*, RC 8356.

Carroll, J. M. and Thomas, J. C. (1982). Metaphor and the cognitive representation of computing systems. *IEEE Transactions on Systems, Man, and Cybernetics*.

Carroll, J. M., Thomas, J. C. and Malhotra, A. (1981). Presentation and representation in design problem solving. *British Journal of Psychology* 71, 143–153.

Ceraso, J. and Provitera, A. (1971). Sources of error in syllogistic reasoning. *Cognitive Psychology* 2, 400–410.

Chapanis, A. (1971). Prelude to 2001: explorations in human communication. *American Psychologist* 26, 949–961.

Chapanis, A. (1976). Interactive human communication: some lessons learned from laboratory experiments. Paper presented at NATO Advanced Study Institute on "Man–Computer Interaction". Mati, Greece.

Clark, I. (1981). Software simulation as a tool for usable product design. *IBM Systems Journal* 20(3), 272–293.

Codd, E. F. (1970). A relational model of data for large shared data bases. *Communications of the ACM* 13(6), 377–387.

Codd, E. F. (1971). Relational completeness of data base sublanguages. *Data Base Systems*. Currant Computer Science Symposia, Vol. 6. Prentice-Hall, New York.

Curtis, B., Sheppard, S., Milliman, P., Borst, M. and Love, T. (1979). Measuring the psychological complexity of software maintenance tasks with the Halstead and McCabe metrics. *IEEE Transactions on Software Engineering*, SE-5 (2), 96–104.

Durding, B., Becker, C. and Gould, J. D. (1977). Data Organization. *Human Factors* 19(1), 1–14.

Engel, S. E. and Granda, R. E. (1975). Guidelines for man/display interfaces. *IBM Technical Report*, TR 00.2720.

Fields, C. and Negroponte, N. (1977). Using new clues to find data. *Proceedings of the Third International Conference on Very Large Data Bases*. AFIPS Press, New York.

Fozard, J. L. and Thomas, J. C. (1975). Psychology of aging: basic findings and some psychiatric implications. *In* J. Howells (Ed.), *Modern Perspectives in the Psychiatry of Old Age*. Bruner/Mazel, New York.

Gould, J. D. (1968). Visual features in the design of computer-controlled CRT displays. *Human Factors* 10, 359–376.

Gould, J. D. and Ascher, R. (1975). Use of an IQF-like query language by non-programmers. *IBM Research Report*, RC-5279.

Green, T. R. G. (1977). Conditional program statements and their comprehensibility to professional programmers. *Journal of Occupational Psychology* 50, 93–109.

Greenblatt, D. and Waxman, J. (1978). A study of three database query languages. *In* B. Shneiderman (Ed.), *Databases: Improving Usability and Responsiveness*. Academic Press, New York and London.

Grice, H. P. (1975). Logic and conversation. *In* D. Davidson and G. Harman (Eds), *The Logic of Grammar*, Dickenson, En Cino.

Halstead, H. M. (1977). *Elements of Software Science*. Elsevier, New York.

Hulicka, I. and Grossman, J. Age-group comparisons for the use of mediators in paired-associate learning. *Journal of Gerontology* 1967, 22, 46–51.

IBM Interactive Query Facility (IQF) for IMS/360, Publication Number GH20-1074, IBM Corporation, White Plains, New York.

Kamman, R. (1975). The comprehensibility of printed instructions and flowchart alternative. *Human Factors* 17, 183–191.

Land, F. (1977). Evaluation of systems goals in determining a design strategy for a computer based information system. *The Computer Journal* 19(4).

Lindsay, P. and Norman, D. (1972). *Human Information Processing*. Academic Press, New York and London.

London, K. R. (1976). *The People Side of Systems*. McGraw-Hill, London.

Love, L. T. Relating individual differences in computer programming performance to human information processing abilities. Ph.D. dissertation, Department of Psychology, University of Washington.

Malhotra, A. (1975). On problem diagnosis. *IBM Research Report*, RC-5498.

Malhotra, A. and Sheridan, P. (1976). Experimental determination of design requirements for a program explanation system. *IBM Research Report*, RC-5831.

Martin, J. (1973). *Design of Man–Computer Dialogues*. Prentice-Hall, Englewood Cliffs, New Jersey.

Mayer, R. (1976). Different problem-solving competencies established in learning computer programming with and without meaningful models. *Journal of Educational Psychology* **68**, 143–150.

McLaughlin, R. (1973). Alphanumeric display terminal survey. *Datamation*, Nov., 71–92.

Meister, D. (1976). *Behavioral Foundations of System Development*. Wiley, New York.

Miller, L. A. and Thomas, J. C. (1977). Behavioral issues in the use of interactive systems. *International Journal of Man–Machine Studies* **9**, 509–536.

Miller, L. H. (1976). An investigation of the effects of output variability and output bandwidth on user performance in interactive computer systems. *ISI Research Report*, 76–80.

Miller, R. B. (1968). Response times in computer conversations. *Proceedings of the Fall Joint Computer Conference*. AFIPS Press, New York.

Newell, A. and Simon, H. A. (1972). *Human Problem Solving*. Prentice-Hall, Englewood Cliffs, New Jersey.

Nickerson, R., Elkind, J. and Carbonell, J. (1968). Human factors and the design of time sharing computer systems. *Human Factors* **10**(2), 127–137.

O'Dierno, E. (1976). Designing computer systems for people. Paper presented at the Symposium, "The role of human factors in computers". Baruch College, New York.

Papanek, V. (1971). *Designing for the Real World*. Pantheon Books, New York.

Reisner, P. (1977). Use of psychological experimentation as an aid to development of a query language. *IEEE Transactions on Software Engineering*, SE-3 (3), 218–229.

Reisner, P., Boyce, R. and Chamberlin, D. (1974). Human factors evaluation of two data-base query languages: SQUARE and SEQUEL. *IBM Research Report*, RJ 1478.

Roberge, J. (1970). A reexamination of the interpretation of errors in formal syllogistic reasoning. *Psychonomic Science* **19**(6), 331–333.

Sheridan, T. and Ferrell, W. (1974). *Man–Machine Systems: Information, Control, and Decision Models of Human Performance*. MIT Press, Cambridge, Mass.

Shneiderman, B. (1976). Exploratory experiments in programmer behavior. *International Journal of Computer and Information Science* **5**(2), 123–143.

Shneiderman, B. (1977). Measuring computer program quality and comprehension. *Information Systems Management Technical Report*, 16.

Shneiderman, B. (1978). Improving the human factors aspect of database interactions. *ACM Transactions on Database Systems* **3**(4), 417–439.

Shneiderman, B. (1979). *Software Psychology*. Winthrop, Cambridge, Mass.

Shneiderman, B. (1982). System message design: guidelines and experimental results. *In* A. Badre and B. Shneiderman (Eds), *Directions in Computer Interactions*. Ablex, Norwood, NJ.

Shneiderman, B., Mayer, R., McKay, D. and Heller, P. (1977). Experimental investigations of the utility of detailed flowcharts in a program. *Communications of the ACM* **20**(6), 373–381.

Sime, M. E., Green, T. R. G. and Guest, D. J. (1973). Psychological evaluation of two conditional constructions used in computer languages. *International Journal of Man–Machine Studies* **5**, 105–113.

Sommer, R. (1972). *Design Awareness*. Holt, Rinehart and Winston, San Francisco.

Stein, M. (1974). *Stimulating Creativity*. Academic Press, New York and London.

Thomas, J. (1976a). A method for studying natural language dialogue. *IBM Research Report*, RC-5882.

Thomas, J. (1976b). Quantifiers and question-asking. *IBM Research Report*, RC-5886.

Thomas, J. (1977). Psychological issues in data base management. *Proceedings of the Third International Conference on Very Large Data Bases* **9**(2), 169–185.

Thomas, J. (1978). A design-interpretation analysis of natural english with applications to man–computer interactions. *International Journal of Man–Machine Studies* **10**, 651–668.

Thomas, J. C. and Carroll, J. M. (1979). The psychological study of design. *Design Studies* **1**(1), 5–11.

Thomas, J. C. and Carroll, J. M. (1981). Human factors in communication. *IBM Systems Journal* **20**(2), 237–263.

Thomas, J. and Gould, J. (1975). A psychological study of Query By Example. *National Computer Conference Proceedings* **44**, 439–445. AFIPS Press, New York.

Weinberg, G. M. (1971). *The Psychology of Computer Programming*. Nostrand Reinhold, New York.

Welford, A. (1958). *Aging and Human Skill*. Oxford University Press, New York.

Welty, C. and Stemple, D. (1978). A human factors comparison of a procedural and a non-procedural query language. COINS Technical Report 78-24, University of Massachusetts, Amherst.

Wheeler, D. (1970). Processes in word recognition. *Cognitive Psychology* **1**, 59–85.

Woodfield, S. (1979). An experiment on unit increase in problem complexity. *IEEE Transactions on Software Engineering*, SE-5 (2), 76–78.

Wright, P. and Fox, K. (1970). Presenting information in tables. *Applied Ergonomics* **1**(4), 234–242.

Wright, P. and Reid, R. (1973). Written information: some alternatives to prose for expressing the outcomes of complex contingencies. *Journal of Applied Psychology* **57**, 160–166.

Zloof, M. (1977). Query By Example: A data base language. *IBM Systems Journal*.

Part 2

The task interface

8. Medical consultation systems: designing for doctors*

E. H. SHORTLIFFE†

Heuristic Programming Project, Stanford University, California, USA

I. Introduction

Although computers have had an increasing impact on the practice of medicine over the last decade, the successful applications have tended to be in domains where physicians have not been asked to interact at the terminal themselves. Few potential user populations are as demanding of computer-based decision aids as are doctors. This is due to a variety of factors which include their traditional independence as lone decision makers, the seriousness with which they view actions that may have life and death significance, and the overwhelming time demands that tend to make them impatient with any innovation that breaks up the finely-tuned flow of their daily routines.

This chapter examines some of the issues that have tended to limit the acceptance of programs for "hands-on" use by physicians.‡ It emphasizes programs intended to give advice in clinical settings, commonly referred to as consultation systems. The goal is to present design criteria which, if adequately considered, may facilitate the use of computer programs by physicians. I shall also show that the computer science subfield known as

---

* This article is based on a paper presented at the annual meeting of the Canadian Society for Computer Simulation of Intelligence, Victoria, British Columbia, May 1980.

† The author is recipient of research career development award LM00048 from the National Library of Medicine.

‡ Interactive clinical programs may also be useful to physicians if an assistant is the one who actually interacts with the system. In such settings the physician might use the program only at the end of the session after data entry is completed. Alternatively the physician might simply receive a computer listing with recommendations. For the purposes of this discussion, however, our specific concern is the design of programs to be used by the physicians themselves. In some applications this may not be the preferred approach.

DESIGNING FOR HUMAN–COMPUTER COMMUNICATION
ISBN 0 12 643820 X

artificial intelligence (AI) offers some particularly pertinent methods for responding to the design criteria outlined. Although the emphasis is medical throughout, many of the issues occur equally often in other user communities where the introduction of computer methods must confront similar psychological and technological barriers.

The chapter begins with a look at medicine itself—the nature of clinical reasoning and the ways in which physicians currently obtain the information that they need for patient management decisions. Acceptability issues are then examined in Section II; they provide a basis for the delineation of suggested design criteria discussed in Section III.* The field of artificial intelligence is introduced in Section IV where I describe the ways in which basic computer science research is attempting to respond to many of the design considerations outlined in Section III. Section V describes a specific medical consultation system, termed MYCIN, that was developed in response to the acceptability criteria discussed. The concluding section then looks to the future, commenting on some modern technological limitations that will need to be overcome, and suggesting alternate approaches that may meld with artificial intelligence to create the kinds of powerful and accepted tools that have been envisioned for years but have thus far not been realized (Shortliffe *et al.*, 1979).

A. The nature of medical reasoning

It is frequently observed that clinical medicine is more an "art" than a "science". Complex and varied factors are considered in medical decision making; any practitioner knows that well-trained experts with considerable specialized experience may still reach very different conclusions about how to treat a patient or proceed with a diagnostic evaluation. The reasons for such discrepancies are complex. For example, there may be observer variation in physical examination or laboratory testing, some physicians are more responsive to the patient's preferences than are others, the financial costs and risks of procedures or treatments may be given different import by different clinicians, and studies in the medical literature on which clinical decisions are based are often subject to varied interpretations.

Another factor which may contribute to observed discrepancies, even among experts, is the tendency of medical education to emphasize the teaching of *facts*, with little formal advice regarding the *reasoning processes* that are most appropriate for decision making. There has been a traditional

---

* It must be emphasized that the opinions expressed regarding design criteria are mostly personal ones. Until recently (Teach and Shortliffe, 1982) there have been remarkably few formal data to support the observations. They are, rather, largely based on my own observations and intuitions.

assumption that future physicians should learn to make decisions by observing other doctors in action and by acquiring as much basic knowledge as possible. More recently, however, there has been interest in studying the ways in which expert physicians reach decisions in the hope that a more structured approach to the teaching of medical decision making can be developed (Kassirer and Gorry, 1978; Elstein *et al.*, 1978).

Until recently computer programs for assisting with medical decision making have not emphasized models of clinical reasoning. Instead, they have tended to assign structure to a domain using statistical techniques such as Bayes' Theorem (deDombal *et al.*, 1972) or formal decision analysis (Gorry *et al.*, 1973). More recently a number of programs have attempted to draw lessons from analyses of actual human reasoning in clinical settings (Wortman, 1972; Pauker *et al.*, 1976). In all cases the motivations for attempting to formalize clinical decisions have been similar:

(1) to improve the *accuracy* of clinical diagnosis through approaches that are systematic, complete, and able to utilize data from diverse sources;
(2) to improve the *reliability* of clinical decisions by avoiding unwarranted influences;
(3) to make the *selection of tests and therapies* efficient;
(4) to improve our *understanding of clinical decision making* so that students can be better taught and future programs better designed.

One goal of this chapter is to demonstrate that, although a variety of methodologies may lead to excellent decisions in the clinical areas to which they have been applied, the programs with greater dependence on models of expert clinical reasoning may have heightened acceptance by the physicians for whom they are designed.

B. The consultation process

It is generally recognized that accelerated growth in medical knowledge has necessitated greater sub-specialization among physicians and more dependence upon assistance from other experts when a patient presents with a complex problem outside one's own area of expertise. Such consultations are acceptable to doctors in part because they maintain the primary physician's role as ultimate decision maker. The consultation generally involves a dialog between the two physicians, with the expert explaining the basis for advice that is given and the non-expert seeking justification of points found puzzling or questionable. Consultants who offered dogmatic advice that they were unwilling to discuss or defend would find that their opinions were seldom sought.

Thus there are a variety of kinds of information flow that a primary physician has come to expect when an expert consultation is obtained:

(1) There are the data about the patient which the physician imparts to the consultant; these data are generally factual but are often subject to interpretations placed upon them by the primary physician.

(2) There are the direct observations made by the expert in visiting the patient's bedside, examining X-rays or pathologic specimens, or reviewing the patient's chart in detail; the more observations of this kind made by the experts, the less dependent they are on the data interpretations offered by the primary physicians.

(3) There are the conclusions and recommendations conveyed by the expert; these may suggest a single diagnosis, a list of possible diagnoses, or a set of likely concurrent diseases; they may withhold diagnosis and instead suggest getting more data; they may recommend a specific drug regimen for a patient or suggest other forms of patient management such as surgery, bed-rest, or fluid replacement.

(4) There are the explanations and justifications offered by the consultant to support the advice; these may be simple statements of fact or a reconstructed chain of reasoning that includes the expert's own judgmental inferential knowledge.

After this interchange has occurred, the primary physician generally has the ultimate decision of whether to follow the consultant's recommendation, seek a second opinion, or proceed in some other fashion. When the consultant's advice is followed it is frequently because the patient's doctor has been genuinely educated about the particular complex problem for which advice was sought.

Because such consultations are accepted largely because the process described allows the primary physician to remain the ultimate decision maker, it can be argued that medical consultation programs must mimic this human process if they are to be accepted by the physicians for whom they are designed. Computer-based decision aids have typically emphasized only the first and third kinds of information flow cited, i.e. the obtaining of patient data and the generation of advice (Shortliffe *et al.*, 1979). Direct patient observations by computer may occur in certain specialized settings such as intensive-care units (Goldwyn *et al.*, 1971), and image processing techniques are supporting research in X-ray or pathology slide analysis, but the technology for more involved observations such as physical examinations is not even seriously contemplated at present. On the other hand, the fourth kind of information flow, explanation of decisions, may be incorporated into computer-based decision aids if the system is given an adequate internal model of the logic that it uses and can convey this intelligibly to the physician-user. At least three of the four aspects of the human consultation process can therefore be approached using currently available computing techniques, and the addition of explanation capabilities may be an important step towards effectively encouraging a system's use by physicians.

II. Acceptability issues

Studies have shown that physicians tend to have an inherent reluctance to use computers in their practice (Startsman and Robinson, 1972). It is sometimes feared that such psychological barriers to computer use are insurmountable, but we are beginning to see systems that have had considerable success in encouraging "hands-on" terminal use by physicians (Watson, 1974). The key seems to be to provide adequate benefits while creating an environment in which the physician can feel comfortable. A similar viewpoint has been noted by Rosati; he asserts that increasing numbers of physicians will welcome computer-based decision aids when they become aware that colleagues who *are* using the machine have a clear advantage in their practice.

Physicians tend to ask at least six questions when a new system is presented to them:

(1) *Is its performance reliable?* This issue may be the primary criterion of a system's acceptability. Physicians demand not only consistently valid decisions, but also reliable hardware so that system availability can be uniformly assured.

(2) *Do I need this system?* A system is useful to physicians if it permits them to accomplish tasks they previously could not attempt, enables them to perform familiar chores in less time than they would normally require, or facilitates better quality decisions with minimal extra time expenditure.

(3) *Is it fast and easy to use?* Physicians generally work under severe time constraints. They would like programs to take no more time than they currently spend when accomplishing the same task on their own. It is not necessarily true that physicians will be uniformly willing to expend extra time if they can be shown that a system will improve the quality of care they deliver. For example, many outpatient clinics typically require that physicians devote less time to

each patient than is ideal; financial costs and limited numbers of physicians may necessitate shortening the length of appointments so that all patients who need care can be seen.

(4) *Does it help me without being dogmatic?* Condescension alienates physicians regardless of whether it comes from a human consultant or a computer system. Care in the choice of words used in computer-generated advice is therefore crucial; the programs must be tactful.

(5) *Does it justify its recommendations so that I can decide for myself what to do?* Physicians tend not to seek advice if it is assumed that they will follow it blindly and hence have no need for their own knowledge or reasoning powers. The concept of computer-based *aids* or *assistants* is thus crucial; physicians welcome clinical *tools* that permit them to maintain their role as ultimate decision makers.

(6) *Is it designed to make me feel comfortable when I use it?* For many physicians computer technology is foreign and somewhat threatening (Startsman and Robinson, 1972). Thus the simple mechanics of interaction with a computer-based tool may be of paramount importance, especially soon after a system's introduction when it is viewed as experimental and unproven.

Experience has shown that reliability alone may not be enough to ensure system acceptance (Shortliffe *et al.*, 1979); the additional issues cited here may also be central to the question of how to design consultation systems that doctors will be willing to use.

III. Design criteria

The preceding discussion allows specification of a number of considerations that are pertinent for the design of consultation systems to be used by physicians. These design criteria can be divided into three main categories: mechanical, epistemological, and psychological.

A. Mechanical issues

It is clear that the best of systems will eventually fail if the process for getting information in or out of the machine is too arduous, frustrating, or complicated. Owen and Moseley (1977) have used the term "congenial" to describe the ideal relationship between physician and computer terminal. They describe a novel device designed with the physician-user specifically in mind, and several other engineering groups have also experimented with customized terminals (Watson, 1974).

Eventually human–computer interaction may involve voice communication by telephone or microphone. This would of course most closely simulate the human consultation process, but the automated methods for understanding and generating spoken words are in their infancy and cannot realistically be applied to the complex dialogs of medical consultation any time in the foreseeable future. Thus some kind of manual interaction by the physician is likely to be required for years to come.

Light pens, drawing tablets, push buttons, and touch-sensitive screens are devices that simplify the interactive process and have the advantage of avoiding the need for typing by the physician. When typing is required, either because these other techniques are unavailable, unreliable, or inappropriate,* it becomes crucial to assume that the physician may not be an experienced typist. Thus spelling or typographical errors should ideally be corrected programmatically if the intended meaning is obvious, and the amount of typing required should be kept to a minimum.

The program's displays must also be carefully designed; attention to detail can have major benefits in encouraging system use. The organization of the dialog should be made clear by spacing, indentation, capitalization, or the use of colour. Computer jargon and unfamiliar abbreviations should generally be avoided. Ideally the terminal will operate at high transmission rates so that full sentences can be displayed with minimal time delay. On the other hand, short form responses from the physician or automatic recognition of abbreviated responses should be encouraged so that the user's typing is kept to a minimum as mentioned above.

It must be easy for new users to learn how to obtain the information that they need. This means an effective approach to educating the novice on system use, but also suggests the need for simple methods of interaction. The programs should ideally be self-documenting and it should be impossible for the new user inadvertently to cause a program crash or a system failure.

Finally, the speed of program execution and the time required for a full consultation must be carefully considered. As was described above, time constraints perceived by physicians will generally prevent them from using a program that requires an inordinate amount of time compared to a phone call to a human consultant or a trip to the library. Similarly, the consultation system must be reliably available. This means both pre-

---

* The great disadvantage of light pens and the other devices mentioned is their inflexibility. They must generally be used in conjunction with keyboards to allow free-text input when the physician wishes to enter information or comments that had not been anticipated.

dictable computer availability and an adequate number of terminals so that queuing can be avoided. A closely related issue is the need for hardware reliability. Because neither computers nor terminals can be guaranteed free of mechanical breakdown, redundancy of all equipment to provide backup may be the only reasonable (although expensive) solution.

B. Epistemological issues

Proper attention to mechanical issues alone is of course not sufficient to guarantee a program's acceptance by physicians. System knowledge and the way in which it is utilized and conveyed to users are also pertinent and help define another group of design criteria.

As has been discussed, the quality of a program's performance at its decision making task is a basic acceptability criterion. A variety of techniques for automated advice systems have been developed and many perform admirably (Shortliffe *et al.*, 1979). Thus the capturing of knowledge and data, plus a system for using them in a coherent and consistent manner, are the design considerations that have traditionally received the most attention.

Other potential uses of system knowledge must also be recognized, however. As has been noted, physicians often expect to be educated when they request a human consultation, and a computer-based consultant should also be an effective teaching tool. On the other hand, physicians would quickly reject a pedantic program that attempted to convey every pertinent fact in its knowledge base, many of which the physician might already be familiar with. Thus it is appropriate to design programs that convey *knowledge* as well as advice, but which serve this educational function only when asked to do so by the physician-user.

As has been mentioned, physicians also prefer to understand the basis for a consultant's advice so that they can decide for themselves whether to follow the recommendation. Hence the educational role of the consultation program can also be seen as providing an explanation or justification capability. When asked to do so, the system should be able to retrieve and display any relevant fact or reasoning step that was brought to bear in considering a given case. It is also important that such explanations be expressed in terms that are easily comprehensible to the physician.

Because it would be unacceptable for a consultation program to explain *every* relevant reasoning step or fact, it is important that the user be able to specifically request justification for points found to be puzzling. Yet an ability to *ask* for explanations generally requires that the program be able to understand free-form queries entered by the user. A reasonable design consideration, then, is to attempt to develop an interface whereby simple questions expressed in English can be understood by the system and appropriately answered.

It is perhaps inevitable that consultation programs dealing with complex clinical problems will occasionally reveal errors or knowledge gaps, even after they have been implemented for ongoing use. A common source of frustration is the frequent inability to correct such errors quickly so that they will not recur in subsequent consultation sessions. There is often a lapse of several months between "releases" of a system, with an annoying error recurring persistently in the meantime. It is therefore ideal to design systems in which knowledge is easily modified and integrated; then errors can be rapidly rectified once the missing or erroneous knowledge is identified. This requires a flexible knowledge representation and powerful methods for assessing the interactions of new knowledge with other facts already in the system.

Finally, the acquisition of knowledge itself can be an arduous task for system developers, and it may be wise to consider from the outset ways in which this process can be facilitated. In some applications the knowledge may be based largely on statistical data, but in others it may be necessary to extract judgmental information from the minds of experts. Thus another design consideration is the development of interactive techniques to permit acquisition of knowledge from primary data or directly from an expert without requiring that a computer programmer function as an intermediary.

C. Psychological issues

The most difficult problems in designing consultation programs may be the frequently encountered psychological barriers to the use of computers among physicians (Startsman and Robinson, 1972; Croft, 1972; Melhorn *et al.*, 1979; Teach and Shortliffe, 1981). Many of these barriers are reflected in the mechanical and epistemological design criteria discussed above. However, there are several other observations that may be pertinent:

(1) It is probably a mistake to expect the physician to adapt to changes imposed by a consultation system. As much as is possible, the system should fit into the physician's usual routine. Furthermore, every effort should be made to respond to the suggestions or requests of the intended users, and it is ideal to have representatives of the eventual users involved in a program's design from the outset.

(2) A system's acceptance may be greatly heightened if ways are identified to permit physicians to perform tasks that they have wanted

to do but had previously been unable to do (Mesel *et al.*, 1976; Watson, 1974).

(3) It is important to avoid premature introduction of a system while it is still "experimental". The biases that tend to develop against a program that functions less than optimally may be impossible to overcome later, even when system performance improves. This consideration must be balanced, however, against the recognition that a system (like a human consultant) is not likely ever to be "perfect".

(4) System acceptance may be heightened if physicians know that a human expert is available to back up the program when problems arise. Particularly during early implementation stages, this means providing easily accessible consultants who can answer questions that may arise regarding the program or its advice.

(5) Physicians are used to assessing research and new techniques on the basis of rigorous evaluations, and they expect no less from clinical computer programs. Because there is little precedent for formally evaluating the decision making performance of the aids we are discussing, novel approaches to assessing both performance and clinical impact are required.

IV. Artificial intelligence

The computer science subfield known as artificial intelligence (AI) involves research closely related to many of the design considerations mentioned above. Although the term has never been uniformly defined, AI is generally accepted to include those computer applications in which the tasks require largely symbolic inference rather than numeric calculations. Examples include programs that reason about mineral exploration, organic chemistry, or molecular biology; programs that converse in English and understand spoken words; and programs that generate theories from observations.

In a recent survey of the field (Winston, 1977), one researcher has characterized AI as the study of ideas that enable computers to do the things that make humans seem intelligent. He also points out that understanding computer intelligence is a useful way to study human intelligence, and indeed many psychologists have been drawn to the study of AI for that reason. The following characteristics are among those which make humans seem intelligent and which are being studied by AI researchers:

(1) the ability to reason symbolically;
(2) the ability to manipulate and communicate ideas; and
(3) the ability to acquire and apply knowledge.

In this section we briefly examine these three general areas of AI research.

A. Symbolic reasoning

AI programs gain much of their power from qualitative, experimental judgements, codified in so-called "rules of thumb" or "heuristics", in contrast to numerical calculation programs whose power derives from the analytical equations used. The heuristics focus the attention of a reasoning program on parts of the problem that seem most critical and parts of the knowledge base that seem most relevant. They also guide the application of the domain knowledge to an individual case by deleting items from consideration as well as focusing on others. The result is that these programs pursue a line of reasoning as opposed to following a sequence of steps in a calculation.

Methods for reasoning symbolically are inherently linked to the knowledge representation that is used by a program. Thus there is no uniform approach common to all AI systems. A recurring theme, however, is that the problems AI programs tackle tend to have a large number of possible decisions or actions. A frequent example is the large number of possible moves at most points during a game of chess. Because each move may in turn lead to several additional potential moves, the number of possible decisions two or more steps into the future often becomes unmanageable. Humans have developed strategies for quickly discounting or eliminating possible actions that they can easily see are less desirable than the two or three best potential decisions. Programs for solving symbolic problems must be given similar strategies so that the machine's computational power can be efficiently spent concentrating on a small number of possible actions. The application of strategies for limiting alternatives to be considered, without eliminating what is in fact the best choice, is known in AI as the problem of "heuristic search"; it is a central theme in computer-based symbolic reasoning.

B. Communication

Computer-based understanding of English, either spoken or written, has fascinated computer scientists ever since attempts were first made, in the 1950s, to write programs for translating from one human language to another. Researchers in this AI application area are closely involved with the field of linguistics, and have been forced to try to understand the nature of language itself. Their problems include analysis of syntax, disambiguation of words with multiple meanings, and analysis of the semantics of language, especially during a lengthy discourse when the overall context determines the meaning of individual words. Understanding language typed into a machine by computer terminal has been extended recently to research into programs that understand spoken words. Speech understanding is particularly complex in that the program must first analyse electrical signals from a microphone in order to determine what has been said. Then an attempt is made to understand the meaning of the words and to have the machine respond appropriately.

C. Knowledge engineering

The acquisition and application of knowledge, although central to AI research since the field's beginnings, have recently been viewed somewhat separately in the context of "expert systems" or "knowledge-based systems". These terms have been coined to describe programs that contain large amounts of specialized expertise that they convey to system users in the form of consultative advice. The phrase "knowledge engineering" has been devised to describe the basic AI problem areas that support the development of expert systems (Feigenbaum, 1978). There are several associated research themes:

(1) *Representation of knowledge.* A variety of methods for computer-based representation of human knowledge have been devised, each of which is directed at facilitating the associated symbolic reasoning and at permitting the codification and application of "common sense" knowledge of the domain. Some commonly used representation schemes include production rules (Davis and King, 1976), frames (Minsky, 1975), and the predicate calculus (Green, 1969).

(2) *Acquisition of knowledge.* Obtaining the knowledge needed by an expert program is often a complex task. In certain domains, programs may be able to "learn" through experience (Samuel, 1967; Winston, 1970), but typically the system designers and the experts being modelled must work closely together to identify and verify the knowledge of the domain. Recently there has been some early experience devising programs that actually bring the expert to the computer terminal where a "teaching session" can result in direct transfer of knowledge from the expert to the system itself (Davis, 1976).*

---

* See also the chapter by Davis in this volume.

(3) *Methods of inference.* Closely linked to the issue of knowledge representation is the mechanism for devising a line of reasoning for a given consultation. Techniques for hypothesis generation and testing are required, as are focusing techniques such as the heuristic search methods mentioned above. A particularly challenging associated problem is the development of techniques for quantifying and manipulating uncertainty. Although inferences can sometimes be based on established techniques such as Bayes' Theorem or decision analysis (Raiffa, 1968), utilization of expert judgmental knowledge typically leads to the development of alternate methods for symbolically manipulating inexact knowledge (Zadeh, 1965; Shortliffe and Buchanan, 1975).

(4) *Explanation capabilities.* For reasons we have explained for the medical context above, knowledge engineering has come to include the development of techniques for making explicit the basis for recommendations or decisions. This requirement tends to constrain the methods of inference and the knowledge representation that is used by a complex reasoning program.

(5) *The knowledge interface.* There are a variety of issues that fall in this general category. One is the mechanical interface between the expert program and the individual who is using it; this problem has been discussed in detail for the medical user, and many of the observations there can be applied directly to the users in other knowledge engineering application domains. Researchers on these systems are also looking for ways to combine AI techniques with more traditional numerical approaches to produce enhanced system performance. There is growing recognition that the greatest power in knowledge-based expert systems may lie in the melding of AI techniques and other computer science methodologies (Shortliffe *et al.*, 1979).

Thus it should be clear that artificial intelligence, and specifically knowledge engineering, are inherently involved with several of the design considerations that were presented in Section III for medical consultation systems. In the next section we will discuss how one medical AI program has attempted to respond to the design criteria that have been cited.

V. An example: the MYCIN system

From 1972 to 1978 our research group at Stanford University was involved in the development of a computer-based consultation system to assist physicians with the selection of antibiotics for patients with serious infections (Shortliffe *et al.*, 1974). The program has been termed MYCIN after the suffix used in the names of many common antimicrobial agents. MYCIN is an experimental system that has spawned several additional projects;* its continuing relevance lies in its attention to most of the issues described in Section III above. The details of the system have been discussed in several publications (Shortliffe, 1976; Shortliffe *et al.*, 1973, 1975; Davis *et al.*, 1977; Scott *et al.*, 1977), but I will briefly describe it here to illustrate the ways in which its structure reflects the design considerations of Section III.

A. Knowledge representation and acquisition

All infectious disease knowledge in MYCIN is contained in "packets" of inferential knowledge known as production rules (Davis and King, 1976). These rules were acquired from collaborating clinical experts during detailed discussions of specific complex cases on the wards at Stanford Medical Center. The system was also given the capability to acquire such rules directly through interaction with the clinical expert.†

A production rule is an inferential statement that consists of a "premise" and an "action". The premise is a list of conditional expressions; if each is true then the conclusions specified in the action portion of the rule can be drawn. MYCIN currently contains some 700 rules that deal with the diagnosis and treatment of bacteremia (bacteria in the blood) and meningitis (bacteria in the cerebrospinal fluid). These rules are stored in the computer using the format of the Interlisp programming language that we use. However, routines have been written to translate all rules into simple English so that they can be displayed and understood by the user. For example, one simple rule which relates a patient's clinical situation with the likely bacteria causing the patient's illness is shown in Fig. 1. The premise conditions are numbered and occur in the "if" portion of the rule; the conclusion to be drawn if the premise holds true is displayed in the "then" portion of the rule. The strengths with which the specified inferences can be drawn are indicated by numerical weights, or certainty factors, that are described further below. This production rule representation scheme is not new to MYCIN and has been used by such diverse

---

* Our current ONCOCIN project at Stanford (Shortliffe *et al.*, 1981) uses techniques developed in the context of MYCIN and is applying them to consultations regarding cancer chemotherapy. ONCOCIN is currently in use on a limited basis in the oncology clinic at Stanford University Medical Center.

† This capability was implemented in rudimentary form in early versions of the system (Shortliffe, 1976) but was substantially broadened and strengthened by Davis in his TEIRESIAS program (Davis, 1976). His approach to implementing such capabilities is discussed in his chapter in this volume and will not be described further here.

RULE300

        [This rule applies to all cultures and suspected infections, and is tried in order to find out about the organisms (other than those seen on cultures or smears) which might be causing the infection]

If: 1) The infection which requires therapy is meningitis, and
      2) The patient does have evidence of serious skin or soft tissue infection, and
      3) Organisms were not seen on the stain of the culture, and
      4) The type of the infection is bacterial

Then: There is evidence that the organisms (other than those seen on cultures or smears) which might be causing the infection is staphylococcus-coag-pos (.75) streptococcus-group-a (.5)

Author: Victor Yu, M.D.

Fig. 1. A sample MYCIN rule, with additional stored information.

programs as a system to play poker (Waterman, 1970) and a system to infer chemical structures from mass-spectral data (Buchanan and Feigenbaum, 1978).

B. Inference methods

1. Reasoning model

The production rule methodology provides powerful mechanisms for selecting the rules that apply to a given consultation. In MYCIN's case the rules are only loosely related to one another before a consultation begins; the program selects the relevant rules and chains them together as it considers a particular patient. The resulting reasoning network, then, is created dynamically and can be seen as a model of one approach to the patient's problem. Two rules chain together if the action portion of one helps determine the truth value of a condition in the premise of the other:

Rule(1): P1 & P2 --> P0
Rule(2): P3 & P4 --> P1

Here rule(1) and rule(2) "chain" together because rule(2) can provide evidence (P1) which contributes to the assessment of rule(1).

    The overall strategy used by MYCIN in rule selection is termed "goal-oriented" and is similar to the consequent-theorem approach used in Hewitt's PLANNER (Hewitt, 1972). MYCIN "reasons backwards" from its recognized goal of determining therapy for a patient. It therefore starts by considering rules for therapy selection, but the premise portion of each of those rules in turn sets up new questions or subgoals. These new goals then cause new rules to be invoked and a reasoning network is thereby developed. When the truth of a premise condition is best determined by asking the physician rather than by applying rules (e.g. to determine the value of a laboratory test), a question is displayed. The physician enters the appropriate response and the program continues to select additional rules. Once information on the patient is obtained, some rules will fail to be applicable; in this way the invoked applicable rules will provide a customized patient-specific reasoning network for the case under consideration.

Portions of a sample consultation session are shown in Fig. 2. The physician's responses are in capital letters and follow a double asterisk. Note that the physician can indicate that he does not know the answer to a question (question 13) and MYCIN will proceed to do the best it can on the basis of the data available. Typographical or spelling errors are automatically corrected (question 12) with the presumed meaning printed at the left margin so that the physician knows what assumption has been made. Note also that the physician's responses are generally single words.

In Fig. 3 the form of MYCIN's final conclusions and therapy recommendations are demonstrated. Note that the program specifies what organisms are likely to be causing the patient's infection and then suggests a therapeutic regimen appropriate for them. There are also specialized routines to calculate recommended drug doses depending upon the patient's size and kidney function.

2. Management of uncertainty

The knowledge expressed in a MYCIN rule is seldom definite but tends to include "suggestive" or "strongly suggestive" evidence in favour of a given conclusion. In order to combine evidence regarding a single hypothesis but derived from a number of different rules, it has been necessary to devise a numeric system for capturing and representing an expert's measure of belief regarding the inference stated in a rule. Although this problem may at first seem amenable to the use of conditional probabilities and Bayes' Theorem, a probabilistic model fails to be adequate for a number of reasons we have detailed elsewhere (Shortliffe and Buchanan, 1975). Instead, MYCIN uses a model influenced by the theory of confirmation; it is based on a system of belief measures known as certainty factors. These numbers lie on a -1 to $+1$ scale with -1 indicating absolute disproof of an hypothesis, $+1$ indicating its proof, and 0 indicating the absence of evidence for or against the hypothesis (or equally weighted evidence in both directions). The relationship of the model to formal probability

--------PATIENT-538--------

1) Patient's name:
** PT538
2) Age:
** 45
3) Sex:
** MALE
4) Race:
** CAUC
= CAUCASIAN
5) Are there any cultures for Pt538 which may be related to the present illness, and from which organisms have been grown successfully in the microbiology laboratory?
** NO
6) Are there any pending cultures of Pt538?
** YES

--------CULTURE-1--------

7) From what site was the specimen for CULTURE-1 taken?
** CSF
8) Please give the date and time when the pending csf culture (CULTURE-1) was obtained. (mo/da/yr time)
** 11/28/78
9) Was a smear examined at the time that the specimen for the pending csf culture (CULTURE-1) was obtained?
** YES
10) Were any organisms seen on the smear of the specimen submitted as the pending csf culture (CULTURE-1)?
** YES

--------ORGANISM-1--------

11) The stain (Gram, India ink, or Ziehl-Neelsen acid-fast) of ORGANISM-1:
** GRAMNEG
12) Is ORGANISM-1 a rod or coccus (etc.):
** ROOD
= ROD
13) What is the form of the individual organisms (e.g. Lancet-shaped for cocci, fusiform for rods, etc.)?
** ??
Expected responses are: FUSIFORM, PLUMP or DUMBBELL-SHAPED
Enter HELP for list of user options.
** UNKNOWN

Fig. 2. The beginning of a sample consultation session.

My therapy recommendations will be designed to treat for organisms that either are very likely or, although less likely, would have a significant effect on therapy selection if they were present. It is important to cover for the following probable infection(s) and associated organism(s):

INFECTION-1 is MENINGITIS

+ <ITEM-1>   E.COLI [from clinical evidence only]
+ <ITEM-2>   PSEUDOMONAS-AERUGINOSA [from clinical evidence only]
+ <ITEM-3>   KLEBSIELLA-PNEUMONIAE [from clinical evidence only]
+ <ITEM-4>   DIPLOCOCCUS-PNEUMONIAE [from clinical evidence only]

  41) Does Pt538 have a clinically significant allergic reaction to any anti-microbial agent?
  ** NO

[Considering   AMPICILLIN-AND-GENTAMICIN   for   use   against INFECTION-1 ...]

  42) Do you have reason to suspect that Pt538 may have impaired renal function?
  ** NO
  43) Pt538's weight in kilograms (or <number> POUNDS):
  ** 70

[REC-1] My preferred therapy recommendation is as follows:
  In order to cover for Items <1 2 3 4>:
                    Give the following in combination:
                    1) AMPICILLIN
                    Dose: 3.5g (28.0 ml) q4h IV [calculated on basis of 50 mg/kg]
                    2) GENTAMICIN
                    Dose: 119 mg (3.0 ml, 80mg/2ml ampule) q8h IV [calculated on basis of 1.7 mg/kg] plus consider giving 5 mg q24h Intrathecal
  Comments: Monitor serum concentrations

  Since high concentrations of penicillins can inactivate amino-glycosides, do not mix these two antibiotics in the same IV bottle.

Fig. 3.   Example of MYCIN's therapy recommendations.

theory and the methods for combining evidence from diverse sources (rules and user estimates) have been described (Shortliffe and Buchanan, 1975) and analysed by others (Adams, 1976). Although the system has served us well to date, it does have several recognized inadequacies (Adams, 1976) and can be seen only as a first step towards the development of a coherent theory for the management of uncertainty in complex reasoning domains.

C. Explanation

Perhaps the greatest advantage of the production rule methodology utilized in MYCIN is the way in which it facilitates the development of powerful mechanisms for explaining and justifying system performance. These capabilities have also contributed to the development of an instructional version of MYCIN known as GUIDON (Clancey, 1979). The explanation program has two options, one of which is limited in scope but fast and easy to use. This option is used during a consultation session and allows examination of the reasoning steps that have generated a specific question. The second option is more powerful but it involves language processing and is therefore less reliable and more time consuming. This question-answering capability is designed to allow full access to *all* system knowledge, both static (i.e. facts and rules obtained from experts) and dynamic (i.e. conclusions reached by the program for the specific consultation session). Each system is briefly described below.

1. Answers to questions about the reasoning status

During the consultation, MYCIN may ask questions which the physician finds puzzling, either because they appear irrelevant or because the details of their applicability are unclear. When this occurs, the physician can digress momentarily and seek an explanation of the question.* Instead of answering the question MYCIN has asked, the user enters the word "WHY" and the program responds with a translation of the rule which generated the question. An example of this feature is shown in Fig. 4. Note that MYCIN begins its response by phrasing in English its understanding of the "WHY question" asked by the physician. It then displays the relevant rule, specifying which conditions in the premise are already known to be true and which conditions remain to be investigated. In many cases this single rule display is an adequate explanation of the current line of reasoning and the physician can then proceed with the consultation by answering the question.

The user can alternatively continue to investigate the current reasoning chain by repeating the "WHY" command several times. Each additional "WHY" is interpreted by MYCIN as a request for display of the next highest rule in the current reasoning chain. For example, in Fig. 4 another "WHY" would be equivalent to asking "Well then, why are you trying to determine the organisms (other than those seen on cultures or smears) which might be causing the infection?" After responding to each "WHY",

---

* The mechanisms for examining the reasoning status using "WHY" and "HOW" commands was largely the work of Davis in his TEIRESIAS program (Davis, 1976). The techniques he developed are general in their applicability and are further detailed by Davis in his chapter in this volume.

35) Is the meningitis a hospital-acquired infection?
** WHY

[i.e. WHY is it important to determine whether the infection was acquired while the patient was hospitalized?]

[2.0] This will aid in determining the organisms (other than those seen on cultures or smears) which might be causing the infection.

It has already been established that

    [2.1] the infection which requires therapy is meningitis, and

    [2.2] organisms were not seen on the stain of this pending csf culture, and

    [2.3] the type of the infection is bacterial, and

    [2.4] neurosurgery is not one of the relevant items from the history of pt538, and

    [2.5] the age of pt538 is greater than 10 days

Therefore, if

    [2.6] the infection was acquired while the patient was hospitalized

then:

there is evidence that the organisms (other than those seen on cultures or smears) which might be causing the infection is e.coli (.75) staphylococcus-coag-pos (.3) pseudomonas-aeruginosa (.3) klebsiella-pneumoniae (.5)

[RULE545]

[back to question 35 ...]

**

Fig. 4. Example of the WHY command.

MYCIN returns to the current question and awaits the physician's response.

The "HOW" command is used in conjunction with the "WHY" command. Note that MYCIN places a unique number before each condition in the premise of a displayed rule (Fig. 4). If the user does not understand *how* a specified condition was met (or will be met), the "HOW" command, followed by the identifying number of the premise clause in question, can be used. Hence "HOW" requires an argument as shown in Fig. 5. This example follows immediately on the "WHY" example in Fig. 4; thus the argument "2.3" refers to the third condition in the premise of RULE545 in Fig. 4 and "2.5" refers to the fifth. MYCIN's responses to "HOW" commands are self-explanatory. Note also that components of all explanations are given identifiers so that, in Fig. 5, the command "HOW 3.1" would have resulted in a display of RULE526.

There are other features of this capability for assessing the reasoning status during a consultation; they are described elsewhere (Davis, 1976; Davis *et al.*, 1977; Scott *et al.*, 1977; Shortliffe *et al.*, 1975). Two points

[back to question 35 ...]

★★ HOW 2.3

[i.e. HOW was it established that the type of the infection is bacterial?]

The following rules concluded about:

the likelihood that the type of the infection is bacterial

	Rule	Yes	No
[2.7]	RULE148	(.19)	
[2.8]	RULE500	(.51)	
[2.9]	RULE501	(.95)	
[3.0]	RULE502	(.97)	
[3.1]	RULE526	(.98)	
[3.2]	RULE504	(.97)	
[3.3]	RULE524	(.98)	

Thus, it has been established that the type of the infection is bacterial.

[back to question 35 ...]

★★ HOW 2.5

[i.e. HOW was it established that the age of pt538 is greater than 10 days?]

In answer to question 2 you said that the age of pt538 is 34 years

Thus, it has been established that the age of pt538 is greater than 10 days.

[back to question 35 ...]

★★ YES

Fig. 5. Examples of the HOW command.

require emphasis here, however. First, these features require no English language processing since the user gives simple single-word commands; hence the capability is fast, efficient, and reliable. On the other hand, questions are limited to the immediate reasoning environment surrounding the question asked by MYCIN. Hence general access to other system knowledge or other conclusions previously made by the program is not possible. To provide a more general explanation capability, MYCIN must be able to respond to questions expressed in simple English as described in the next section.

2. Answers to questions about the consultation and knowledge base

MYCIN's general question-answering feature is automatically made available to the user at the end of each consultation session. After a therapy recommendation has been given, the physician may still have several questions regarding details of the consultation and the basis for diagnostic and therapeutic advice. Figure 6 shows an example of a simple English

** WHY DID YOU TREAT E.COLI?

ITEM-1 is E.coli associated with meningitis. I decided to treat ITEM-1 on the basis of clinical evidence only.

The following rules concluded about:
> the likelihood that e.coli is one of the organisms (other than those seen on cultures or smears) which might be causing the infection

RULE545 was used to conclude that e.coli is one of the organisms (other than those seen on cultures or smears) which might be causing the infection (.74). The last question asked before the conclusion was made was 35.

RULE557 was used to conclude that e.coli is one of the organisms (other than those seen on cultures or smears) which might be causing the infection (.93). The last question asked before the conclusion was made was 37.

The parameters most frequently used in these rules were:
> the infection which requires therapy
> whether a smear of the culture was examined
> whether organisms were seen on the stain of the culture
> the type of the infection

Would you like a summary of ALL the parameters used by these rules?
> ** YES

> Parameter   (rules with this parameter)

the white count from the patient's peripheral CBC (in thousands) (557)
whether the results of a recent CBC of the patient are available (557)
whether the infection was acquired while the patient was hospitalized (545)
the age of the patient (545)
the relevant items from the history of the patient (545)
the type of the infection (545, 557)
whether organisms were seen on the stain of the culture (545, 557)
whether a smear of the culture was examined (545, 557)
the infection which requires therapy (545, 557)

Fig. 6. Detailed response to a free text question.

question which MYCIN understands and attempts to answer. Our approach to natural language understanding is very simple (Scott *et al.*, 1977) but often adequate if questions are kept short without subordinate clauses. In many cases questions are best answered simply by retrieving relevant rules and displaying them in a format suitable for the question being asked. In Fig. 6 MYCIN offers a detailed explanation of how it had decided that the patient might be infected with an *E. coli*. All rules are specified by number so that the physician can have them displayed if full details are desired (see Fig. 9 for an example of this feature).

Figure 7 demonstrates the way in which a physician can ask general

** HOW DO YOU DECIDE THAT AN ORGANISM MAY BE AN E.COLI?

The following rules conclude about:

the likelihood that the identity of the organism is E.coli
555, 304, 243, 3

The parameters most frequently used in these rules are:

the infection which requires therapy
the stain of the organism
the morphology of the organism
the genus of the organism

Which of the rules do you wish to see?

** 3

RULE003
___

If: 1) The infection which requires therapy is not meningitis,
       2) The genus of the organism is not known with certainty,
       3) The site of the culture is one of: those sites that are normally sterile,
       4) The stain of the organism is Gramneg,
       5) The morphology of the organism is rod, and
       6) The aerobicity of the organism is facultative

Then: There is evidence that the identity of the organism is e.coli (.4)
       klebsiella-pneumoniae (.3) proteus-mirabilis (.3) proteus-non-mirabilis (.3) enterobacter (.2) serratia (.1) salmonella-typhi (.1) shigella-dysenteriae (.05) citrobacter-freundii (.05)

** HOW DO YOU TREAT PNEUMOCOCCAL PNEUMONIA

The MYCIN system currently can treat the following infections: BACTEREMIA MENINGITIS CYSTITIS. Because the knowledge base is incomplete, all other infections will be treated like bacteremia.

For treatment of DIPLOCOCCUS-PNEUMONIAE in BACTEREMIA

The drugs of choice (ranked by relative efficacy, assuming sensitivity):
1st choice:

PENICILLIN or AMPICILLIN

2nd choice:

NAFCILLIN, CEPHALOTHIN, ERYTHROMYCIN, or CLINDAMYCIN

3rd|choice:

TETRACYCLINE, CHLORAMPHENICOL, or VANCOMYCIN

** WHAT DOSE OF ERYTHROMYCIN DO YOU RECOMMEND?

When ERYTHROMYCIN is given for BACTEREMIA, the recommended dosage is:

if age is > 12 yrs then 12 mg/kg q6h IV
    else if age is > .08 yrs then 5 mg/kg q6h IV
    else if age is > .02 yrs then 5 mg/kg q12h IV

Fig. 7. Requests for the system's general knowledge.

questions of the knowledge base (static knowledge); neither the questions nor MYCIN's responses refer to any specific consultation session. Note that MYCIN has a sense of its limitations and makes it clear that it has no knowledge specific to pneumonia. Also, a large dictionary includes synonyms and hence permits MYCIN to recognize that "pneumococcal" refers to "pneumococcus", which in turn is the same as "diplococcus-pneumoniae".

Figure 8 shows MYCIN's ability to explain the basis for its therapy

---

** WHY DID YOU GIVE AMPICILLIN AND CHLORAMPHENICOL IN REC-1?

AMPICILLIN-AND-CHLORAMPHENICOL was not prescribed for ITEM-1 or ITEM-3
   For ITEM-1 no drug was prescribed.
   For ITEM-3 AMPICILLIN was prescribed.
AMPICILLIN-AND-CHLORAMPHENICOL was prescribed for ITEM-2 in RECOMMENDATION-1 because:
   -- AMPICILLIN-AND-CHLORAMPHENICOL is used for treating hemophilus-influenzae in meningitis
   -- AMPICILLIN-AND-CHLORAMPHENICOL was considered for treating ITEM-2 because it is more appropriate than AMPICILLIN for this patient.
   [RULE066]
   -- ITEM-2 is sensitive to AMPICILLIN-AND-CHLORAMPHENICOL
   -- there were no contraindications for it
   -- it was part of the recommendation which covers for all of the items, using the fewest number of drugs.

Would you like to see some details?** YES

The following decision(s) are relevant:
   The drugs considered for the hemophilus-influenzae ranked according to desirability are ampicillin-and-chloramphenicol (.95) chloramphenicol (.89) carbenicillin (.79) tetracycline (.76) erythromycin (.75) cephalothin (.7) [RULE101 RULE066]

   The drugs to which the hemophilus-influenzae is sensitive are ampicillin-and-chloramphenicol (1.0) chloramphenicol (1.0) carbenicillin (1.0) tetracycline (1.0) erythromycin (1.0) cephalothin (1.0) [RULE098 RULE445]
   For the conclusion concerning ampicillin-and-chloramphenicol see RULE445.

   The meningitis is one of the infections for which ampicillin-and-chloramphenicol is appropriate [RULE441]

Fig. 8. An explanation of therapy selection.

selection. It is not uncommon to accept the program's list of likely organisms but then to wonder how a specific regimen was chosen; this feature allows the drug choice to be justified. Note that RULE066 is apparently central to the drug selection explained in Fig. 8. Hence the physician can request a display of RULE066 using the simple printing command demonstrated in Fig. 9. Not only is the rule retrieved, but relevant literature references are provided along with a prose justification.

Despite their potential power, the language understanding features demonstrated in Figs 6–9 have significant limitations. Most of these relate

⋆⋆ PRINT 66

RULE066

If: 1) Ampicillin is one of the drugs considered for the item ranked according to desirability, and
2) The diagnosis of the infection is meningitis, and
3) The age of the patient is greater than or equal to 1 week, and
4) The identity corresponding to the item is hemophilus-influenzae, and
5) The item is one of the most likely (top cluster) identities causing an infection in the patient, and
6) It is not known whether ampicillin is one of the drugs to which the item is sensitive in vitro, and
7) A: The patient is not allergic to one or more antibiotics, or
B: Chloramphenicol is not one of the drugs to which the patient is allergic

Then: It is definite (1.0) that the combination of ampicillin with chloramphenicol is a more appropriate therapy for use against the item

Justification: Due to the increasing number of Ampicillin-resistant Hemophilus influenzae isolated in the last few years a combination of ampicillin and chloramphenicol is recommended until sensitivities of the organism are known. At that time, chloramphenicol should be discontinued unless the organism is ampicillin-resistant, in which case, ampicillin is discontinued.

Literature:
1. Katz SL: Ampicillin-resistant Hemophilus influenzae type B: A status report. Pediat. 55:66, 1975.
2. Katz SL et.al.: Ampicillin-resistant strains of Hemophilus influenzae type b, Pediat. 55:145, 1975.
3. Nelson JD: Should ampicillin be abandoned for treatment of Hemophilus influenzae disease? JAMA 229:322, 1974.

Author: Victor Yu, M.D.

Fig. 9. Displaying a relevant rule on request.

to the state-of-the-art in AI research regarding the understanding of free text. The associated computer code is large, complex, and very slow. Furthermore, we have found that it takes novice users several sessions before they learn the best ways to phrase questions so that MYCIN will interpret them properly. Even the most advanced research in natural language processing still has significant conceptual and performance barriers to overcome.

D. Evaluating MYCIN

As work on MYCIN progressed, we devised techniques for analysing formally the system's performance. It must be emphasized, however, that decision making performance is only one aspect of overall system acceptability; as we have discussed, many of the most significant problems occur when attempts are made to encourage physicians to use a program, even if it is known to reach good decisions.

The details of the evaluation studies will not be presented here,* but a number of specific points are of interest. First, *any* evaluation is difficult because there is so much difference of opinion in this domain, *even among experts*. Hence, it is unclear how to select a "gold standard" by which to measure the system's performance. Actual clinical outcome cannot be used because each patient of course is treated in only one way and because a poor outcome in a gravely ill patient cannot necessarily be blamed on the therapy that had been selected.

Secondly, although MYCIN has performed at or near expert level in almost all cases, the evaluating experts in one study (Yu *et al.*, 1979a) had serious reservations about the clinical utility of the program. It is difficult to assess how much of this opinion is due to actual inadequacies in system knowledge or design and how much is related to inherent bias against *any* computer-based consultation aid. In a subsequent study we attempted to eliminate this bias from the study by having the evaluators unaware of which recommendations were MYCIN's and which came from actual physicians (Yu *et al.*, 1979b). In that setting MYCIN's recommendations were uniformly judged preferable to, or equivalent to, those of five infectious disease experts who recommended therapy for the same patients.

Finally, those cases in which MYCIN has tended to do least well are those in which serious infections have been simultaneously present at sites in the body about which the program has been given no rules. It makes sense, of course, that the program should fail in areas where it has no

---

* See Yu *et al.* (1979a) for the details of the bacteremia evaluation, and Yu *et al.* (1979b) for the data on MYCIN's performance selecting therapy for patients with meningitis.

knowledge. However, a useful antimicrobial consultation system must know about a broad range of infectious diseases, just as its human counterpart does. Even with excellent performance managing isolated bacteremias and meningitis, the program is therefore not ready for clinical implementation.

There will eventually be several other important evaluation questions regarding the clinical impact of systems like MYCIN. Are they used? If so, do the physicians follow the program's advice? If so, does patient welfare improve? Is the system cost-effective when no longer in an experimental form? What are the legal implications in the use of, or failure to use, such systems? The answers to all these questions are years away for most consultation systems, but it must be recognized that all these issues are ultimately just as important as whether the decision making methodology manages to lead the computer to accurate and reliable advice.

VI. Conclusion

Although I have asserted that AI research offers potential solutions to many of the important problems confronting researchers in computer-based clinical decision making, the field is not without its serious limitations. These principally result because AI is still a young field with most of the work seen as basic research rather than the application of established computer science techniques. A glance at the list of current AI research areas reveals how far we are from the definitive answers: knowledge representation, symbolic reasoning, natural language processing, speech understanding, methods of inference, intelligent computer-aided instruction, robotics, automatic programming and program verification.

On the other hand, AI has reached a level of development where it is both appropriate and productive to begin applying the techniques to important real-world problems rather than purely theoretical issues. The difficulty lies in the fact that such efforts must still dwell largely in research environments where short-term development of high-performance systems is not likely to occur. The research machines have generally been large, and the programs often slow. Furthermore, the programs themselves tend to be large and to utilize complex data structures. The next several years are likely to see several major changes in technology that will affect the logistics of introducing AI systems into clinical settings. Of particular importance is the development of "personal workstations", stand-alone machines designed for professionals and capable of running large AI programs in a single-user environment. The first generation of such machines was introduced to the marketplace by several vendors in 1981.

It is also important to recognize that other computational techniques may meld very naturally with AI approaches as the fields mature. Thus we may see, for example, more direct links between AI methods and statistical procedures, decision analysis, pattern recognition techniques, and large databanks. As researchers in other areas become more familiar with AI, it may gradually be brought increasingly into fruitful combination with these alternate methodologies. The need for physician acceptance of medical consultation programs is likely to make AI approaches particularly attractive, at least in those settings where hands-on computer use by physicians is desired or necessary. This chapter has explained why the wedding of AI and medical consultation systems is a natural one and has shown, in the setting of the MYCIN system, how one early application responded to design criteria identified for a user community of physicians.

VII. References

Adams, J. B. (1976). A probability model of medical reasoning and the MYCIN model. *Math. Biosci.* **32**, 177–186.

Buchanan, B. G. and Feigenbaum, E. A. (1978). Dendral and Meta-Dendral: their applications dimension. *Artificial Intelligence* **11**, 5–24.

Clancey, W. J. (1979). Tutoring rules for guiding a case method dialog. *Int. J. Man–Machine Studies* **11**, 25–49.

Croft, D. J. (1972). Is computerized diagnosis possible? *Comp. Biomed. Res.* **5**, 351–367.

Davis, R. (1976). Applications of Meta Level Knowledge to the Construction, Maintenance, and Use of Large Knowledge Bases. Ph.D. Thesis, AI Memo 283, Computer Science Department, Stanford University, Stanford, California, July.

Davis, R. and King, J. (1976). An overview of production systems. *In* E. W. Elcock and D. Michie (Eds), *Machine Representation of Knowledge*. Wiley, New York.

Davis, R., Buchanan, B. G. and Shortliffe, E. H. (1977). Production rules as a representation for a knowledge-based consultation system. *Artificial Intelligence* **8**, 15–45.

deDombal, F. T., Leaper, D. J., Staniland, J. R. *et al.* (1972). Computer-aided diagnosis of acute abdominal pain. *Brit. Med. J.* **2**, 9–13.

Elstein, A. S., Shulman, L. S. and Sprafka, S. A. (1978). *Medical Problem Solving: An Analysis of Clinical Reasoning*. Harvard University Press, Cambridge, Mass.

Feigenbaum, E. A. (1978). The art of artificial intelligence: Themes and case studies of knowledge engineering. *AFIPS Conference Proc. NCC 1978*, Vol. 47, p. 227. AFIPS Press, Montvale, N.J.

Goldwyn, R. M., Friedman, H. P. and Siegel, J. H. (1971). Iteration and interaction in computer data bank analysis: a case study in the physiologic classification and assessment of the critically ill. *Comp. Biomed. Res.* **4**, 607–622.

Gorry, G. A., Kassirer, J. P., Essig, A. and Schwartz, W. B. (1973). Decision analysis as the basis for computer-aided management of acute renal failure. *Amer. J. Med.* **55**, 473–484.

Green, C. C. (1969). *The Application of Theorem Proving to Question-Answering Systems.* Ph.D. Thesis, Tech. Report CS 138, Computer Science Department, Stanford University, Stanford, California, June.

Hewitt, C. (1972). *Description and Theoretical Analysis (Using Schemata) of PLANNER: A Language for Proving Theorems and Manipulating Models in a Robot.* Ph.D. Dissertation, Department of Mathematics, Massachusetts Institute of Technology, Cambridge, Mass.

Kassirer, J. P. and Gorry, G. A. (1978). Clinical problem solving: a behavioral analysis. *Anns. Int. Med.* **89**, 245–255.

Melhorn, J. M., Warren, K. L. and Clark, G. M. (1979). Current attitudes of medical personnel towards computers. *Comput. Biomed. Res.* **12**, 327–334.

Mesel, E., Wirtschafter, D. D., Carpenter, J. T. *et al.* (1976). Clinical algorithms for cancer chemotherapy—systems for community-based consultant-extenders and oncology centers. *Meth. Inform. Med.* **15**, 168–173.

Minsky, M. (1975). A framework for representing knowledge. *In* P. H. Winston (Ed.), *The Psychology of Computer Vision.* McGraw Hill, New York.

Owen, E. W. and Moseley, E. C. (1977). A user-compatible terminal for medical applications. *Comput. Biol. Med.* **7**, 165–178.

Pauker, S. G., Gorry, G. A., Kassirer, J. P. and Schwartz, W. B. (1976). Towards the simulation of clinical cognition: taking a present illness by computer. *Amer. J. Med.* **60**, 981–996.

Raiffa, H. (1968). *Decision Analysis: Introductory Lectures on Choices Under Uncertainty.* Addison Wesley, Reading, Mass.

Samuel, A. L. (1967). Some studies in machine learning using the game of checkers: II—recent progress. *IBM J. Res. Dev.* **II**, 601–617.

Scott, A. C., Clancey, W., Davis, R. and Shortliffe, E. H. (1977). Explanation capabilities of knowledge-based production systems. *Amer. J. Computational Linguistics*, Microfiche 62.

Shortliffe, E. H. (1976). *Computer-Based Medical Consultations: MYCIN.* Elsevier/North Holland, New York.

Shortliffe, E. H. and Buchanan, B. G. (1975). A model of inexact reasoning in medicine. *Math. Biosci.* **23**, 351–379.

Shortliffe, E. H., Axline, S. G., Buchanan, B. G., Merigan, T. C. and Cohen, S. N. (1973). An artificial intelligence program to advise physicians regarding antimicrobial therapy. *Comput. Biomed. Res.* **6**, 544–560.

Shortliffe, E. H., Axline, S. G., Buchanan, B. G. and Cohen, S. N. (1974). Design considerations for a program to provide consultations in clinical therapeutics. *Proc. 13th San Diego Biomedical Symposium*, pp. 311–319. San Diego, California, February.

Shortliffe, E. H., Davis, R., Axline, S. G., Buchanan, B. G., Green, C. C. and Cohen, S. N. (1975). Computer-based consultations in clinical therapeutics: explanation and rule-acquisition capabilities of the MYCIN system. *Comput. Biomed. Res.* **8**, 303–320.

Shortliffe, E. H., Buchanan, B. G. and Feigenbaum, E. A. (1979). Knowledge engineering for medical decision making: a review of computer-based clinical decision aids. *Proceedings of the IEEE* **67**, 1207–1224.

Shortliffe, E. H., Scott, A. C., Bischoff, M. B., Campbell, A. B., van Melle, W. and Jacobs, C. D. (1981). ONCOCIN: An expert system for oncology protocol management. *Proceedings 7th International Joint Conference on Artificial Intelligence*. Vancouver, British Columbia, August.

Startsman, T. S. and Robinson, R. E. (1972). The attitudes of medical and paramedical personnel towards computers. *Comp. Biomed. Res.* **5**, 218–227.

Teach, R. L. and Shortliffe, E. H. (1981). An analysis of physician attitudes regarding computer-based clinical consultation systems. *Comput. Biomed. Res.* **14**, 542–558.

Waterman, D. A. (1970). Generalization learning techniques for automating the learning of heuristics. *Artificial Intelligence* **1**, Nos 1 and 2.

Watson, R. J. (1974). Medical staff response to a medical information system with direct physician-computer interface. *MEDINFO 74*, pp. 299–302. North-Holland, Amsterdam.

Winston, P. H. (1970). *Learning Structural Descriptions from Examples*. Ph.D. Thesis, Project MAC TR-76, Massachusetts Institute of Technology, Cambridge, Mass.

Winston, P. H. (1977). *Artificial Intelligence*. Addison-Wesley, Reading, Mass.

Wortman, P. M. (1972). Medical diagnosis: an information processing approach. *Comput. Biomed. Res.* **5**, 315–328.

Yu, V. L., Buchanan, B. G., Shortliffe, E. H. *et al.* (1979a). An evaluation of the performance of a computer-based consultant. *Comput. Prog. Biomed.* **9**, 95–102.

Yu, V. L., Fagan, L. M., Wraith, S. M. *et al.* (1979b). Antimicrobial selection by a computer—a blinded evaluation by infectious disease experts. *J. Amer. Med. Assoc.* **242**, 1279–1282.

Zadeh, L. A. (1965). Fuzzy sets. *Information and Control* **8**, 338–353.

9. Doctors using computers: a case study

M. J. FITTER and P. J. CRUICKSHANK

MRS/SSRC Social and Applied Psychology Unit, Department of Psychology, The University, Sheffield, England

I. Introduction

We are not surprised to discover microtechnology in the offices and on the shop floor of today's "progressive" organizations. The use of the technology has become commonplace and the logic of its introduction is rarely questioned or challenged. Yet, in the UK at least, people react with a degree of surprise if one suggests that their own doctor has a computer in his/her consulting room—or even that the doctor's office is "computerized". But the tasks that doctors and their staff perform have no immunity from the computer revolution! Certainly doctors are highly skilled individuals; but the history of technology itself is the history of redefining tasks so that their skill content is radically changed (often deskilled) either by mechanization or more recently automation. Even tasks requiring intellectual skill, for example those of the designer and draughtsperson, are now routinely aided by computer technology. Is it not merely a matter of time before the doctors' tasks are, to a significant extent, formally defined and incorporated in a computer system? If not, what are the inhibiting factors that distinguish medical skills from other skills? If it is so, what are the consequences likely to be?

This chapter does not attempt to provide a comprehensive analysis of such issues but, by focusing on a specific example of doctors using a history taking and symptom processing system in their consulting rooms, it does aspire to shed some light on issues of wide interest. We will begin by looking at the role of the doctor, then consider the uses to which computers are likely to be put, the ways that the use of such systems can be integrated with the doctor's role, and then we will examine skill requirements and consider the implications of the systems being used by the doctors

DESIGNING FOR HUMAN–COMPUTER COMMUNICATION
ISBN 0 12 643820 X

themselves, by specially trained paramedics, or even by direct interaction with patients.

A. Consultations—the doctor's role

One inhibiting factor, which may slow or even forestall the use of computers in the consulting room, is the doctor's role as *counsellor*. This is a task seen as requiring considerable interpersonal skills, requiring the patience and sensitivity to listen to patients relating their experiences, and providing support, reassurance and advice. This is not a task that would normally be seen as amenable to computerization though there are exceptions. It has been shown that patients like interacting with a computer terminal and providing it with information themselves (Lucas, 1977; Lucas *et al.*, 1977). Moreover, they may be more honest than they would be with a doctor if the topic is one that is embarrassing for them to talk about. Colby *et al.* (1966) developed a computer method of psychotherapy (based on ELIZA—Weizenbaum, 1965). Teach and Shortliffe (1981) have surveyed clinicians on their expectations of the use of computers in medical applications. Overall they found a positive attitude for applications to enhance patient management with an anticipation of real benefits for doctor and patient. Substantial emphasis was placed on the need for humanistic interactive capabilities. Nevertheless, despite the counter instances, in Britain at least, there is a concern that computers may in some way inhibit the doctor–patient relationship. For example, although the Royal College of General Practitioners, in a recently published report on computers in Primary Care (RCGP, 1980), has welcomed the benefits that are likely to result from using computers, they also expressed concern over the unknown effects on doctor–patient communication. This concern, however, should perhaps be considered in relation to the extremely small proportion of time that the average Medical School devotes to training doctors in interpersonal and interviewing skills. Thus, on this evidence, concern for the undermining of doctors' interpersonal skills is unlikely to be a decisive factor in the introduction of computer systems.

In fact, Medical School training places great emphasis on diagnostic skills and the doctors' role as *decision-maker*. Nevertheless, it has been argued (e.g. de Dombal, 1979) that it is in this area of medical decision making that there is considerable room for improvement in performance, and that this is where computers will make their mark.

The diagnostic process has been described by many authors and succinctly summarized by de Dombal (1979) (see Fig. 1). In essence, the patient (presumed ill) has the passive role of providing information for the doctor (the expert) to process, reach a decision and feedback to the patient.

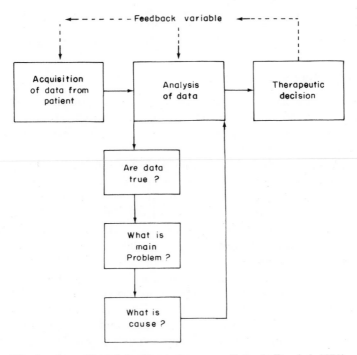

Fig. 1.   An outline of the diagnostic process (from de Dombal, 1979).

The decision making itself is likely to result in a number of outcomes including a diagnosis, a request for laboratory tests, referral to a specialist, and prescription of medication, surgery and/or advice. Although de Dombal argues that "Deciding whether a patient is telling the truth and linking the patient to a particular problem class are currently done rather well by doctors and extremely badly by computers", he also states, "Nevertheless if there is one single change that would assist the development of computing and information science it would be the adoption of more standard, more reproducible terminology" (de Dombal, 1979, p. 38). It is precisely such standardization that has had a major impact (both as precursor for, and consequence of, computer systems) in almost all areas of work organization. Moreover, de Dombal has demonstrated that the accuracy of clinical diagnosis is improved by the requirement to feed symptoms systematically into the computer, irrespective of whether any feedback is provided by the computer.

Clearly there will be considerable variation in the emphasis which doctors place on counselling skills and on rational decision procedures, with more emphasis on the former in Primary Care and on the latter in hospital medicine. We have performed our case study in both environments.

B. The computer's role

The use of computers in medicine, as in other applications, is as a means of systematically enhancing the processing of information. Thus we need to consider the computer's role in the gathering, the analysis, and the presentation of information.

Information may be input to the computer on patient histories and current encounters. This includes symptoms, tests requested and the results, previous diagnoses, advice and medication prescribed, etc. The system might permit entirely free text as input material, which would more or less directly mimic the blank cards on which doctors can write their notes or, at the other extreme, might require a highly structured and detailed form to be completed by the doctor. These two extremities vary on the degree to which the computer imposes *structure* on the doctor's data gathering and the degree to which detail in terms of predefined *categories* are specified by the computer system. We believe each has its own corresponding advantages and disadvantages, and that a wide variety of information gathering alternatives are available. For example, patient management protocols, for use with certain chronic illnesses, provide structure for the consultation without necessarily defining in detail the alternative inputs that can be made to the system; free text is still possible within a particular topic. The advantage of the structure would be to prompt the doctor on what was regarded as the "optimum" management for the particular illness. Its disadvantage to the doctor would depend on the extent to which the doctor was constrained to follow the protocol and his/her judgement as to its appropriateness, i.e. protocols standardize structure.

Alternatively, a system which provided a check list for the doctor to tick off categories as deemed appropriate would *categorize* the input without necessarily imposing structure on the consultation. The list might be in alphabetical order with no obligation to cover all topics completely or in no particular order. Thus the structure of the list (alphabetical) would not impose any medical structure but would constrain the doctor to use the predefined categories, i.e. check lists standardize terminology. If the doctors fully understand and use the terminology, communication is likely to be improved, although it may be difficult to achieve a detailed consensus on terms, given current medical practices. Also, the level of detail (e.g. on a disease categorization or on a symptom) may be regarded as insufficient by the doctor, i.e. potentially important information is being thrown away.

From a computational point of view categorization of input simplifies the information processing. Otherwise, before any symptom or disease analysis can be carried out, the system must perform its own categorization. This can be extremely complex and error prone given the wide variety of names and synonyms (and spelling!) in current use.

The analysis of information falls into three types:

(a) look-up tables
(b) statistical analysis
(c) "knowledge-based" analysis

Look-up tables are the simplest and, as their name suggests, given one or more inputs, a list or table of associations provides the output. For example, the patient management protocol mentioned above might perform simple analyses on the input and skip to the relevant section of the protocol. Alternatively, a drug interaction chart would indicate which drugs should not be prescribed with the one under consideration.

Statistical analyses have a lengthy history in medical computing and use formal statistical theory (e.g. Bayesian statistics or a logistic regression model) and an acturial database (e.g. of previous symptom histories and disease classification) to process the input (e.g. the current patient's symptoms).

Knowledge-based systems are more recent, and also more complex, in that they attempt to "capture" the practitioner's mental skills inside the computer program. To the extent that they succeed, they process the information in a manner similar to the human decision maker or at least in a manner comprehensible to the decision maker (e.g. Shortliffe, 1976). However, they might also provide a faster and/or more accurate analysis because of the internal computational logic and an infallible memory. The relative merits of statistical and knowledge-based techniques have been discussed by Fitter and Sime (1979) and will be returned to in the next section.

The presentation of information (i.e. the computer's output) relates back to its gathering. The computer may be being used as an information storage and retrieval system able to present an orderly patient history, list of current medication, test results, etc. Additionally, it may be providing the results of computer analysis; in this latter sense the doctor may be using the computer as an alternative form of (non-invasive) test. The feedback of such analyses and the orderly presentation of information are likely to have a significant impact on the doctor's decision processes. One of the common criticisms made by doctors of their own (and their colleagues') notes is that it can be extremely difficult to find *relevant* information because of their lack of structure and an abundance of redundant and almost certainly irrelevant information. However, some doctors have commented to us that there are many "clues" in their own handwritten notes which would be difficult to specify precisely, but which indicate, for example, their emotional reaction to the patient at the time the information was collected. As we noted at the outset, computers succeed to the extent that it is possible to standardize and formally define what is relevant and thereby produce useful summaries.

C. Mixing doctors and computers

We have argued that the strength of computers is the imposition of a formalized and structured environment that they bring about—or more precisely, that the systems designers create and the computer system itself enforces. That is not to say of course that the doctor is totally constrained and without choice in his/her activities. Quite the reverse, a well designed system will leave the user with considerable flexibility and freedom to choose how and when to use it. Nevertheless, the actual *benefits* result from the doctor accepting the options available and then working within the system's constraints. We have observed that in group Primary Care practices doctors work relatively independently of one another—there are relatively few procedures on which they need to reach a consensus of opinion. The introduction of a computerized system, for say patient records, creates the need for a consensus on data gathering methods, terminology, priorities, etc. Without such agreement some intended benefits (e.g. morbidity analysis, analysis of prescribing patterns) are not likely to result.

It is not difficult to see how the role of the doctor as decision maker can be supplemented by computers, although the problems of achieving an integration of human and machine are by no means trivial. The role of counsellor appears, initially at least, not to match well with the doctor as provider of information for the computer, and evaluator of feedback. The case study which follows will provide concrete examples of problems that arise and attempts at resolution.

The doctor is not a "logical" or algorithmic decision maker, nor a natural user of tightly defined terminology. Many practitioners would call their skill a craft, some would call it an art. One of our interests in this study is therefore the way in which doctors manage to integrate their own decision making techniques with those incorporated in a formal information system. If the system is, for example, receiving and analysing symptom data and then providing feedback on disease likelihoods, how is the feedback and the requirement for further input incorporated into the doctors "informal" model of the decision process? The mechanisms of statistical analyses are not likely to be comprehensible. One accepts the result or rejects it. The opportunity to question the rationale for a particular decision/recommendation does not exist. Knowledge-based systems, on the other hand, do allow the doctor to interrogate the decision mechanism and ask for explanations. Such systems, however, still require the doctor to work within a predetermined framework and terminology.

A further important issue is the question of who is the most appropriate user of such systems. Should it be the highly skilled doctor or is it possible, and desirable, to train paramedics to act as operators, extracting information from the patient and inputting it to the system? The doctor can then receive a print-out of the computer's analysis prior to seeing the patient. Issues raised here concern the skills required by the paramedic (is it easier for a paramedic to learn and use a specific terminology?—it would certainly be cheaper) and the effect on clinical performance and on patient satisfaction. Another alternative is for the patient to interact directly with the computer system, answering questions put to him/her and, even though this would involve a shift in medical ideology, receiving feedback of medical information.

The concerns and possibilities outlined in this introduction can be summed up by two views, the first by a leading exponent of clinical information systems, and the second a summary of a working party of the Council for Science and Society making a historical analysis of the impact of technology on work.

There is not a competition between computer and doctor. When competitive systems have been tried, they have failed. A well designed diagnostic support system should do for the doctor what a well designed golf course does for the golfer. It should further his strengths, reward his good efforts, and instead of harshly penalizing his errors—so motivate him that he himself seeks to improve his own performance. In short, it should play like Augusta rather than Pine Valley or Oakmont (de Dombal, 1979).

Yet the historical parallels would also support a less encouraging interpretation. Crompton invented his hand mule to ease his own labour and make it more productive, yet 50 years after, by a natural development, it was turned against the spinner to eliminate his skill and destroy the control which this gave him over his work. CAD seems very likely to eliminate in a similar way the skill of the design draughtsman. Could expert systems be used for the same purpose against a professional level of skill? And if they could be, at some future time, what safeguard can there be against this use? Even if this does not happen, there is a further kind of question that should be asked. When all spray painting is done by robots who will have the skill to program them? When medical diagnosis is delegated to computers, who will extend this skill by practising it, and who will be alert to the first signs of side effect from some new drug? This is an extension of comments which were made earlier about the separation of manual and mental work. It has to be recognised that in giving up the interplay between knowledge and its regular practical exercise, we are departing from the only conditions we know for the successful development of art and science. It is not clear that they can continue to progress without these conditions (Council for Science and Society, 1981, p. 68).

II. The case study

It seems likely that in the near future computer terminals will become commonplace in the consulting room, in both primary care and hospital environments. By studying the effect of the computer on the doctor and patient, we hope our approach will lead to a better understanding of the psychological issues involved in the interactions between patient, doctor and computer, and result in more appropriate interfaces between the doctor and computer.

Thus our objective is to establish a conceptual framework for assessing the impact of computer terminals and to determine criteria for the design of future consulting room systems. The particular application we have chosen to study is history taking and symptom processing of dyspepsia patients, and we provide some results outlining the impact of a computer in this environment. However, we hope our framework and techniques will be relevant to a much wider range of applications, including the use of computer-based patient records and protocols for the management of health care.

Previous studies have demonstrated the high diagnostic performance that can result from the statistical processing of symptom histories, both when doctors take the symptom history, which is afterwards fed into the computer by a clerical assistant (see, for example, de Dombal (1979)), and when patients interact directly with a computer terminal by answering questions about their symptoms (see, for example, Knill-Jones (1981)). Our system is similar in that it produces a probabilistic analysis, but is designed to be used interactively by the doctor during the consultation. This would appear to be a direction in which medicine is moving with cheaper hardware and better user interfaces.

A. The computer system

The symptom processing system we have observed and analysed in use (FIRST-AID) was developed with the need for acceptability in the demanding clinical environment very much in mind (Barber and Fox,

1981). The system is designed to a functional rather than a procedural specification. That is, users have available a collection of facilities which they can decide to use individually and incorporate the computer into their interviewing and decision procedure. Minimal constraints are imposed on how and when to use the system so we can learn the ways in which doctors choose to incorporate the computer, given a fairly free choice. This approach is reflected in the training given to the doctors. The symptom terminology is introduced initially, followed by training on how to use each of the functions available. Minimal guidance is given on when, or in what sequence, to use facilities.

In the consulting room, on a trolley beside the desk, there is a visual display unit and keyboard which the doctor uses as a prompt on symptoms available, to select and enter symptoms and to get feedback on disease probabilities. In addition, there is a printer on the desk which provides structured history sheets on which the doctor can write notes. One of these sheets contains a list of symptoms entered by the doctor and the resulting disease probabilities. An outline of the system is given in Fig. 2 (see Barber and Fox (1981) for a full specification of the system and its design criteria).

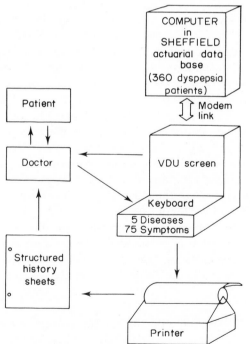

Fig. 2. Outline of the information links between computer system and consultation. Reproduced from *Behaviour and Information Technology* **1**, 1, 89–92 (1982).

B. The research environment

The system has been used in two environments. Over a period of 12 months it has been used in the gastroenterology outpatient clinic of a local hospital during the patients' first visit. The study was carried out in collaboration with the consultant, Dr K. D. Bardhan—his medical staff have been the system's users. The consultation is with the Registrar or Senior House Officer and its purpose is to take a history, do a physical examination, and request investigations prior to the patients' next visit to see the consultant. We have video-taped consultations of nearly 100 patients seeing one of the three doctors who have used the computer. In addition we have about 60 video-taped consultations of the same three doctors recorded prior to the installation of the computer for a "before and after" comparison. Patients were interviewed by a researcher (P.J.C.) and completed questionnaires immediately before and after their consultation to make an assessment of their orientation to medicine, expectations of, and reaction to, the consultation, their mood, and awareness of the computer (if used). Some months after their consultation a sample of 300 patients (both computer and non-computer) was surveyed by post about their attitude to computers in medicine.

The second environment in which the system has been tested is very different. In collaboration with Professor Metcalfe of Manchester University, we set up an experimental design to assess the impact of the computer on GP consultations. Four doctors, all members of the Department of General Practice at Manchester University and experienced in consultation skills, each interviewed six patients (half the consultations were with computer assistance and half without). The patients were played by professional actors, experienced at playing patients for the purpose of training doctors, and their roles were written by Professor Metcalfe. Consultations were video-recorded and "patients" and doctors made an assessment of each consultation immediately afterwards and also a wider assessment of the impact of the computer at the end of the day.

The objective and style of the hospital and GP consultations are different, the hospital one being rather more specifically disease-oriented. The hospital consultation also has more clearly defined objectives and a higher level of routine. An outline of the two environments in which the system has been tested and the design of the study are given in Figs 3 and 4.

C. The computer's influence on the doctor's information processing

In this chapter our main purpose is to outline the *issues* under consideration; a later publication deals with the empirical evidence in greater depth.

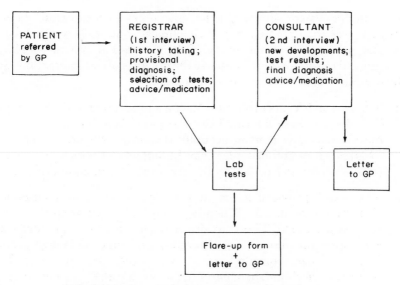

At the *1st interview* consultations are video recorded and patients
interviewed by researcher before and after the consultation.

Data collected for 3 doctors and 152 patients
    59 consultations without (pre) computer
    & 93 consultations with computer.

Fig. 3. Environment 1: hospital outpatient clinic. Reproduced from *Behaviour and Information Technology* **1**, 1, 89–92 (1982).

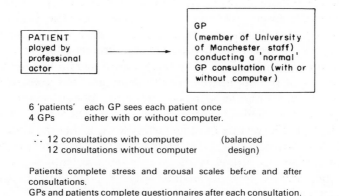

6 'patients'   each GP sees each patient once
4 GPs   either with or without computer.

∴ 12 consultations with computer   (balanced
    12 consultations without computer   design)

Patients complete stress and arousal scales before and after
consultations.
GPs and patients complete questionnaires after each consultation.
All consultations video recorded.

Fig. 4. Environment 2: GP consultation. Reproduced from *Behaviour and Information Technology* **1**, 1, 89–92 (1982).

The computer system was designed to give users a considerable choice in the way it was incorporated into their clinical routine. Nevertheless, the computer provides a formal (predefined) information system which may constrain and to some extent formalize the doctor–patient interaction. Such influence may occur for the following reasons:

(1) The system accepts symptom data on a predefined number of topics. The doctors were informed that the more data that are entered the more likely it is that an accurate diagnosis will result. Thus the *coverage* of symptom topics may be influenced with a tendency to pursue "computer topics" at the expense of "non-computer topics".

(2) The VDU provides a list of the topics, which is continuously available to the doctor. When he/she inputs a symptom the topic is marked as entered. This provides visual feedback of topics dealt with and topics remaining. The discrete topics may encourage users to structure their consultation so that topics are discussed more separately and independently from each other, rather than by informal integration of information which seems to typify the normal medical consultation and result in a lack of clear boundaries between consultation topics.

(3) In addition, the ordered list of topics may encourage the doctor to adopt a corresponding *sequence* for gathering symptom data, although the topics were listed in an order that, it was hoped, would be a "natural" sequence for the doctor.

(4) When entering symptoms the doctor is required to *categorize* the information into one of a small number of alternatives (often binary-present or absent) for each topic. This may lead the doctor to phrase questions to the patient in a way that will result in unambiguous answers "to meet the computer's requirements". Moreover, even though the doctor may have his/her own symptom categories (e.g. the patient has nightpains or not), these may not necessarily be the same as the computer's categories, i.e. the doctor's *terminology* may not coincide with the terminology used when the database was collected. The result of a mismatch is clear. Either the doctor will use his/her own terminology, in which case the computer symptoms are potentially inaccurate, or the doctor must attempt to gather information and use it in two distinct ways, i.e. one terminology for data entry and another for decision making.

(5) At any time during the entry of symptoms the user can ask for *feedback* in the form of the "computer's probabilities" resulting from

the symptoms thus far entered. Clearly, this feedback may influence the future course of the consultation by alerting the doctor to other possibilities.

All these possible effects result from the role of the doctor as an "information filter"; that is, the doctor extracts information from the patient and then on the basis of medical and social knowledge interprets the information and categorizes it into a form suitable for the formal information system. This potential for increased structuring of the information gathering is likely also to have an impact on the doctor's decision processes. Although the use of the computer by a paramedic would be in the sole capacity of information gatherer, the *doctor* also has the responsibility for the management of the patient and all the decisions therein entailed. To what extent can the "formal model" implied by the requirements of the information system integrate with the doctor's usual and typically "informal model" of the decision process? This question is of considerable psychological interest and is general to all decision-based information processing systems.

Increased structure and the routinization of the consultation are not necessarily undesirable. In fact there are compelling *a priori* grounds, and supporting empirical evidence, to suggest that formalizing the interview leads to better medical decisions. (The argument has been cogently put by de Dombal (1979).) It may be that it is the requirement to provide information for a computer system, rather than the feedback it gives, which results in better decisions.

A preliminary analysis indicates that the computer does have a considerable impact in the areas outlined above, although there are considerable methodological difficulties in providing clear evidence. The coverage of topics and the structure of the consultation appear to become noticeably "computer oriented" when the computer is used, although there is no indication that the *sequence* of the history taking is influenced. The doctors do not actually extend the coverage of topics to include all "computer topics" although some do enter symptoms for more topics than they have explicitly discussed with the patient. This is usually for negative symptoms (i.e. ones that the patient is believed not to have) which the doctor apparently decides on by a process of "reasonable inference" based on medical knowledge. There is also strong evidence that for some symptoms doctors tend to enter data based on their own terminology which is at variance with computer terminology. Thus the data has been collected to meet their own information requirements but an inference (or additional information) is then required to select the appropriate computer category. It appears that, for various reasons, some symptoms are more "fragile" than others, and are, therefore, less reliable for use in a formal information system.

The doctors appear to be influenced only to a *minor extent* by the feedback of disease probabilities, they make very little use of feedback *during* the consultation but tend to check it against their own judgement at the end. One influence is through being alerted to a moderate probability for a disease which they had thought to be relatively unlikely.

Most of the above issues are influenced by the general strategy that the doctor adopts for handling a computer system and patient in the consultation. In the next section we outline the various ways in which the doctors coped with the complex dynamics of this interaction.

D. Patterns of computer use

The system has been used in the consulting room by seven doctors (three hospital doctors and four GPs). There is considerable variation in the ways that each doctor used the terminal. However, there are distinct patterns that emerge, and consequences that follow from the choices made. This section provides a framework for examining the various patterns of use and looks at the advantages and disadvantages to the doctor of using a particular method.

A major variable is the extent to which the doctors chose to use the terminal *while the patient was present*. One strategy, adopted by some, was to attempt to minimize the use during the consultation. This could be achieved by inputting basic details (age, sex, etc.) *before* the patient entered, and then inputting symptoms elicited during the history taking when the patient had gone to undress ready for the physical examination. At the other extreme, some doctors attempted to use the terminal "conversationally". That is, they obtained a symptom from the patient, turned to the terminal and input it, and then returned to the patient for more information. This pattern of use requires frequent alterations of attention between patient and computer. It is somewhat akin to attempting to hold a conversation with two people, each of whom has no direct contact with the other. A third strategy, again used by doctors on some occasions, was a compromise between the first two. The doctor would elicit information on a number of symptoms and then turn to the terminal and enter them all in a "block" of computer activity. This required the patient to sit inactive for the duration of the terminal use.

Although the doctors experimented with the terminal, each tended to settle down into one of these patterns of use. There was no obvious sign that the GPs or hospital doctors as a group, preferred one particular strategy, each of which appears to have its own advantages and disadvantages. The first (minimal use) has the benefit of keeping the consultation simple for the doctor (it requires no switching of attention) and does not let the computer technology overtly intrude upon the patient. However, it requires the doctor to save up information (increasing memory load), and thus when the symptoms are eventually entered they are likely to be more influenced by the medical decision process itself. One of the doctors commented

> it was easy to forget the answers, and I wonder really how accurate our histories are if they are written down at the end of a consultation, because if you've what, ten points, it's very easy to forget some of the points or inaccurately remember the answers so that, say for example, length of history which you get, say at 2 years at the beginning of the interview; if you wrote it down at the end of the interview it might well have been altered.

Although this problem clearly would also exist for hand-written notes if made *after* the consultation, the act of entering data into the computer seems to raise the status of these "facts" and thus make more prominent the question of their accuracy. A further drawback of using the terminal after the history taking is completed is that the doctor cannot use the menu of symptom topics as a checklist or be influenced by feedback of computer probabilities during the history taking.

The "conversational" strategy has the correspondingly opposite pros and cons. It is less susceptible to memory load and interpretation, but requires the mental load of frequently switching attention between two different tasks. This itself appears to make significant demands on the doctor's interaction skills, by creating a pressure to formalize the interaction with the patient. For example, it was predominantly when the computer was being used interactively that we observed on video the doctor saying, "we'll come to that later", when the patient raised a new point that was lower down the topic list. The response times of the system became very critical when used conversationally. The doctor wants to complete one topic before going on to the next, which means successfully entering the relevant symptom. This might entail getting the computer to display the relevant topic menu and symptom codes, inputting the code and checking it has been accepted without error. The response times to provide a menu and to process a symptom were around 8–10 s. Although such time may be satisfactory in the context of the user working alone at a terminal, in the complex dynamics of a consultation, 10 s is a very long time. The doctor waiting in silence is usually a very clear invitation for the patient to "open-up". Moreover, in a normal consultation the doctor would invariably regulate any interruptions and control the course of the consultation and the use of time. Thus, to have an enforced "dead-time" of 10 s is very unusual.

We have observed a number of strategies for coping with this delay:

(1) Ask the patient to confirm the symptom about to be entered.
(2) Stare intently at the screen to indicate the doctor is busy.
(3) Stare into space between the patient and screen "as if in thought".
(4) Return to the patient and pursue the next topic.

This last strategy seemed to create difficulties for the doctor who had to decide whether to break off discussion of the new topic prematurely to complete the previous one, or to continue to the end and then enter both together.

The compromise strategy, as one might expect, carries with it to a lesser degree the pros and cons of the other strategies. Our initial assessment is that it is the more successful of the strategies in that it makes good use of the information system while at the same time allowing the doctor to, by and large, conduct his/her usual "patient-centred" consultation, interspersed with short periods of "computer-centred" activity. Thus the doctors were able to incorporate this in a way that made it clear to patients that they were now about to devote their attention somewhere else; in the same way that one might apologize before turning to talk to someone else for a few moments.

During a period of computer use an enforced delay of 10 s would be likely to end the period and return the doctor to the patient. It was only the GPs who used the system in this way in blocks because for them we managed to avoid the delay of having to wait for a menu and symptom codes to be displayed. During the block, the doctor did on occasions turn to the patient to confirm a symptom before entering it—"You did say you've had the pain for about 6 months?" At these times the doctor was still "computer-centred", though momentarily diverted to the patient purely as an "information source"; yet during the rest of the consultation the doctor could be as "patient-centred" as he/she wished.

E. The patient and the computer

Many doctors are concerned that computers will "dehumanize" medicine. Many patients too have this fear, regretting the demise of the "family doctor" in exchange for large impersonal group practices where a different doctor is encountered on each visit. Such patients complain that they see little enough of the doctor as it is, without a computer reducing the personal contact even further. On the other hand, many patients are more selfless in this respect, and say that if doctors want or need computers then it should be their choice, not the patients'. They are sympathetic to the stress faced by overworked clinicians and hope that computers can help to lighten the load. A less common response is the feeling that all computers are a bad thing because they contribute to unemployment.

This overview was obtained from interviewing 69 new patients who had some experience of one of the three hospital doctors using the computer. In addition, information was obtained from a postal questionnaire survey of 302 patients from the hospital outpatients clinic and from a questionnaire and interview survey of 416 patients in a large group practice of six doctors. (These data are described more fully in Cruickshank (1981).) It was found that the patients who had experienced the computer being used were more favourable in their attitudes towards the use of computers in medicine than patients who were not using personal experience as a basis for opinion. Furthermore, the 69 general practice patients who claimed to have used a computer themselves were also more favourably disposed towards doctors using them. Table I tabulates these questionnaire survey results.

Table I

Patient scores on a 26-item questionnaire measuring attitudes to doctors using computers. Each item is scored 0–4, with high scores being favourable to the use of the computer, and a maximum score of 104 points (incomplete questionnaires not included)

Outpatient clinic[a]		General practice[b]	
Computer used by doctor	Computer not used by doctor	Personal computer experience	No personal computer experience
71·3	62·2	73·9	64·0
($n = 85$)	($n = 208$)	($n = 69$)	($n = 270$)

[a] $t = 2·14$; $p = 0·007$.
[b] $t = 4·39$; $p = 0·000$.

The result might suggest that for patients, the experience of doctors using computers in the consulting room was a favourable one. However, there is evidence to the contrary. A study was made of patient stress both before and after seeing the hospital doctors. It is believed to be medically undesirable for patients to leave a consultation feeling tense, anxious and nervous, since Ley and Spelman (1965) showed that anxious patients tended to forget the doctor's instructions. In fact, most patients are considerably calmer when they leave the consultation than when they are waiting for it to begin. However, a proportion of patients leave the consultation more tense than they were when they entered it, and we found that this proportion was higher when the computer was used. Tenseness was assessed using the mood-adjective checklist developed by MacKay *et al.* (1978).

Table II shows the proportion of patients showing increases or decreases in stress; more patients than would be expected by chance show an increase in stress when the computer was used. Overall, non-computer patients were found to show a greater drop in stress at the end of the consultation than did computer patients. This pattern was repeated in the simulation study at the Department of General Practice in Manchester, where, ingeniously, actors reported their feelings "in character" at the end of each consultation. The 12 consultations (two for each character) employing the computer showed a smaller drop in stress overall than did the 12 consultations without computer.

Table II

Table of frequencies of patient change in stress, comparing before seeing the doctor with after seeing the doctor, for computer and non-computer patients

	Increase	Decrease	No change	Total
Computer	15	45	7	67
No computer	7	56	16	79
Total	22	101	23	146

$X^2 = 6\cdot69$, df $= 2$, $p < 0\cdot05$.

It appears paradoxical that the computer has an adverse effect on patient stress but a favourable influence on the patients' attitude to computers. It was necessary to compare the importance of the stress of the patient, which was seemingly adversely affected, against the experience of the computer, which appeared to be favourable as reflected in the attitudes survey. However, a multiple regression showed that stress on leaving the consultation was a better predictor of attitude to computers than actual contact with the computer. Patients who left feeling tense and worried were less in favour of the idea of doctors using computers. This was irrespective of whether the computer had been used for them or not. Thus, patients for whom the visit to the doctor is stressful do not welcome computers into the consultation. These may be patients who feel that the doctor does not pay them sufficient attention or allow them enough of his/her time, and who do not envisage the computer improving the situation. The above findings are fully described in Cruickshank (1981).

With regard to differing strategies of computer use adopted by doctors, this seemed to have little differential impact upon patients. Using a seven-point scale, ranging from "not at all" to "a very great deal" and categorizing two of the hospital doctors as "minimal users" of the computer in the presence of the patient, and the third as a "conversational user", it was found that patients of the two "minimal" doctors reported noticing the computer significantly less than did the patients of the "conversational" doctor. Some of the "minimal" doctors' patients even asked where the computer had been, when interviewed after the consultation. Yet this dimension, that of noticing the computer, is the only patient variable at the present stage of analysis that had been affected by the doctors' pattern of use. We have deliberately not conducted a controlled study of the impact of different patterns of use because we preferred to allow doctors to choose the style that they felt most comfortable with, hoping that this would ensure their best performance *vis-à-vis* the patient. Yet it happens that even doctors who have made a special study of consulting skills (the members of the Department of General Practice) show the previously mentioned decrement in their ability to reduce patient stress when using an interactive computer system. It also appears that even doctors not employing the most intrusive "conversational" style of computer use still show this effect.

It may be hoped that if doctors become aware of this possible side-effect of interactive computer use and also take special precautions with anxious patients who may not be well-disposed towards medical computer use, they may be able to compensate in their behaviour and overcome it.

It is also possible that when patients become more used to the idea of doctors using computers (still a novel concept to many) they may no longer show this effect. All the patients in the hospital study were new referrals, and we have had no opportunity to study long-term patient management using computers. Similarly, with much more intensive use of the system by doctors, they might develop their own coping strategies. However, findings so far serve as pointers to the directions in which computer-using doctors should be moving, and towards which future systems designers should work.

III. Conclusions

We have raised a number of research issues and drawn some initial conclusions which we believe have general relevance for the introduction of computer technology into the consulting room.

(1) Computers have the effect of "formalizing" the consultation both at the level of information filtering and in the structuring of the consultation.

(2) The computer can be usefully regarded as a member of a three-way (triad) relationship between patient, doctor and computer. The doctor is required to switch his/her attention between patient and computer. For the doctor, communication with each is a very different task needing different skills and requires an additional mental load to manage the alternation of attention.

(3) Traditional human factors research on user interface design needs supplementing to cope with the additional complexities of the three-way interaction in a sensitive environment. In particular, system response can be highly critical in a situation in which even a few seconds of silent inactivity is highly meaningful. Although some of the effects of using a terminal are no more than the problems of using a notepad, there are also qualitatively different aspects. The computer is active, the notepad passive. Doctors are used to being in control of the situation and determining the pace of the action. They never have to wait for their notepads to say "ready".

(4) It is important to consider the dynamics of the three-way (professional, client, computer) interaction further. In the conventional pattern of use there is no direct contact between patient and computer. Therefore, how can the doctor best integrate between the two and create a reassuring environment for the patient? It is suggested the doctor should use the computer in fairly short blocks of concentrated activity. What are the implications of completing the three-way relationship and allowing direct contact between patient and computer? This would have a fundamental effect on the consultation.

(5) In these early stages of computer use patients appear to be slightly more stressed if their doctor is using a computer, but on the whole accept its use. The prospects for longer term computer use are as yet unknown. Increased familiarity with computers may improve matters, but more complex and demanding systems may worsen them from the viewpoint of the doctor–patient relationship. The patient must not be allowed to come off second best in a competition with the computer for the doctor's attention.

(6) For the computer system to give real benefits, it is probably going *to change* the doctor's current work methods. For this to happen, doctors must be motivated to change, want the benefits available, and have the confidence to handle a novel task whilst at the same time maintaining a satisfactory rapport with the patient. Most patients have implicit trust in their doctors and most doctors would not wish to place this at risk.

IV. Acknowledgements

We are grateful to many people who have participated in this project. Dr K. D. Bardhan, his staff and the nurses and reception staff in the outpatients' department of Montagu Hospital, Mexborough; the Rotherham Area Health Authority; Professor D. Metcalfe and his staff at the Department of General Practice, University of Manchester; and our colleagues, Max Sime, John Fox, David Barber and Garry Brownbridge.

This chapter develops and expands on issues discussed in "The computer in the consulting room: a psychological framework". *Behaviour and Information Technology* **1**, 81–92 (1982).

V. References

Barber, D. C. and Fox, J. (1981). First Aid: A design philosophy and program for on-line symptom processing. *International Journal of Bio Medical Computing* **12**, 249–265.

Colby, K. M., Watt, J. B. and Gilbert, J. P. (1966). A computer method of psychotherapy: preliminary communication. *Journal of Nervous and Mental Disease* **142**, 148–152.

Cruickshank, P. J. (1981). Patient stress and the computer in the consulting room. *Social Science and Medicine* **16**, 1371–1376.

Council for Science and Society Report (1981). *New Technology: Society, Employment and Skill*, London.

de Dombal, F. T. (1979). Computers and the surgeon—a matter of decision. *Surgery Annual* **11**, 33–57.

Fitter, M. J. and Sime, M. E. (1980). Creating responsive computers: responsibility and shared decision making. *In* H. T. Smith and T. R. G. Green (Eds), *Human Interaction with Computers*. Academic Press, London and New York.

Knill-Jones, R. P. (1981). A computer assisted diagnostic system for dyspepsia. Paper presented at British Computer Society Medical Specialist Groups. One day symposium on Computers and the Clinician. Royal Hallamshire Hospital, Sheffield.

Ley, P. and Spelman, M. S. (1965). Communications in an outpatient setting. *British Journal of Social and Clinical Psychology* **4**, 114.

Lucas, R. W. (1977). Questioning Patients by computer: who will benefit? *Health Bulletin* **35**, 296–302.

Lucas, R. W., Mullin, P. J., Luna, C. B. X. and McInroy, D. C. (1977). Psychiatrists and a computer as interrogators of patients with alcohol–related illnesses: a comparison. *British Journal of Psychiatry* **131**, 160–167.

Mackay, C., Cox, T., Burrows, G. and Lazzerini, T. (1978). An inventory for the measurement of self-reported stress and arousal. *British Journal Social & Clinical Psychology* **17**, 283–284.

Royal College of General Practitioners: Report of the Computer Working Party (1980). *Computers in Primary Care*, London.

Shortliffe, E. H. (1976). *Computer Based Medical Consultations : MYCIN*. Elsevier, New York.

Teach, R. L. and Shortcliffe, E. H. (1981). An analysis of Physician Attitudes, regarding Computer-Based Clinical Consultation Systems. *Computers & Biomedical Research* **14**, 542–558.

Weizenbaum, J. (1965). ELIZA—A computer program for the study of natural language communication between man and machine. *Communications of the ACM* **9**, 1, 36–45.

10. Interactive conflict resolution in air traffic control

R. G. BALL and G. ORD

Royal Signals and Radar Establishment, Great Malvern, England

I. Introduction

A system such as air traffic control (ATC), which involves many technologically advanced components, would seem to be a prime candidate for a high degree of automation. However, at present, the level of automation introduced into any ATC system in the world has been small; the human controller, who is an integral part of the system, not only makes the decisions himself but also carries out a great deal of processing in his head. Such a conservative approach is due to the high level of safety demanded of the system, an excellent safety record being a strong argument to exercising extreme caution in introducing any major change. Completely computer-controlled systems have yet to show themselves capable of providing such integrity. But there are work-load limits to the traffic handling capacity of controllers, and thus of the present type of system, and these limits are now being reached.

How might computers help? It would seem that their introduction must be a gradual process and that one step in the right direction is to provide computer aids which stop short of invading the controller's realm of decision making but provide him with every assistance up to this point. Interactive Conflict Resolution (ICR), as yet at an experimental stage, could be one such aid. To understand its role it is necessary to have some appreciation why ATC is necessary and how it is done.

II. The need for air traffic control

The purpose of ATC is to ensure a "safe, orderly and expeditious" flow of air traffic from point of origin to destination. It might appear that, with all the sky to choose from, there would be little difficulty in achieving these objectives. In practice, there are a number of constraints which mean that expedition and, to a lesser extent, orderliness have frequently to be sacrificed to the paramount requirement for safety.

Some of the constraints are functions of the way that aircraft fly, how airlines operate them, the routes they have to follow, the timetables that passengers wish to adhere to, the weather, etc. The general effect of these is to produce a demand for quite a large number of aircraft to fly along the same narrow strips of sky (airways), at the same restricted range of height, at the same times of day and taking off from and bound for the relatively few airfields capable of handling them. The result is a situation analogous to the motorway which ends in a bottleneck! This would be hazardous without control. Other constraints tend to be of a political nature and include such problems as environmental factors (particularly with regard to noise abatement), international boundary handover restrictions and any other legislation that a national administration imposes on air traffic making use of its airspace and runways. Such considerations are a substantial complicating factor in the orderly and expeditious flow of traffic.

Although the control of each individual aircraft rests ultimately with the pilot, it is difficult to see how overall supervision can be exercised except from the ground, where decisions can be based on much fuller information than is currently available to individual pilots.

III. Methods of air traffic control

A. Sectorization

In practice, in a busy area, the control task is carried out by a team of Air Traffic Controllers. To keep the workload on each individual controller within reasonable bounds, the airspace under the control of any large-scale ATC authority is divided into "sectors". There are terminal area sectors around major airports and en-route sectors concerned with airways. Considering the latter as an example, the entry and exit points of each sector are marked by ground-based navigational beacons, the exit beacon of one sector being the entry beacon of the adjacent one. Sector lengths are such that the average transport aircraft will take between 10 and 30 min to fly from entry to exit. Hence, the controller's job is to assist aircraft to fly from point to point in the air route network, preferably by allowing them to "do their own thing", whilst keeping them safely separated from each other.

B. The controller's task

To carry out this task the controller has a variety of information presented to him, the most important parts being the flight plans for the aircraft under his control and the present air situation as seen by radar. The flight plans, which are filed by pilots, usually before take-off, become available to a controller several minutes before the aircraft enter his sector. The plans give flight identification, aircraft type, estimated arrival times at the beacons, route, speed, desired en-route height and destination. About the time that an aircraft is actually handed over to him from the previous sector, he will update the estimated arrival times. Then, on the basis of the present position and height as seen by radar, he will mentally predict where the aircraft will be in the future. The accuracy with which this can be done depends on the flight plan information, the controller's experience of this type of aircraft, on his knowledge of the way the air operator requires its pilots to fly the aircraft, the length of the flight, and the MET conditions. The future time for which he will be prepared to make the prediction will depend on what other potentially conflicting traffic there is. If the traffic density is high he may only trust his prediction ability to look 2 or 3 min into the future, particularly if the aircraft are climbing or descending. At the end of this time a further assessment of the situation is necessary, resulting in a heavy workload for the controller.

C. Problems of increased traffic

The sector lengths mentioned above have, in the past, allowed a reasonable number of aircraft per controller without too much proliferation of inter-sector co-ordination. Unfortunately, as traffic has increased, there has been not only an increase in the number of aircraft that a controller may be responsible for at any given time, but there has also been an effective transfer of some of the aircraft's navigation from the pilot to the controller, e.g. when he advises action to avoid a potentially hazardous situation which the pilot could not possibly foresee. Thus, there are now not only more aircraft per controller but there is also an increase in the amount of control activity per aircraft, rapidly tending towards the point where the controller becomes overloaded.

The solution to this situation is not simply to plug in more controllers (e.g. by further sectorization)—the rapid escalation of communication required between them soon nullifies any benefit so gained. Rather, the aim should be to try and reduce the scale of the control function to the point where the controller is working well within his limits, whilst remaining effectively in control of the situation. This could be done by relieving him of tasks which are more properly carried out elsewhere, e.g. on the flight deck (navigation) or by a computer provided to help him. Is such a transfer of tasks possible?

D. A predictive aid to exploit accurate aircraft navigation

Over the last decade it has become possible for a pilot to navigate his aircraft, both horizontally and vertically, with a high degree of predictability, i.e. to follow a well-defined "profile". This navigation ability is not being fully exploited by ATC systems as yet. The controller has only the flight plan to go on and, although he may have a good idea of future progress in the horizontal plane, the plan is only a coarse guide for predicting in the vertical plane and thus for making decisions and advising the pilot of a future safe course (a process known as "issuing a clearance"). An experienced controller may have a reasonable idea of how a particular airline will perform a manoeuvre but he will rapidly lose the ability to visualize the future relative positions of a number of aircraft as traffic density increases. This inability to accurately predict future aircraft positions results in a failure to fully exploit the actual navigation capabilities of the aircraft. In the overriding interests of safety the controller frequently has to insert some kind of delay or give a series of partial clearances, and is thus unable to ensure that the pilots can fly uninterrupted profiles. The result is that the original flight plan is modified in a way which penalizes the air operator. The minimum effect that can be expected of such measures is that there will be an increase in workload on the ground and in the air; it could lead to the disruption of the schedules of many other aircraft.

There is no doubt that there are many occasions when controller intervention of this kind is unavoidable, but there are also a substantial number of cases when he could issue a more satisfactory clearance, thereby reducing workload all round, if he had a better prediction of what was liable to happen. Furthermore, where some modification of flight plan(s) is inevitable, the ability to assess accurately the likely outcome of a particular course of action before actually initiating it could significantly reduce the severity of any such intervention. To achieve these ends the controller needs two aids in addition to those he may have already. These are:

(a) a "predictive display" to present him with the probable future development of the current situation, and

(b) a means of interacting rapidly with the system which drives this display so that he can try out the likely effects of any modification to clearances that he may decide to recommend.

The components under (a) and (b) form, when taken together, what is known as a "what if?" facility. Such a facility could be of use in many control and other problem-solving areas, providing that the dynamics of the system are amenable to analysis and formalization (Benoit and Martin, 1972), and that the response time of the "what if?" components is short compared with the real-time response of the system being modelled by them.

IV. An overview of a control system including prediction

In order to provide a predictive aid it is necessary to feed the computer with more detailed information about an aircraft's performance than is currently available from the present type of flight plans. Once such information is available, and is introduced into the ATC computer, a great deal of computation, some relevant to prediction, becomes possible. For example, by being able to associate the flight intention data with present radar position on a computer driven display, a wide range of methods of predictive display to a controller can be used. In addition, automatic detection of possible future infringements of safety standards (conflicts), together with manual and automatic ways of resolving the conflicts, become possible (Ball and Ord, 1976; Ball *et al.*, 1976). Computer assistance can also help with the task of monitoring the progress of aircraft, as well as with the automatic transfer of data between sectors.

It was on account of the emphasis on conflict resolution and the controllers' interaction with such resolution that the work became known by the title of Interactive Conflict Resolution (ICR for short). It will be referred to as such throughout the remainder of this chapter.

Figure 1 shows schematically the way that the twin streams of information, one about the present position of the aircraft as seen by radar and the other concerning the intention of the aircraft, can be associated and processed to drive displays showing the present and predicted states. The information displayed can be either in diagrammatic or tabular form, and one or both displays can be used to provide the output from the computer when it is engaged in an interactive mode with the controller.

It is not difficult to provide a great deal of computation to assist the controller and allow him to give better clearances to aircraft; the question is rather to decide how much assistance is desirable. This, and some of the other interesting concepts involved in the controller–computer relationship, will be discussed in more detail in the next section. This discussion of concepts will be followed by a section which will describe one particular implementation of the ideas. The chapter concludes with a description, in

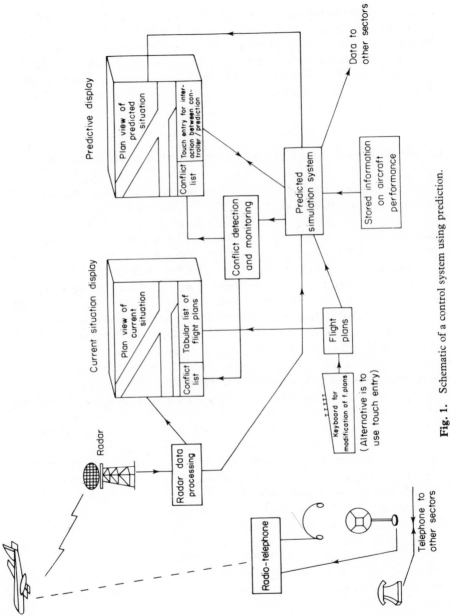

Fig. 1. Schematic of a control system using prediction.

broad outline, of experiments which set out to evaluate the concepts and the results which were obtained.

V. The controller–computer relationship

A. Achieving the right balance

As has been stated, in present-day ATC systems the controller works on the basis of flight plans, which give him an idea of aircraft intention, supported by a radar display, which informs him about the actual current situation. To these must be added radio contact with aircraft actually under control and communication with other controllers—frequently by telephone. From all these sources an experienced controller can build up a pretty good "picture" of what is likely to happen in his sector over the next few minutes—provided that there is a reasonable balance between the number of aircraft and the complexity of their future interactions. The ICR system adds a "what-if?" facility to extend his forward-looking capabilities, and thus enables him to control more traffic without loss of quality of service. Also, because ICR requires that a machine has access to most of the information that is available to the controller, it can relieve him of some of the more mundane aspects of his present activities. However, there is a penalty in that more man–machine interaction is required and an attendant danger that the controller will, at some point, begin to "lose the picture" of what is likely to develop. Since, for the foreseeable future, it is axiomatic that responsibility for safety will remain solely with the controller, this raises the following fundamental problems.

(a) What is the correct distribution of function between man and machine? In particular, how is the man to remain effectively in the picture and in control?

(b) If man and machine are truly to complement each other, how are they to communicate? How can one ensure that the man gets sufficient benefit from the machine to justify the effort of communication with it?

In his efforts to satisfy the second of these requirements the system designer must avoid the pitfall of tending to reduce the role of the man to that of a button-pressing accessory to an omniscient machine. If the controller is to be held responsible for any decisions taken, he must know in some detail how they are reached. Furthermore, he must be able to work on in the event of a machine failure—though with a reduction in the maximum rate of acceptable traffic flow. Consequently, what is envisaged is a cooperative system in which the number-crunching abilities of the machine are available to enhance the experiential pattern-recognition abilities of the man, who will have the benefit of knowing that the machine is making quantitative assessments of his proposed tactics in a way that he could not by himself. Clearly, he must generally be able to trust the machine, but must also be able to judge whether or not the advice that it gives him is reasonable. This he should increasingly be able to do with continued association in a synergic activity.

B. Communication between controller and computer

It must be borne in mind that any given task of the controller is but one of many that are competing for his attention. Therefore, the man–machine communication problem effectively reduces to minimizing the data exchange between them, and making it as natural as possible.

The output from the computer is, for the systems of the immediate future, likely to remain in the form of visual data. In most present-day ATC systems the two basic sources of this data are the labelled plan display (lpd) and the flight progress board (fpb). The lpd shows in diagrammatic form the real position of aircraft and is at present used for radar monitoring; a similar form of presentation is likely to be useful for predicting future position. The fpb is made up of flight progress strips, each of which carries some essential information regarding a particular aircraft's flight through a single sector on its route. The strips are usually printed by machine and may be manipulated in a number of ways which are of great significance to the controller. With increasing automatic aid, there has been a tendency to replace the fpb with an electronic data display (edd), which may be updated by the computer, though it is very difficult to produce an edd which is as versatile as the fpb. Because of the potentiality of the ICR system to maintain up-to-date flight plans, an edd was included in the system from the start.

Input from controllers has, up till now, usually been by pressing buttons or keys. With the introduction of a powerful computing facility, a dialog (or conversation) between computer and controller becomes a possibility. In the context of ICR, there is a restricted repertoire of (a) questions which the controller can ask the computer, and (b) instructions which he can issue to it. And, conversely, there is some restriction in the way the computer can reply. Advantage can be taken of this to minimize the number of input errors against which precautions have to be taken in the software program. A powerful method is that of "menu-selection" used in a dynamic form. When a controller wishes to provide an input, he is presented by the computer with a menu of the options which the computer can accept. When the controller has accepted one of them, the computer then presents him with a further series of options which are the logical outcome of his previous selection. This process can continue until a complete meaningful message is built up. Even when dealing with numerical inputs it is possible to restrict the options to only those which are credible from an operational point of view. It is very desirable, in order to avoid errors, for the controller to be able to have a means of input which selects, unequivocally, one of the options. One way of doing this is to display the options visually, say, in a table and make the controller point to the one he wants. A light pen or a touch-wire system could have been employed (Johnson, 1967). ICR employed a device developed in-house, known as the touchpad, which facilitates remote interaction with the menu-selection display (Matthews, 1979). The way in which it is used will be described in Section VIB.

C. Planning and monitoring

Before postulating a division of tasks between controller and computer it is necessary to consider the two main phases of work involved in tactical ATC.

The planning phase involves deciding what clearances are to be offered to pilots, based on the ability of the ground-based controller to predict and evaluate the future air situation. The monitoring phase consists of keeping a watch on the way that the present situation is developing and how aircraft actually relate to each other. These two phases are not totally independent in that the present actual situation provides the baseline for any current planning activity which, in turn, will modify the future observed situation. Thus the controller has to work in two time domains—he must always be aware of the present situation and he must constantly be planning ahead. Therefore, if the machine is to be a real aid to him, he must be able to discriminate easily between current and predicted information on his displays.

D. A suggested division of tasks

Bearing in mind some of the points considered in the previous paragraphs, a division of tasks has been attempted. No claim is made that an ideal has been achieved—in fact, much of what was done was constrained by the equipment available in a general experimental environment. In general, the controller has been given the tasks which involve pattern recognition and overall appreciation of the traffic situation; the computer, the tasks which involve continuous updating of information and detailed trend analysis. The division is as follows:

(a) Planning—man.
   (i) Assessing future trends.
   (ii) Allocating priorities.
   (iii) Deciding tactics.
   (iv) Informing the machine of proposed changes in flight plans.
   (v) Making decisions and issuing clearances to pilots.
   (vi) Co-ordinating with other sectors.

(b) Planning—machine.
   (i) Presenting flight plan and radar data in an easily assimilable form.
   (ii) Making detailed trend analyses (conflict searches) and issuing appropriate warnings to the controller.
   (iii) Transmitting controller decisions to other sectors.
   (iv) Allowing the controller to check machine predictions at his own rate.
   (v) Possibly offering simple suggestions regarding modifications of profiles (automatic resolution).

(c) Monitoring—man.
   (i) Ensuring legal separation standards are not likely to be infringed in the short term.
   (ii) Keeping a look-out for emergencies.
   (iii) Maintaining essential contact with pilots.

(d) Monitoring—machine.
   (i) Ensuring separation standards are not likely to be infringed over a longer term than the controller, to give him some room to manoeuvre.
   (ii) Updating the basic data for future predictions.
   (iii) Providing a back-up, or "safety-net", to warn the controller in the unlikely event of his having overlooked a potential hazard.

Though it was with this sort of breakdown in mind that the man–machine interface of the ICR system was designed, automatic resolution (b(v) above), which was included earlier in the research programme, has been omitted at the current stage of development. The reasons for this omission are referred to in the concluding section.

E. Computer aid in controller-to-controller communication

So far we have concentrated on the relationship between one man and a computer and have considered this in the context of a single complex airways sector. If long-term clearances are to be given involving a complete manoeuvre (e.g. a complete descent from a cruising level to enter a terminal area at a fixed level), it is advisable for the complete manoeuvre to take place within a sector; otherwise the task of co-ordinating the manoeuvre over more than one sector may prove to be impossible. This implies that the sector cannot be a short one and may, under heavy traffic conditions, contain more aircraft than a single man can handle. Splitting up sector control between two men is difficult—it is necessary for both controllers to know what the plan is, and for each to be aware of any variations made to accommodate deviating aircraft. However, once a plan has been agreed between them and entered into the computer, it can readily be displayed to either controller without any further controller input. The exact mechanism for this interchange of information needs to be investigated (see Section VIC).

VI. Experimental implementation of ICR

In order to investigate the technique of predictive displays, a series of experiments was carried out at the Royal Signals and Radar Establishment (RSRE) as part of a programme sponsored by the UK Civil Aviation Authority. The computer-driven display system available enabled a simulation to be made of an en-route sector under the control of a one- or two-man team. The reaction time of the system was quick enough to give a fair measure of realism to the simulation—an essential feature in any man–computer experiments. During the experiments various different ideas were assessed by the RSRE team, with the help of members of the staff of the Applied Psychology Department of the University of Aston in Birmingham. Having filtered out the less promising ideas, more realistic experiments were then mounted at the Air Traffic Control Evaluation Unit (ATCEU) at Hurn Airport using teams of controllers.

One particular form of the data display and of the controller–computer conversation facility is now described in some detail. It is followed by a description of an interface which was used for two-man operation.

A. The controller–computer interface—data display

As mentioned in Section VB there are two basic sources of visual data—an electronic data display (edd) and a labelled plan display (lpd). The latest form of edd is shown in the lower part of Fig. 2. This contains essential information regarding present and future progress of every aircraft in the system, past progress being deleted from the display as an aid to the controller's own filtering processes.

The radar monitor had the format shown in the upper part of Fig. 2. It simulated two converging two-way airways with an assumed airport complex just beyond the south-east corner. The area under control was marked by the four triangular navigation beacons and, during the main ICR experiment, was treated as a single sector. This could be considered to be complex by present standards, but allowed a high demand to be placed on the controller without requiring an unrealistic rate of traffic-flow along any given track. The northern track on each airway was mainly concerned with south- and east-bound traffic, much of which would seek to descend into the airport terminal area. The southern tracks were largely allocated to north- and west-bound traffic, mostly climbing out of the terminal area. Particular problem points are those marked A, where the two inbound air-routes converge, and B, where north-bound climbing traffic had to cross east-bound descending traffic.

As can be seen from Fig. 2, the flight progress edd and the radar display were combined on one tube to provide what was known as the "situation display", because it referred to the current state of the system.

Alongside the situation display was the "planning" display, shown in Fig. 3, which was also divided into two main areas. The upper part was a replica of the radar monitor, but was capable of being used in a forward-looking mode. It was possible to control the time of prediction in this mode by means of a rolling ball which allowed the controller to advance predicted time at a rate under his own control and so examine the probable future situation in a highly flexible way. The likely consequences of any tactics postulated by the controller could therefore be displayed and examined before he was committed to act on them. The penalty was that the radar never appeared on the planning display at all—although it was, of course, still available on the situation display. This caused some problems in that it compelled the controller to relate information from both the planning and situation displays.

The lower section of the planning display was occupied by the tellback area of the interactive input facility. This is described in Section VIB.

A small area which was common to both the situation and the planning displays can be seen just below half-way down on the left in Figs 2 and 3. This displayed the result of the latest conflict search performed by the main (or "global") part of the ICR system. Global search was carried out very frequently and included all possible pairs of aircraft. It was based on flight plans which had been modified by confirmed controller decisions, together

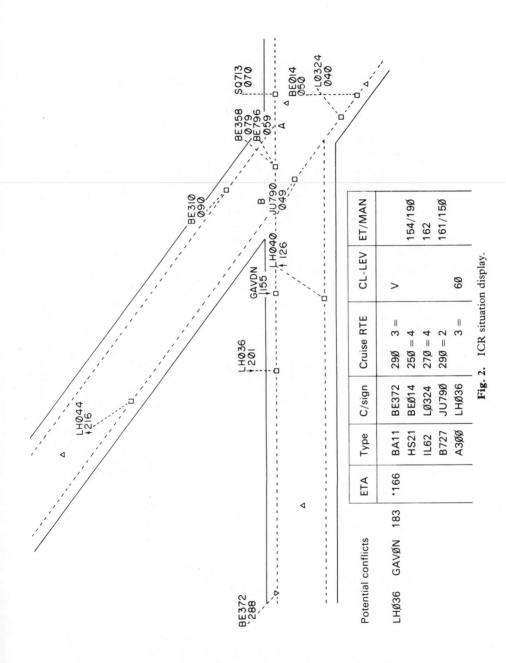

Fig. 2. ICR situation display.

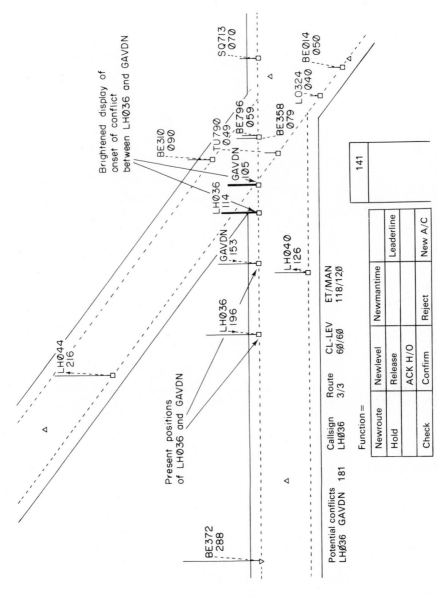

Fig. 3. ICR planning display (at second stage of menu selection).

with the preferred flight profiles of any aircraft for which he had not yet exercized any explicit control function. All flight plans were updated regularly by the system, using radar derived data. If any conflict recorded in the list had an imminence of 3 min or less then it flashed to attract the controller's attention, thus reminding him that some urgent action might be necessary.

B. Controller–computer interface—conversation

The main input device used in the ICR system was the in-house development called the touchpad. This was let into the surface of the desk below the displays and provided 16 discrete areas which corresponded with the 16 areas on the "menu-card" shown at the foot of Fig. 3. In practice, it was unnecessary to look at the touch-sensitive surface and so the touchpad had no delineation to show where the individual menu items were situated. An item was selected by running the fingers over the surface, which caused a cross to move around the tellback area on the planning display, thus telling the user which item was currently being selected. Before a menu-selection sequence was started the cross was not displayed so, when it was, it also indicated that a sequence had been started and not correctly terminated. When the tellback indicated that the desired item was being selected, the user could signal this to the machine by operating an "accept" key with the ball of the thumb, without removing the fingers from the menu-selection area of the pad.

An important feature of the man–machine conversation was that it was carried out on two levels. These could broadly be divided into machine response to controller suggestions and to controller decisions. With suggestions, the conversation was immediate—rather in the nature of a quick consultation—and was localized between the man and his planning display. The rest of the system knew nothing about it until the controller signalled that a decision had been made. This would then be entered into the main system database, and be reflected in the way that the system carried out its future predictions and, eventually, in the developing real-time situation. Thus, the system assisted the man in his planning task by displaying the predicted consequences of his decisions, as well as monitoring actual aircraft behaviour.

Figure 4 gives an example of how the controller could examine his suggestion that an aircraft's sector exit height be changed. Figure 4(a) shows the rest position of the menu, with a cross indicating that LH∅36 is the selected aircraft. Upon accepting this, three things happened, as shown in Figs 4(b) and 3. First, the aircraft's current flight plan was displayed in

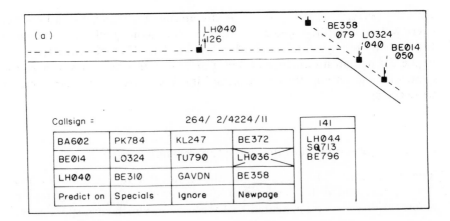

(a)

LH040
↑126

BE358
079 L0324
040 BE014
050

Callsign =		264/ 2/4224/11		141
BA602	PK784	KL247	BE372	LH044 SQ713 BE796
BE014	L0324	TU790	LH036	
LH040	BE310	GAVDN	BE358	
Predict on	Specials	Ignore	Newpage	

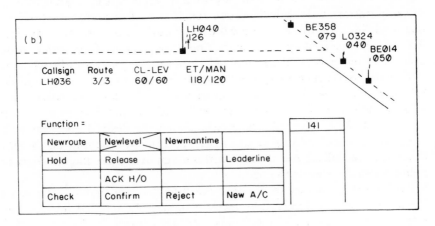

(b)

LH040
↑126

BE358
079 L0324
040 BE014
050

Callsign	Route	CL-LEV	ET/MAN
LH036	3/3	60/60	118/120

Function =

Newroute	Newlevel	Newmantime	
Hold	Release		Leaderline
	ACK H/O		
Check	Confirm	Reject	New A/C

141

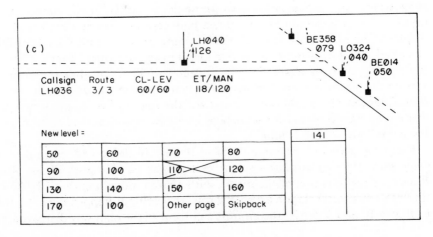

(c)

LH040
↑126

BE358
079 L0324
040 BE014
050

Callsign	Route	CL-LEV	ET/MAN
LH036	3/3	60/60	118/120

New level =

50	60	70	80
90	100	110	120
130	140	150	160
170	100	Other page	Skipback

141

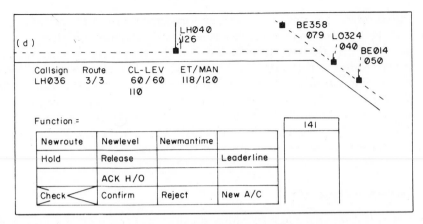

Fig. 4. Specimen menu-selection sequence. (a) Selection of aircraft—accept LH036. (b) Selection of function—accept change in flight level. (c) Selection of value—accept flight level 110 (i.e. 11,000 feet). (d) Selection of function—check for conflict.

shortened form above the tellback area. It will be seen that each item has two values—the actual clearance currently stored by the machine followed by the value requested by the air operator in order to fly the optimum profile. Secondly, if the aircraft was the subject of a potential conflict as a result of the last global conflict search, this fact was indicated symbolically on the "lpd" area of the planning display as a bright paint against the background of the current prediction (see Fig. 3). The third response to confirmation of the selected aircraft was to replace the list of callsigns in the tellback area with a "menu-card" containing the next set of options. This offered a number of functions which could be performed on the aircraft's flight plan, and also a means by which other decisions could be made concerning the nominated aircraft.

The second and third stages of postulating a change of flight level to 110 ($= 11,000$ feet) are shown in Figs 4(b) and (c). Note that the controller's suggestion appears underneath the appropriate entry in the reduced flight plan above the tellback area of Fig. 4(d) which shows the fourth stage, the menu being a repeat of Fig. 4(b). It was possible at this stage to add another amendment to the flight plan, such as a change in the time of manoeuvre, or, if the controller was confident that his original suggestion was a sound one, he could confirm the amendment to the flight plan without seeking any further aid from the machine. In this case the "what-if?" facility would be pre-empted by the controller. However, if he wished to have further assurance that what he was suggesting was safe, he could instruct the machine to perform a "local" conflict search, which concentrated on the aircraft of interest, and informed him of the results very rapidly. If the result of this search was unsatisfactory, he could then make a fresh attempt. If the search indicated that the suggestion was sound, he would confirm it to the system and the menu would then revert to the rest position—Fig. 4(a) without the cross. It is important to note that, up to this point, the controller and the predictive display have been engaged in a game of "let's pretend". It is only when the "confirm" instruction is inserted that the suggestion becomes a decision to the machine, and is incorporated into the main database of the system.

C. Two-man operation

Section VE discussed the possibility of using the computer as a means of communication between two or more controllers. Taking account of the airway structure (see Fig. 2) it might appear that the obvious division of responsibility would be for one man to take the east–west airway and another man to take the north–south airway. Alternatively, one could control inbound traffic and the other outbound. Both these possibilities suffer from the difficulty of allocating control of the common south-east corner, since only one sector controller at a time can be responsible for any given volume of airspace. Hence, the solution adopted was to divide the tasks, basically, between planning and executive control. The planning controller (known in ATC nomenclature as the "support" controller), would carry out most of the clearance optimization and would pass the results on as recommendations to the sector (or "executive") controller, who could accept or modify them, as he saw fit, before actually passing instructions to the aircraft. (It is the executive controller who carries out monitoring as part of his role.) The support controller was provided with a set of displays and input devices similar to those of the executive controller and communicated with the machine in the manner described above. However, when he confirmed his suggested modification to a flight plan it went into the main part of the system purely as a suggestion to his executive colleague, who then had to signal his acceptance to the machine at the time that the aircraft became his responsibility. Thus there were a number of degrees of aircraft "status", of which the controllers had to be aware, and which were of the following nature.

(1) Not yet processed by the support controller.
(2) Processed by the support man but not yet in sector.
(3) Entering sector.
(4) Acknowledged by the executive controller.
(5) Aircraft given a less than optimum clearance.

With the exception of number 3, these were indicated symbolically on the callsign level of the menu. Number 3, because it involved a change of responsibility from the previous sector, was the only status which demanded an immediate response and was, therefore, signalled to both controllers by flashing the callsign on the menu-card. This warned the support controller that his involvement with that aircraft was coming to an end, and alerted the executive controller to the fact that he was about to become responsible for it.

With the facilities described it should be possible for much of the communication between controllers to take place through the machine—though it is not argued that this is always a good thing.

VII. Evaluation—experimental aims, design and measurements

After initial experiments at the research establishment, fuller experiments were conducted at the Air Traffic Control Evaluation Unit at Hurn Airport. The general aim of the latter was to gain an early indication of the feasibility and possible future applications of the ICR concept and to observe the strategies and preferences of practising controllers under varying workloads. The feasibility of using a computer to help when control is split up between two controllers was also of considerable interest.

The most recent experiment at ATCEU was conducted over a period of four weeks and six controllers took part, arranged in three teams. After some introductory training each team undertook 28 runs of 45 min each, with heavier traffic samples being used as the experiment progressed. Each pair of controllers changed over in the planning and monitoring roles after every seven runs. The most important results are summarized below (for fuller details see Russell-Smith *et al.*, 1977; Whitfield and Bird, 1977; Whitfield *et al.*, 1980).

(1) All three forms of prediction—global search, local search, and manual prediction—were used extensively. The computer records show that the support controller, especially, made frequent use of local search and manual prediction. As an example, Table I is a

Table I

Mean frequency of use of manual prediction per run

	Support	Executive
1st set of runs	14·6	8·5
2nd set of runs	11·4	6·0

record of the use of manual prediction. The frequency of use of this facility was logged for each controller in each run, and comparisons are presented here between the mean frequencies of use per run, in the two roles of support and executive, and in the first and second sets of seven runs in which each controller undertook each role.

The subjective comments were very much in favour of the facilities. There was some suggestion that manual prediction was used less in busy situations, but there were several comments on its usefulness for analysing predicted conflicts.

(2) The support/executive team arrangement worked very well. Effective co-ordination between the two was very high. Table II shows the relationship between the flight plan modifications made by the executive (E) and/or the support (S) controllers to inbound aircraft during the last seven runs of each team. As an example, the top-right quadrant records the plans which were modified (M) by the support controller but subsequently were not modified (NM) further by the executive controller. (It is not necessary to assume that the modifications made by the executive controller were needed to remove conflicts; some were given so that the aircraft should have a more economic clearance.)

The table indicates the low frequency of modifications by both controllers to the same aircraft. Other measurements showed that only a small number of conflicts were "passed on" by the support controller to the executive controller. It appeared that the support controller was able to make full use of the predictive facilities, insulated from the immediate demands of traffic, while the executive controller could rely on the support controller's forward planning and concentrate on more immediate monitoring and control. Few difficulties arose between the two members of the team, and little actual verbal communication was required to attain smooth cooperation.

Table II
Relationship between flight plan modifications by S and E controllers

| | | Executive | |
		M	NM
Support	M	34	130
	NM	7	114

(3) The traffic levels handled during the experiment were quite high. Some of the samples contained the equivalent of up to 46 aircraft per hour, and they appeared to be dealt with efficiently by the teams. Moreover, from an analysis of controller/pilot communication messages recorded by the computer, it is clear that there were relatively few cases of revised clearances once the aircraft had entered the sector.

Subjective estimates of workload were obtained in the checklists completed by each subject after each run. Subjects were asked to rate their perceived workload on a five-point scale, ranging from "very low" to "very high".

Table III
Subjective workload—percentages averaged across responses by
six subjects on each of their runs

Very low	Rather low	Moderate	Rather high	Very high
12%	23%	41%	17%	7%

Table III suggests that workload was within reasonable limits on most occasions. The relatively small number of "very high" ratings is associated with heavy samples. Perhaps more important is the high frequency of ratings less than "moderate". This is a pertinent reminder that any computer aid should promote an optimum level of workload for the controller.

(4) There are two approaches to the subject of monitoring. Either the computer can be made to indicate when an aircraft is deviating from the intended plan and the controller left to judge whether any further action is needed—or it can be programmed to keep a continuous check on the total state of the air situation and warn him if a future conflict is likely. The evaluation showed that the controllers were more interested in the computer providing warnings of future conflicts due to aircraft deviations, than to the actual deviations themselves.

(5) The controller's "picture" of the overall traffic situation was raised spontaneously by the controllers as an area of concern. There seems to be a danger that his appreciation of the situation may be reduced at the higher levels of traffic made feasible by the computer aid.

VIII. Conclusions

The following conclusions can be drawn from the observations and evaluations of the ICR technique at RSRE and at ATCEU.

(1) An aid such as ICR should allow controllers to issue long-term clearances in heavy traffic conditions, thus reducing workload.

(2) Although controllers had the task of inputting to the computer the information about both trial and confirmed clearances, they seemed to consider that the assistance they received was well worth their effort.

(3) The automatic monitoring of an aircraft's progress was so successful that controllers came to rely on it, perhaps unduly so.

(4) The technique provided a facility by which several controllers could interact with the method of control in a way which gave a satisfactory, flexible and safe division of responsibility between them.

(5) The general difficulty of keeping the controller abreast with the air situation implies that it might be difficult for him to understand the solutions provided by any but the simplest form of automatic resolution algorithm.

(6) The technique looks as though it can be applied to other air situations beside the en-route example employed in the experiments.

IX. Acknowledgements

The authors wish to acknowledge the help of their colleagues at RSRE, the participation in the work of Mr D. Whitfield and his staff from the Applied Psychology Department of the University of Aston in Birmingham, and the assistance given by the staff of ATCEU in mounting and running the larger experiments. They are also grateful to the controllers who acted as subjects.

The work was sponsored and financed by the Civil Aviation Authority and facilities were also provided by the Ministry of Defence (Procurement Executive).

X. References

Ball, R. G. and Ord, G. (1976). Co-operative ATC using a medium-term predictive aid. *Proc. Eurocontrol Seminar on Conflict Detection and Resolution*, Luxembourg.

Ball, R. G., Lloyd, R. B. and Ord, G. (1976). Interactive conflict resolution in air traffic control. *Proc. AGARD Conference on Plans & Developments for Air Traffic Systems: Proceedings No. 188*, Cambridge, Mass.

Benoit, A. and Martin, R. H. G. (1972). On the generation of accurate trajectory prediction for air traffic control purposes. *Proc. 19th Technical Conference, International Air Transport Association*, Dublin.

Johnson, E. A. (1967). Touch displays: a programmed man–machine interface. *Ergonomics* **10**, 271.

Matthews, A. V. (1979). Touch pad—a computer input device. *RSRE Memo. 3208*. Royal Signals and Radar Establishment, Malvern, UK.

Russell-Smith, F. P., Ord, G. and Whitfield, D. (1977). An experiment to examine the concept of interactive conflict resolution (phase II). *Report No. 454*, Air Traffic Evaluation Unit, National Air Traffic Services, Hurn, UK.

Whitfield, D. and Bird, J. M. (1977). Interactive conflict resolution: a second experimental study: human factors assessment. *AP Report No. 79*, Applied Psychology Department, University of Aston in Birmingham.

Whitfield, D., Ball, R. G. and Ord, G. (1980). Some human factors aspects of computer-aiding concepts for air traffic controllers. *Human Factors* **22**(5), 569–580.

11. The Query-by-Example concept for user-oriented business systems

M. M. ZLOOF

IBM, T. J. Watson Research Center, Yorktown Heights, New York, USA

I. Introduction

As computers get cheaper and more available, small- and medium-size businesses are increasingly automating their manual operations, and one can easily predict that computers will soon infiltrate such domains of our lives as offices, schools, and homes. Thus a new set of users is emerging, the "non-programmer professional". Our definition of such a class of users is those who know their applications and have been carrying it through manually. Those users would want to automate their job by interacting directly with the computer without the intervention of a professional programmer; therefore, a need for high-level user-friendly languages is becoming quite apparent. Furthermore, a language for expressing a simple query against a database is no longer sufficient, but rather there is a requirement for more elaborate language facilities in order to accommodate setting up entire applications. One should point out that perhaps there is no one simple language that is suitable to all application domains. It is more likely that one language will fit a particular domain better than others.

In this chapter we concentrate on the domain of business applications and we will attempt to show that the two-dimensional programming approach of Query-by-Example (Zloof, 1975a,b,c, 1976, 1977, 1978) and its supersets SBA and OBE (Zloof, 1981, 1982; Zloof and deJong, 1977) is a suitable language for non-programmers who wish to automate their manual procedures. Emphasis will be given to the human factor aspects of the language.

Because we are trying to address the community of non-programmers, we will avoid as much as possible using any computer jargon.

DESIGNING FOR HUMAN–COMPUTER COMMUNICATION
ISBN 0 12 643820 X

II. Business objects operations

Long before the invention of computers, business objects were introduced to facilitate the communication of information among the different business outfits. These objects include tables, forms, charts, reports and documents, etc., ranging from a very structured object such as a table to entirely unstructured ones such as a letter. The operations that were manually performed with respect to these objects can be summarized as follows:

(1) Create an object.
   (Example: Defining a table with all its attributes, or composing a letter.)
(2) Insert into, delete from, or update an object.
   (Example: Insertion of a new record into a table, or editing an existing letter.)
(3) Move data from one object to another.
   (Example: Mapping data from a database table to a report, or mapping data from a database table to a document such as address, etc.)
(4) Retrieve data from an object.
   (Example: Queries on structured database which may include matching fields between objects, or text search if the object is free text.)
(5) Send and receive objects.
   An object may be sent only if a certain condition occurs in the database, or as a consequence of an event, or at a certain time or date.
(6) Various security features.
   In a manual operation security was merely accomplished by locking the data in a file cabinet, allowing only authorized people to have access. In a computer system, on the other hand, security issues are handled quite differently.

III. The main concept of Query-by-Example

For a language to be powerful enough for business operations, it must at least be able to handle most of the above operations in such a way that a non-programmer professional can express these operations with no difficulty. We believe that Query-by-Example is such a language to the extent that it is powerful enough to cover many business functions and yet easy to learn and use. The main concept behind Query-by-Example and its OBE and SBA extensions is that the user mimics manual operations by "programming" directly within two-dimensional skeletons of the above business objects (displayed on a screen) by entering examples of these operations. Query-by-Example, like ALPHA (Codd, 1971) and QUEL (Stonebraker, 1975), is a relational calculus-based language, whereas other high-level languages are relational algebra-based languages to the extent that they contain relational algebra operators such as PROJECTION, UNION, INTERSECTION, JOIN, DIFFERENCE and SELECTION.

IV. Language design considerations

It is only recently, since the use of computers has infiltrated the non-programmer community, that the words "ease-of-use", "user friendly", and "human factors" have been added to the lexicon of computer sciences terminology. The reasons why these considerations did not receive earlier attention are twofold: first, the use of computers was limited to the professional programmers; and secondly, since computers were relatively expensive, slow, and limited in memory and other storage devices, language designers were (maybe justifiably) mainly concerned with per-formance and implementation considerations. Today, on the other hand, the *ease-of-use* aspect of the language is receiving attention, because a non-programmer user must find it easy to learn and use, otherwise it will be neglected, no matter how fast, efficient, and powerful the system is.

The question now arises: what is ease-of-use and how can one define and quantify it? Ease-of-use and user-friendly are fuzzy variables—far from being rigorously defined. While it is relatively easy, for example, to measure and compare the speed of two machines, it is quite difficult to define ease-of-use, or say that one language is twice as user-friendly as another; the terms are subjective and depend on the user's taste, background, environment, training, etc. Recently (Thomas and Gould, 1975; Reisner *et al.*, 1975; Shneiderman, 1978; Greenblatt and Waxman, 1978) researchers have tried to measure different languages in terms of average time required to formulate a set of queries, percentage of correct queries, confidence ratings, classification of errors, etc. (see Thomas, this volume).

Because Query-by-Example was found to be highly user-friendly (Thomas and Gould, 1975), and because it is being accepted by the non-programmer community, we shall try to give our considerations in designing a language.

We first provide a set of human factor considerations that we found important in designing any language. These resulted partly from psychological studies and partly from feedback from the user community. In our opinion, the extent to which a language satisfies these requirements will determine the degree of user-friendliness of that language.

(1) *Minimum concepts required to get started.* A non-programmer cannot be expected to become familiar with a thick user manual in order to start using the language. Thus for simple operations the user should be required to learn very little.

(2) *Minimum syntax.* The language syntax must be simple and yet cover a variety of complex transactions. It is assumed that a user will not necessarily use the system continuously; therefore, if the language syntax and constructs are not straightforward, he may not be able to retain its concepts for long.

(3) *Consistency.* The language operators must be consistent throughout the various phrase structures. Operators must not change semantics in different contexts.

(4) *Flexibility.* A high-level language must have the flexibility to capture the user's thought process, thus providing many degrees of freedom in formulating a transaction.

(5) *Easy to extend and modify.* Dynamic modification of the database by means of creating new views at any point in time provides the user with flexibility in reorganizing the database.

(6) *Minimum exceptions.* Too many exceptions to the rules imply bad language design and will require the user to be quite familiar with these rules (necessitating longer training time).

(7) *Easy detection of errors.* The language syntax and phrase structure should be such that they minimize the possibility of an error; if, on the other hand, the user formulates an erroneous transaction, a simple and clear error message should be given by the system.

(8) *Unified language.* To minimize syntax change for new concepts, the same query syntax should be used for modification, definition, and control of the database.

V. Language overview

In Query-by-Example we introduce the concept of two-dimensional programming language by means of examples on the following sample database that may be found in the admissions department of a hospital:

PATIENT (NAME, AGE, SEX, ADMISSION DATE, ROOM NO., DEPT., PHYSICIAN, BLOOD TYPE)

LOCATION (ROOM NO., FLOOR)

BLOOD BANK (BLOOD TYPE, QUANTITY)

At this point we will assume that the above database has already been defined and the data has been entered. We now give examples of the language facilities in accordance with the following sequence: retrieval, modification, definition, authority and integrity constraints, triggers, and electronic mail. These examples do not by any means cover the entire language features. The purpose of this overview is to merely have the reader observe the style of the language, stressing the design fundamentals described in the previous section.

A. Retrieval

Let us start with a simple query to retrieve information from a single table:

Get the names and room numbers of all the female patients whose physician is Jones.

Initially, the user is presented with a blank table skeleton displayed on the screen as follows:

Table Name Field				

The user keys in the appropriate table name in the "table name field", in this case, PATIENTS. The user may now either fill in the column headings of the table or let the system generate them automatically. Having established the column headings, the user now "programs" within that skeleton by making the following entries:

PATIENTS	NAME	AGE	SEX	ADMISSION DATE	ROOM NO.	PHYSICIAN	WARD	BLOOD TYPE
	P.		F		P.	JONES		

P. stands for "print", which indicates that the desired output are the names and the corresponding room numbers. F and JONES are called "constant elements" which determine the records selection criteria. This query may be paraphrased as follows: display the names and room numbers of records such that their corresponding sex column contains F and the physician column contains JONES. The formulation of this query mimics the way one would manually scan the table to retrieve the desired data.

Column headings not participating in the query such as AGE, WARD, etc., can be left out, if the user so desires. In relational algebra-type languages, this query is equivalent to SELECTION on SEX and PHYSICIAN, and PROJECTION on NAME and ROOM NO.

Note that to formulate the above query, the user need only remember the P. operator for column selection (row selection is accomplished by the constant element entries, that is to say, few concepts are required to get started).

1. The concept of the "example element"

In addition to constant elements, example elements (variables) are used in Query-by-Example to cover a wide variety of operations, such as:

(1) Matching data between fields.
(2) Expressing conditions on fields.
(3) Moving data from one table to another or from a table to a report.
(4) Derivation of new fields from already existing ones.
(5) Text search.
(6) Inserting, deleting, or updating groups or records simultaneously.
(7) Delegating access authority to groups of users.
(8) Sending electronic mail to groups of users.

To distinguish them from constant elements, in our examples, example elements are underlined strings of characters. Thus X ABC 50 are all example elements (variables).

We will now continue with examples using example elements to demonstrate the above-mentioned operations.

2. Matching data between fields

Consider the following query:

Get the names, ages, and room numbers of all the patients on the 18th floor (you may want to ask such a query in case of an elevator failure). This query involves a scan of two tables, the PATIENTS table and the LOCATION table. Therefore, two skeletons have to be displayed on the screen, filling in both table names; the final formulation of this query is as follows:

PATIENTS	NAME	AGE	ROOM NO.
	P.	P.	P.X

LOCATION	ROOM NO.	FLOOR
	X	18

Here we deleted redundant columns of the PATIETS table from the
screen.

$\underline{X}$, which is an example element, indicates that there must be a match
between the ROOM NO. in the PATIENTS table and the ROOM NO. in
the LOCATION table, the latter corresponding to FLOOR 18. This is
equivalent to a manual operation by which a record is picked up in the
PATIENTS table, if its room number matches a room number in the
LOCATION table where the floor is 18.

This query is equivalent to SELECTION, JOIN, and PROJECTION.
Note that representing the example element by $\underline{X}$ is completely arbitrary,
and any other string of characters could have been used, as long as they are
underlined and both fields match. Once the concept of the example element
is understood, the user can link any number of tables and any number of
rows within a single table, as in the following example.

List the names and ages of patients older than Smith. The formulation is as
follows:

PATIENTS	NAME	AGE
	P.	P > $\underline{A}$
	SMITH	$\underline{A}$

Explanation: If Smith's age is $\underline{A}$ as an example, then we want to display the
names and ages of patients older than $\underline{A}$. The order of the rows is immaterial.
(Note that $\underline{A}$ was arbitrarily used as an example element; we could have used
any other characters.)

3. Conditions on fields

Conditions on one field or multiple fields can be accomplished by
specifying a condition expression involving example elements in a condition box which can be displayed upon request.

Print out the names, ages, and admission dates of patients between the ages of 50
and 65:

PATIENTS	NAME	AGE	ADMISSION DATE	WARD
	P.	P.$\underline{A}$	P.	

CONDITIONS
$65 \geqslant \underline{A} \geqslant 50$

Arithmetic condition expressions such as $\underline{A} + \underline{B} > 50$ where $\underline{A}$ and $\underline{B}$ are example elements drawn from database tables or logical condition expressions such as $(\underline{A} = 50$ or $60)$ are also admissible as entries in a condition box.

4. Moving data from one table to a user-created table

It is sometimes desirable to collect data from more than one table and place it in a new user-created table as an output report. For example, if we wish to see an output containing the names, the room numbers, and the floor of each patient, the formulation of the query is as follows:

PATIENTS	NAME	AGE	SEX	ROOM NO.
	$\underline{N}$			$\underline{R}$

LOCATION	ROOM NO.	FLOOR
	$\underline{R}$	$\underline{F}$

	NAME	ROOM NO.	FLOOR
	P.$\underline{N}$	P.$\underline{R}$	P.$\underline{F}$

The third table is not a database table (table containing data) but rather an output table that the user creates by mapping the data from the base tables, specified by the matching example elements. Because it is a user-created table and does not correspond to stored data, the user can fill in any descriptive headings or leave them blank—in other words, they need not correspond to headings in the base tables.

5. Derivation of new fields

In the previous example we moved data by means of the example element to separate fields. It is also admissible to have any arithmetic expression as an entry to a new field whereby its examples are drawn from database tables.

6. Text search

If an entry to a field is a text, such as contents of an article or physician's comments, it can be searched by means of partial underlinings, because underlining a string of characters renders that string an example element. If we partially underline, the part that is underlined works as an example and the rest remains constant.

If we add, for this example, a comment column to the patient table, we can formulate the following query:

PATIENTS	NAME	AGE	COMMENTS
	P.	P.	X Hypertension Z

which means: get the name and ages of patients whose comments entry contains the word "hypertension" regardless of whether it is at the beginning, middle, or end of the text.

7. Built-in functions

There are five built-in functions in Query-by-Example: CNT., SUM., AVG., MAX., MIN. These functions operate on sets of values specified by the operator ALL.; thus, if we want to count the female patients, it will be expressed as follows:

PATIENTS	NAME	AGE	SEX	ROOM NO.
	P.CNT.ALL.		F	

The ALL. operator indicates a set of all the female patients and the CNT. function counts this set resulting in an integer.

8. Groupings

In order to group records by field values, the operator G. is used. As an example, count the number of patients in each room. This is expressed as follows:

PATIENTS	NAME	AGE	ROOM NO.
	P.CNT.ALL.		P.G.

The G. operator partitions the table by identical room number values and the CNT.ALL. counts the name of the patients having the same room number.

B. Modification

Insertions (I.), deletions (D.), and updates (U.) are done in the same style as the query operations. The only major difference is the use of I., D. or U.

in place of the P. used in the retrieval operations. The user can employ any admissible query expression to select the records to be inserted, deleted or updated. For example, the following will insert a new record into the patient table:

PATIENTS	NAME	AGE	SEX	ADMISSION DATE	ROOM NO.	PHYSICIAN	BLOOD TYPE
I.	HENRY	63	M	5/6/78	A563	HENRY	B

(Note: I. is used here as shorthand for prefixing every entry with I.)
  The following:

PATIENTS	NAME	AGE	SEX	PHYSICIAN
D.				HENRY

deletes *all* patients whose physician is HENRY.

One can also use example elements to specify the records selected to be modified. For example, if a physician, say HENRY, goes on vacation and wants to assign his patients to JONES, this update is accomplished as follows:

PATIENTS	NAME	AGE	SEX	PHYSICIAN
	X			HENRY
	X			U.JONES

The X represents HENRY's patients and the second line updates those records to JONES as Physician. Note that there is no limit on linking this table to other tables to further restrict the selection criteria.

VII. Table creation

An important facility in Query-by-Example is the ability of end users to define their own databases interactively through the screen, mimicking the way tables are created manually. This feature eliminates the need of a professional programmer throughout the entire process of setting up the application and writing programs against it.

In addition to creating new tables, users can extend columns to existing tables, and create "snapshots" (defined later). To create a table the user starts from a blank skeleton in which he inserts the table name (must be unique) and the table headings; for example, the headings of the PATIENT table will be defined as follows:

I. PATIENT	I.	NAME	AGE			DEPT	PHYSICIAN

The I. to the right of PATIENT refers to the entire row of column headings (not all of them are shown).

To continue the definition of the PATIENT table certain system keywords are utilized to specify the field data types, domain, sizes, keys, etc. To help the user, these keywords are attached to all skeletons as row keywords, and the user can issue a query to retrieve them. For example, the following query:

PATIENTS	NAME	AGE			DEPT	PHYSICIAN
P.X̲						

will retrieve the list of the keywords as follows:

PATIENTS	NAME	AGE			DEPT	PHYSICIAN
TYPE KEY DOMAIN ICW						

The user proceeds now to define the attributes of these keywords as follows:

PATIENTS		NAME	AGE	ADMISSION DATE	DEPT	PHYSICIAN
TYPE	I.	CHAR	FIXED	DATE	CHAR	CHAR
KEY	I.	Y	N	Y	N	N
DOMAIN	I.	A	B	C	D	A
ICW	I.	20	2	8	6	20
.						
.						

Keywords Explanation:

· *TYPE* specifies the data entry type such as CHAR, FIXED, FLOAT, DATE, etc.

· *KEY* specifies the fields that are to be considered keyfields (unique values). Y stands for yes and N for no. Note that we used the NAME, ADMISSION DATE combination as keyfields because a patient might be admitted to a hospital more than once.

· *DOMAIN* specifies the name of the underlying domain, the value set from which data elements are drawn. For example, the columns NAME and PHYSICIAN are drawn from the same underlying domain of names. Thus, both have A as domain value.

· *ICW* specifies the width of the column when displayed to the user on the screen.

Having specified all or part of the keyword attributes, the user is now ready to enter data in that table. If the user does not specify any of the keyword attributes, the system picks up various default values to complete the definition. When the table is defined, the user may formulate queries not only against the data records but also against the data definition directory. For example, if a user wishes to find out which are the keyfields, the following query is issued:

PATIENTS	NAME	AGE	ADMISSION DATE	DEPT	PHYSICIAN
KEY P.					

A. Table expansion

The owner of a table may expand an existing table in the same fashion that the original table was created. For example, if we want to add a new column such as BLOOD TYPE to the PATIENT table, this is done as follows:

PATIENTS	I. BLOOD TYPE
TYPE	I. CHAR
KEY	I. N
DOMAIN	I. L
ICW	I. 2

If the PATIENT table already contains data, null values will be assigned to the BLOOD TYPE column until they are updated by the user. Deletions and updates of the table directory are carried out in the same style as the insertions.

B. Creating a "snapshot"

A snapshot is a table whose data is mapped from already existing tables in the database. For example, if we wish to create a table containing the patient names, the room numbers, and the floors they are in, it is done as follows:

I.A	I.	NAME	ROOM NO.	FLOOR
	I.	$\underline{N}$	$\underline{R}$	$\underline{F}$

PATIENTS	NAME	ROOM NO.
	$\underline{N}$	$\underline{R}$

LOCATION	ROOM NO.	FLOOR
	$\underline{R}$	$\underline{F}$

Here we created a table named A. The inserted data is mapped from the PATIENT and the LOCATION tables. Note that there is no need to specify the definition attributes because they will automatically be inherited from the domains of the PATIENT and LOCATION tables.

VII. Security

Security of a database refers to the protection of the database against unauthorized disclosure, alteration or destruction.

In a relational system where the construction of the database is dynamic, with continuous creation of new relations (tables), expansion of existing relations, and destruction of others, it is important to have a wide range of flexible security features to be applied against or dropped from the database. In general, the creator (owner) of a table may place restrictions on the different users' duties and qualifications:

(a) One user may be given an unlimited access to a table for all types of operations: READ, INSERT, DELETE, and UPDATE.
(b) One user may read the table but not alter its content.
(c) Another may be restricted to reading a subset of the table records—for example, only information concerning patients of Department A—or a subset of the table records determined by a general Query-by-Example expression.
(d) The delegation of authority is to one particular user or a group of users defined again by a general Query-by-Example expression—for example, a physician may be allowed to read information concerning his (her) own patients only.

In order to cover this wide range of security statements in a way that business professionals can formulate without the aid of a programmer, we introduce very little new syntax, using as much as possible syntax and concepts that have already been introduced.

Thus a security statement is comprised of two parts:

(1) An authority keyword applied to a row of a table includes the delegated authority level (read, insert, delete, or update, or any combination) followed by the ID of the user to whom the authority is delegated. This ID can be either a constant element which represents one user or an example element which, as we shall see, will represent a group of users. Example of authority keywords:
AUTH(P.)HENRY—which will delegate read authority to the user
ID Henry.
AUTH(P.,I.)$\underline{X}$—which will delegate read and insert authority to a group determined by the example element $\underline{X}$.

(2) The second part of an authority statement is a Query-by-Example expression which will determine which subset of the table the users have access to.

Let us demonstrate this by some examples:

PATIENTS	NAME	AGE	SEX	ADMISSION DATE	ROOM NO.	PHYSICIAN	WARD
AUTH(P.)HENRY	N	A	S	AD	R	PH	CARDIOLOGY

The above expression will delegate authority to Henry to only read (specified by the P.) records of the Cardiology Department. The omission of an example element from a field prevents the user from reading information from this field. For example, if we omit the A under the Age and leave that entry blank, then Henry will not be able to read the patients' ages.

PATIENTS	NAME	AGE	SEX	ADMISSION DATE	ROOM NO.	PHYSICIAN	WARD
AUTH(P.,U.)JONES	X	Y	F	W	L		Z

LOCATION	ROOM NO.	FLOOR
	L	4

This statement delegates to JONES the authority to read and update (but not insert or delete) only records of female patients on the fourth floor only, without the ability to read or update the physicians' names. The point to be stressed here is that any Query-by-Example expression is permissible to select the records for which the authority is delegated.

To delegate authorities to a group of users simultaneously, we use an example element as an ID, and by linking this example element to other fields, the group of users will be determined. For example:

PATIENTS	NAME	AGE	SEX	PHYSICIAN
AUTH(P.)X	N	A	S	X

Here the ID is the example element X which is linked to the physician field in the same row, which means if the users are physicians, they are permitted to only read the name, age, and sex of their own patients.

A. Insertion, deletion, retrieval or update of authority statements

The owner or an authorized user can insert, delete, retrieve or update authority statements by simply prefixing it with I., D., P., or U., respectively. For example:

PATIENTS	NAME	AGE	SEX	ADMISSION DATE	WARD
I.AUTH(P.)HENRY	N	A	S	AD	CARDIOLOGY

will insert the authority keyword together with its query expression, or

PATIENTS	NAME	AGE	SEX	ADMISSION DATE	WARD
D.AUTH(P.)HENRY	N	A	S	AD	CARDIOLOGY

will revoke Henry's authority to read the patients table. Similarly, prefixing the authority keyword by P., will display its corresponding query expression.

B. Comments

(1) With the minimum addition of the authority keyword, a table owner or an authorized user can formulate a wide variety of complicated access statements.

(2) It should be noted that the level of centralization of the database is up to the particular application. The language provides a complete spectrum of control. If, for example, only one person defines tables and does not delegate modification authorities to other users, then the database is completely centralized. On the other hand, if many users are allowed to define tables and they in turn delegate modification authorities to other users, then we have a decentralized operation.

VIII. Integrity

To ensure the integrity of the database, various integrity constraints against the tables can be formulated. As in the security section, integrity constraints are again specified by a constraint keyword applied against a Query-by-Example expression in skeleton tables. With this keyword, and with the standard Query-by-Example expressions, the user can cover a wide variety of integrity constraints, such as:

(a) Static.
(b) Transitional.
(c) Constraints which are enforced only upon the occurrence of a certain storage operation (e.g. constraints which are enforced only upon deletion).
(d) Constraints which are enforced only upon the validity of certain condition(s) (e.g. only female patients are allowed in the maternity ward).
(e) Constraints against single elements.
(f) Constraints against a set of elements.

The integrity constraints keyword starts with the word CONSTR followed (if necessary) by the operation required for the constraint to be enforced. Thus:

CONSTR(I.)   —Ensures the validity of the database only upon insertion.

CONSTR(I.,U.)—Ensures the validity of the database only upon insertion or update.

Examples of integrity constraint expressions are:

PATIENTS	NAME	SEX	AGE
CONSTR(I.,U.)		$\underline{S}$	$\underline{A}$

CONDITIONS
$\underline{S} = (M \text{ or } F)$
$120 > \underline{A} > 0$

This constraint will ensure that a sex field will consist of either M or F entries, and an age field will have patients not older than 120 years.

PATIENTS	NAME	AGE	SEX	PHYSICIAN
CONSTR(I.,U.)	$\underline{X}$			$\neg = \underline{X}$

This constraint will ensure that a patient cannot be his (her) own physician.

PATIENTS	NAME	AGE	SEX	ROOM NO.
CONSTR.	ALL.N̲			G.L̲

CONDITIONS
CNT.ALL.N̲ ≤ 4

This constraint ensures that no room can accommodate more than four patients.

A. Insertion, retrieval, deletion and update of integrity constraints

As in authority prefixing, the constraint with P., I., D., or U., will accomplish one of those operations. For example:

PATIENTS	NAME	AGE	SEX
I.CONSTR	X̲	> 70	F

will insert the entire constraint expression (with its corresponding query expression), or

PATIENTS	NAME	AGE	SEX
P.CONSTR(D.)			

will display all constraints that are enforced upon deletion.

IX. Triggers

The material covered so far provided the user with the facilities of creating, retrieving, modifying and controlling the database. Let us define these facilities as "first-level automation" in the sense that the user must, at any point, formulate and execute programs or execute pre-stored programs.

To automate further a business operation is to automatically let the computer take certain actions whenever a condition or an event or any combination of them occur, thus mimicking the automation of routine business procedures. For example:

(1) Some programs are to be automatically and periodically executed and their output distributed to the appropriate departments.
(2) A database modification occurs automatically if a certain condition is met. (For example, if a patient is admitted more than three times within a year, reduce his daily charge by 10%.)
(3) If a department exceeds its budget, a notice is sent to the appropriate persons.

This kind of automation we call "second-level automation" because actions are taking place without the explicit intervention of the user. In this manner, clerks, secretaries or executives can automate their routine business procedures, and be relieved from having to query constantly the database to look for certain conditions in order to take some actions. Furthermore, one can imbed certain triggers as reminders for some actions that cannot be automated. For example, an executive may want to get a reminder from the system to call the bank manager if the cash on hand went down below a certain level.

As in security and integrity constraints, triggers are expressed by means of a row trigger keyword applied to a query expression. The trigger keyword has parameters that include any of I., D., U., time and date. Thus the expression:

PATIENTS	NAME	AGE	SEX
TR1(I.)	$\underline{X}$	> 70	F

is an example of a valid trigger expression which includes the prefix TR followed by the trigger name (1, in this case) followed by the parameter I.. The meaning of this trigger expression is as follows: TR1 is activated only upon insertion of female patients over 70 years old. (Suppose one is making a survey on this category of patients.)

Associated with every trigger activation, at least one action must take place—either one of insertion, deletion or update. For example, if we create a table called FEMALES OVER 70 with a NAME column, we can let the system automatically insert in this table by entering the following expression:

FEMALE OVER 70	NAME
I(TR1).	$\underline{X}$

which means: insert $\underline{X}$ only if TR1 is activated. Thus if a female patient over 70 is admitted to the hospital, her name will automatically be copied in this last table. (Note that the insert operator is parametrized by the trigger TR1, meaning that the insertion takes place only if TR1 is activated.)

One can view triggers as generalizations of integrity constraints. While expressing a constraint prevents certain operations from taking place if the constraint is activated, issuing a trigger causes another operation to take place.

In general, a trigger can have as parameters other triggers. As an example, consider a hospital where the blood reserve is limited, and we wish to display an alert message if a patient is admitted to the hospital where his blood-type is below a certain quantity, say ten gallons. To express this operation, we must have a trigger which activates upon insertion of any new patient. This trigger is in turn a parameter of another trigger that activates only if that blood-type quantity is below ten gallons. Thus the program will look as follows:

PATIENTS	NAME	BLOOD TYPE
TR1(I.)	<u>N</u>	<u>BL</u>

BLOOD BANK	BLOOD TYPE	QUANTITY
TR2(TR1)	<u>BL</u>	< 10

P(TR2).	This is to alert you that blood type <u>BL</u> is below 10 gallons.

The message in the last table will be displayed only if TR2 is activated. Thus the system is automatically alerting the user whenever the blood quantity of a newly admitted patient is below ten gallons.

As opposed to authority and integrity constraints, trigger statements are not stored one by one, but rather an entire trigger program is stored as a unit. The display of trigger statements is also done through displaying the corresponding program rather than one trigger at a time.

X. Electronic mail

In order for Query-by-Example users to communicate between each other (for example, sending mail), we introduce a new function called SEND. With this minimal additional syntax users can accomplish the following operations:

(1) Send objects to one person or group of people.
(2) Send objects automatically only when a certain condition(s) occurs in the database (for example, a message will be sent only if one exceeds his/her budget limit).
(3) Send objects in specific dates and times.
(4) A combination of the above.

The SEND function when used is followed by the object name, the keyword TO, and the receiver ID. Thus, SEND A TO HENRY means: Object A to be sent to the ID Henry.

When issuing a SEND function, it does not always necessarily mean that the object is physically sent. For example, if two ID's are sending messages to one another and they are sharing the same database, the SEND function will mean letting the receiver have access to the object. On the other hand, if the receiver is at a physical distance from the sender, then the object is actually sent. The point to be made here is that, from a language point of view, there is no difference in formulating a SEND expression whether the receiver is sharing your database or he has a different remote database.

Examples:

(1) Send object A to Henry. The formulation of this operation is as follows:

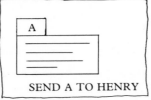

SEND A TO HENRY

Object A (a letter, for example) is created and edited on the screen. The statement on the bottom sends this object to Henry.

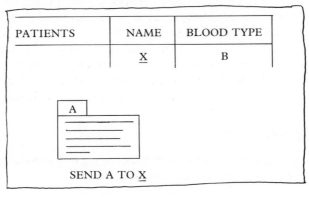

Note that the example element $\underline{X}$ can be part of any Query-by-Example expression.

We can generalize the SEND operation by coupling it with various triggers, i.e. send an object only if certain conditions occur in the database. For example, we wish to send a message A to all the physicians if there is a shortage of a certain blood-type.

BLOOD BANK	BLOOD TYPE	QUANTITY
TR1(U.)	$\underline{BL}$	< 50

PATIENTS	NAME	PHYSICIAN
		$\underline{Z}$

A

This is to notify you that a shortage of blood type $\underline{BL}$ exists. If you have a patient of that blood type, please contact us as soon as possible.

SEND (TR1). A TO $\underline{Z}$

The trigger in parentheses specifies that A is sent only if TR1 is activated. Note that the example element $\underline{BL}$ is mapped from the database to the message sent to all physicians. That is to say, if upon update of the quantity of a particular blood-type, say B, the system will map that blood-type B to the body of the message.

These are just a few examples to indicate the style of combining triggers to electronic mail. In general, one can map any number of example elements to the body of the object which is sent, and can send the object if a number of triggers are activated simultaneously at a specific time and date.

A. Receiving mail

To keep track of the mail, the system keeps a log in a system table called MAIL that contains the following headings:

MAIL	FROM	TO	OBJECT	DATE

When a send operation is executed, the system automatically fills in a record in the mail table indicating from whom the object was sent (because it knows the sender ID), and to whom the object is sent. (Note that if an example element is used as a receiver ID, more than one record is entered.)

The MAIL table is accessible by all users and they can issue a query to find out if they have any mail. For example, if SMITH wishes to find out if he has any mail, he/she will issue the following query:

MAIL	FROM	TO	OBJECT	DATE	TIME
	P.	SMITH	P.	P.	P.

which will result (as an example) with the following output:

MAIL	FROM	OBJECT	DATE	TIME
	THOMAS	ABC	7/5/79	4:00
	HENRY	LMN	7/7/79	12:30

Now if the user SMITH wishes to see the content of the ABC object, he has to issue a print command.

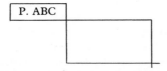

P. ABC

And the system will display the body of the ABC object.

XI. Conclusion

(1) What we attempted here was to show an easy-to-use user-language by which people can interact with the computer. The language goes beyond the scope of simple query statements in that users can define their own applications, and specify authority and trigger expressions, and statements to communicate business objects to other users.

(2) We did not give here a formal definition of the language syntax and semantics because our purpose was to communicate to the reader the

style and the human factors of this approach rather than syntactical details.

Let us now summarize on what is achieved in this two-dimensional approach in contrast to conventional linear string languages.

(1) Most of the mathematical concepts are hidden from the user. For example, entering a variable $\underline{X}$ under the DEPT column implies $\exists \underline{X} \in \text{DEPT}$; and entering two constants (or variables) in the same row implies a conjunction.
(2) The user enjoys the flexibility of formulating a program in any sequence desired, thus easily capturing his thought process.
(3) The use of linking example elements enables the user to express a wide variety of operations, ranging from matching data between fields to sending mail to various users.
(4) Exception rules are kept at a minimum, because the user is free to specify any entry under any column and in any row as long as it conforms to the local syntax.
(5) Syntactical errors are kept at a minimum because the syntax is minimal. Further, if an error does occur, the system can detect the spatial location of that error, i.e. in what table, what column, and what row the error occurs, keeping error messages simpler than those in conventional language.

XII. References

Codd, E. F. (1971). A Data Base Sublanguage Founded on the Relational Calculus. *Proc. ACM SIGFIDET Workshop*, available from ACM.

Greenblatt, D. and Waxman, J. (1978). A study of three database query languages. *In* B. Shneiderman (Ed.), *Data Bases, Improving Viability and Responsiveness*. Academic Press, New York and London.

Stonebraker, M. R. (1975). *Getting Started in INGERS—A Tutorial. ERL-M518*. University of California, Berkeley.

Thomas, J. C. and Gould, J. D. (1975). A Psychological Study of Query-by-Example. *AFIPS Conf. Proc.*, pp. 439–445. National Computer Conf. 44.

Reisner, P. *et al.* (1975). Human Factors Evaluation of Two Data Base Languages—SQUARE and SEQUEL. *AFIPS Conf. Proc.* National Computer Conf. 44.

Shneiderman, B. (1978). Improving the Human Factors Aspects of Database Interactions. *IBM Dept. of Information Systems Management, Technical Report No. 28.*

Zloof, M. M. (1975a). Query-by-Example. *AFIPS Conf. Proc.*, pp. 431–438. National Computer Conf. 44.

Zloof, M. M. (1975b). Query-by-Example: The Invocation and Definition of Tables and Forms. *Proc. of the Int'l. Conf. on Very Large Data Bases*, pp. 1–24. Boston, Massachusetts.

Zloof, M. M. (1975c). Query-by-Example: Operations on the Transitive Closure. *IBM Research Report RC5526*. IBM, Thomas J. Watson Research Center, Yorktown Heights, New York.

Zloof, M. M. (1976). Query-by-Example: Operation on Hierarchical Data Bases. *AFIPS Conf. Proc.* pp. 845–853. National Computer Conf. 45.

Zloof, M. M. (1977). Query-by-Example: A Data Base Language. *IBM Systems J.* **16**(4).

Zloof, M. M. (1978). Security and Integrity Within the Query-by-Example Data Base Management Language. *IBM Research Report RC6982*. IBM, Thomas J. Watson Research Center, Yorktown Heights, New York.

Zloof, M. M. (1981). QBE/OBE: A Language for Office and Business Automation. IEEE *COMPUTER* magazine, May.

Zloof, M. M. (1982). Office-by-Example: A business language that unifies data and word processing and electronic mail. *IBM Systems Journal* **21**(4), 272–304.

Zloof, M. M. and deJong, S. P. (1977). The System for Business Automation (SBA): Programming Language. *Communications of the ACM* **20**(6), 385–396.

any case being too numerous to examine exhaustively in most practical cases). However, the power of the method has been amply demonstrated by other application studies. Thus in DENDRAL, described for example by Buchanan *et al.* (1971), the method is applied to Mass-Spectrometery data and the rules are again implemented as production rules. The reader in any case, has already been introduced in an earlier chapter of this book to Shortliffe's work on MYCIN. In actual fact, a well-established method of programming, one using decision tables, is also an application of rule-based decision making; in this case, using binary logic. Here, perhaps the validity of the rules that make up the decision tables is based less on heuristics and expediency and more on well-established problem knowledge. The tables are also rigorously scrutinized for completeness and consistency.

In control engineering, the conventional method of designing controllers is to start with a precise mathematical model of the process. Thus process dynamics get represented as integro-differential equations. The desired response characteristics of the process are also expressed mathematically. All this mathematical information is combined and the equations can usually be solved to give a mathematical expression of control to be carried out. Usually this solution appears as a function relating plant states or outputs to control action to be effected at the input. That we have today achieved a high degree of automation from aircrafts and spacecrafts to chemical processes is a tribute to the success of this method and its numerous variations. However, this success can mainly be achieved when the models are given as linear equations relating a relatively small number of inputs and outputs. With more complex processes, the primary design relies on the simplification, linearization, and decoupling of input–output loops, etc. of the model, without sacrificing its accuracy too much so as to make their solution tractable. In any case, the modelling of the process mathematically remains the fundamental starting point in the design of the controller.

Many complex processes unfortunately, do not yield to this design procedure and have, therefore, not yet been automated. As such processes are already controlled by skilled human operators, it follows that this is an area where rule-based decision making could usefully be applied. That is then the reasoning behind the work described here. Figure 1 shows the schematic diagram of the rule-based control system. The process in this experimental work was a steam-engine, some of the rules for a part of this process are displayed in Fig. 2, where the caption gives the key to the linguistic labels used and their meaning. Examples of complex processes to which this technique may be applied are cement kilns, steel making furnaces, etc. Peray and Waddell (1972), for instance, give a complete protocol for controlling a cement kiln from which three of the rules are

12. Process control using fuzzy logic

E. H. MAMDANI

Department of Electrical and Electronic Engineering, Queen Mary College, University of London, London, England

I. Introduction

The main theme of this chapter is the application of rule-based decision making. The principle application area described here happens to be the control of industrial processes. Contrary to a conventional approach, the control is carried out by implementing linguistic decision rules, or heuristics. This chapter describes how fuzzy logic can be used for implementing such rules.

The idea of rule-based decision making is not new to this work; many research studies have been carried out on this topic. The central issue in all these studies is to automate a given decision-making process not by first accurately modelling (in a mathematical form) the system involved about which the decisions are required, but instead by trying to implement already available problem knowledge from a human who has demonstrated an ability to make decisions about the system in a problem-solving environment. This problem-knowledge is first acquired from the human by requiring him to articulate it in the form of linguistic rules. The problem environment and the manner in which these rules are implemented then vary from one research study to another. Thus in one of the earliest such works, Waterman (1970) uses production rules to implement rules concerning the game of poker. In fact it should be remarked that the work on process control using fuzzy logic was inspired as much by Waterman and his approach to rule-based decision making as by Zadeh (1973) and his novel theory of fuzzy subsets.

In these studies on rule-based decision it is implicitly accepted as natural that the human supplied rules will have inconsistencies and that these will most usually not be complete (i.e. take account of all eventualities—these in

DESIGNING FOR HUMAN–COMPUTER COMMUNICATION
ISBN 0 12 643820 X

II. Fuzzy logic and implementation of fuzzy rules

The basis of fuzzy logic is the notion of fuzzy subsets. These are generalized subsets of ordinary sets (which will be called the universes of discourse in the sequel). Figure 3 shows a graph whose abscissa represents a *set* of measurements, say representing height. The graph shows several crisp subsets of this set called **short, medium** and **tall**. The graph shows these subsets as a function of χ, which maps each measurement into either 0 or 1 given on the ordinate, so that for example:

$$\chi_{\text{small}} : u \to \{0, 1\} \qquad u \in U$$

If the scale on the abscissa is normalized in some way, say 0–1 m, then **small, medium** and **tall** can be applied to various height variables such as people, buildings or mountains, by multiplying the abscissa scale with a context dependent scaling factor G. Thus, G may be 2, when one is talking about people, and 9000, when talking about mountains. Note that G is applied to the underlying set, the universe of discourse, rather than the subsets which represent linguistic values of the variable in question.

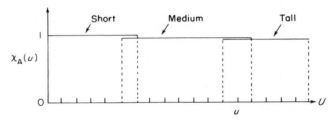

Non-fuzzy subsets:
$\chi_A : U \to \{0, 1\}$ $\chi_A(u) = \begin{cases} 0 & \text{if } u \notin A \\ 1 & \text{if } u \in A \end{cases}$

Operations:

Set union	Set intersection	Set complement
$A \cup B$	$A \cap B$	$\bar{A}$

Properties:

$$A \cup A = A \qquad\qquad A \cap A = A \qquad\qquad \text{Idempotence}$$
$$A \cup B = B \cup A \text{ etc.} \qquad\qquad\qquad\qquad\qquad \text{Commutativity}$$
$$A \cup (B \cup C) = (A \cup B) \cup C \qquad\qquad\qquad \text{Associativity}$$
$$A \cup (B \cap C) = (A \cup B) \cap (A \cup C) \qquad\qquad \text{Distributivity}$$
$$\overline{(A \cup B)} = \bar{A} \cap \bar{B} \qquad\qquad\qquad\qquad \text{De Morgan's Law}$$
$$A \cap \bar{A} = 0; \ A \cup \bar{A} = 1 \qquad\qquad \text{Law of excluded middle}$$

Fig. 3. Crisp subsets and their properties.

Zadeh's proposal of fuzzy subsets is a generalization of the mapping function χ to μ, so that for example:

$$\mu_{small}: u \to [0, 1] \qquad u \in U$$

That is, each element of the universe may belong to the subset small to a varying degree from and including 0 to 1. Thus, according to Zadeh, fuzzy subsets are better able to represent the vagueness inherent in linguistic variables. Figure 4 shows the fuzzy subsets **small**, **medium** and **tall** for the same universe as for Fig. 3. In fuzzy subsets theory one can further easily represent adjectives or hedges such as **very**, **more or less**, **not**, to form for example, **very small**, **not tall**, etc. as mathematical functions of μ_{small} and μ_{tall} (μ for each u are called membership values).

Then

$$\mu_{very\,small}(u) = \mu^2_{small}(u) \qquad \text{for each } u$$

and

$$\mu_{not\,tall}(u) = 1 - \mu_{tall}(u) \qquad \text{for each } u$$

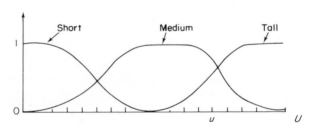

Fuzzy subsets:
$\mu_A: U \to [0, 1]$

$\mu_A(u)$ membership value ranging from 0 to 1

Union $A \bigcup B$:
$\mu_{A \cup B}(u) = \max(\mu_A(u), \mu_B(u))$

Intersection $A \bigcap B$:
$\mu_{A \cap B}(u) = \min(\mu_A(u), \mu_B(u))$

Complement $\bar{A}$:
$\mu_{\bar{A}}(u) = 1 - \mu_A(u)$

All properties as in Fig. 3 *except*:
$A \bigcup \bar{A} \neq 1 \quad \text{and} \quad A \bigcap \bar{A} \neq 0$

Fig. 4. Fuzzy subsets and their operations.

These particular functions are arbitrary, as are the maximum and minimum operations proposed for logical AND and logical OR, to be discussed shortly. This chapter will not deal with the rationale behind the various mathematical forms that have been proposed for use in fuzzy logic. Figures 3 and 4 also give the basic method of forming set union, set intersection and set complement in crisp and fuzzy subset theories respectively. When fuzzy subsets represent linguistic values, then the theory can be used to form a fuzzy logic by letting the set operations stand for logical connectives **OR**, **AND** and **NOT** (Fig. 5).

The above form of logical **AND** may be found meaningless—consider, for example, the meaning of the statement "people are **tall AND short**"— as the compound phrase is made up of two phrases with the same universe of discourse connected with **AND**. More appropriate, semantically, would

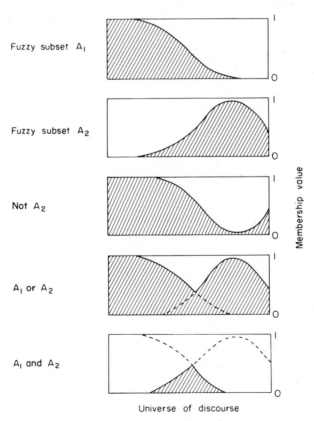

Fig. 5. Simple logical connectives for fuzzy subsets.

be the case where the compound phrase connects phrases in two separate universes of discourse—e.g. "people who are **tall AND very rich**"—the universes in the example being height and wealth. It is interesting that in fuzzy logic the connectives are not restricted to simple ones given above which were obtained from fuzzy versions of operations such as set union, set intersection and set complement. Mathematical operations have also been proposed to implement interactive versions of logical connectives for logical operations like **AND** and **IMPLICATION**. These connectives are useful in forming compound phrases from primary phrases which are fuzzy subsets of two or more separate universes of discourse.

Figure 6 shows how interactive logical connectives may be implemented. The figure shows two fuzzy subsets, A and B, of two separate universes, U and V. The example shows these as continuous curves which, in this case, where the universes are quantized, can be represented as vectors. Thus, U has seven elements and V has eight elements; A is then a seven-element vector [1, 1, 0·7, 0·4, 0·2, 0, 0] and B is an eight-element vector [0, 0·2, 0·6, 1, 1, 0·3, 0·1, 0]. Here A and B are two primary phrases. The compound phrase $A \, \square \, B$ is formed as some mathematical relation between the vectors

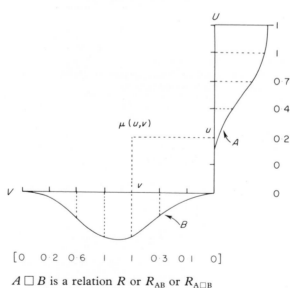

$A \, \square \, B$ is a relation R or R_{AB} or $R_{A\square B}$
  where $\mu_R(u, v) = f_\square(\mu_A(u), \mu_B(v))$

$\square$ may be logical AND or logical IMPLICATION
  f_{AND}; $f_{IMPLICATION}$ must be defined

Fig. 6. The general form of interactive connectives in fuzzy logic.

A and B and is itself denoted R, $R_{A\square B}$. This relation is a fuzzy subset of the universe of discourse $U \times V$, i.e. the universe is all pairs of elements of U and V. The universe of discourse of $R_{A\square B}$ then has $8 \times 7 = 56$ elements, and just as A and B are vectors so $R_{A\square B}$ is a matrix. Each element u, v of the compound universe has associated with it a membership value $\mu(u, v)$, and the set of pairs $\{(u, v), \mu(u, v)\}$ is in fact $R_{A\square B}$, which is equated to the compound phrase $A \square B$. The question is then how to determine the value of $\mu(u, v)$? In general, $\mu_{R_{A\square B}}(u, v)$ can be formed as

$$\mu_{R_{A\square B}}(u, v) = f_{\square}(\mu_A(u), \mu_B(v))$$

i.e. as some mathematical function $f_{\square}$ of $\mu_A(u)$ and $\mu_B(v)$; the function $f_{\square}$ corresponding to each logical operation $\square$.

For logical AND, the proposed mathematical function is min (see Fig. 7). For logical IMPLICATION on the other hand, a variety of functions have been proposed and their properties investigated on various semantic grounds.

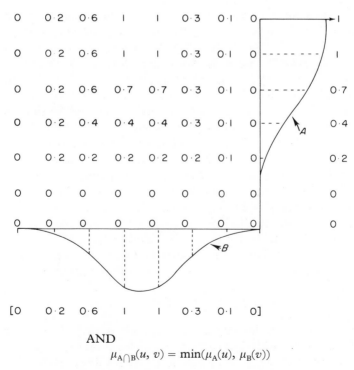

AND
$$\mu_{A\cap B}(u, v) = \min(\mu_A(u), \mu_B(v))$$

Fig. 7. An example of the relation $R_{A\cap B}$ for logical AND.

Three of these functions are:

(a) bounded sum of $\bar{A}$ and B (after Lukasiewicz)

$$\mu_{R_{A\to B}}(u, v) = \min(1, \mu_{\bar{A}}(u) + \mu_B(v))$$
$$= \min(1, (1 - \mu_A(u)) + \mu_B(v))$$

In this form one takes the arithmetic sum of the membership value of B at (v) and that of the complement of A at (u); and this sum is then bounded by 1 (in case it happens to be greater than 1) to obtain the membership value at the point (u, v) in the relation $R_{A\to B}$.

(b) Material implication as $\bar{A} \vee B$ (based on Variant of Standard Sequences)

$$\mu_{R_{A\to B}}(u, v) = \max(\mu_{\bar{A}}(u), \mu_B(v))$$
$$= \max((1 - \mu_A(u)), \mu_B(v))$$

(c) Implication $A \to B$ as $(A$ **AND** $B)$ **OR** (**NOT** (A) **AND** $1)$

$$\mu_{R_{A\to B}}(u, v) = \max[\{\min(\mu_A(u), \mu_B(v))\}, \{\min(1, (1 - \mu_A(u))\}]$$

Form (a) will not be discussed further here. Forms (b) and (c) can be arranged to give two alternative ways of implementing the rules of Fig. 2 on a computer. Before this is done in detail, note that each rule of Fig. 2 can be represented symbolically as $A_k \wedge B_k \to C_k$, where say, the 1st rule, A_1 is **negative big** (**NB**) OR **negative medium** (**NM**) pressure error (PE), B_1 is **negative small** (**NS**) change in pressure errors (CPE) and C_1 is **positive medium** (**PM**) heat change (HC). Thus, the rule $A_1 \wedge B_1 \to C_1$ is a compound phrase with three fuzzy subsets defined on three different universes of discourse: A_1 on U, B_1 on V and C_1 on W. Here U is PE, V is CPE and W is HC. A_1 itself, is a compound fuzzy subset formed by taking a simple OR of NB & NM, each being a primary fuzzy subset of U, i.e. PE. Similarly, B_1 is the fuzzy subset NS of the universe CPE and C_1 is the fuzzy subset PM of the universe HC. The various fuzzy subsets used in Fig. 2 are given in Table II. Thus, each rule is a relation $R_{A_k \wedge B_k \to C_k}$, which is, it will be recalled, itself a fuzzy subset of the cross-product universe of discourse $U \times V \times W$ and in which the membership value at each element $\mu(u, v, w)$ can be calculated as a function of $\mu(u)$, $\mu(v)$ and $\mu(w)$ as described above. For each rule, k, the functions can be represented as

$$\mu_R(u, v, w) = f_\to\{f_\wedge(\mu_{A_k}(u), \mu_{B_k}(v)), \mu_{C_k}(w)\}$$

Furthermore, the complete collection of rules is also a relation R, or a fuzzy subset R, of the same kind as each R_k (i.e. defined on the same universe of discourse as R_k—$U \times V \times W$) obtained by combining together the R_k's by a logical operation which interprets "ALSO" in Fig. 2.

Table II

Fuzzy subsets for the linguistic terms used in Fig. 2. Numbers given are membership values times ten

Error (E)

e	-6	-5	-4	-3	-2	-1	-0	+0	+1	+2	+3	+4	+5	+6
PB[a]	0	0	0	0	0	0	0	0	0	0	0	3	7	10
PM	0	0	0	0	0	0	0	0	0	3	7	10	7	3
PS	0	0	0	0	0	0	0	3	7	10	7	3	0	0
PO	0	0	0	0	0	0	0	10	7	3	0	0	0	0
NO	0	0	0	0	3	7	10	0	0	0	0	0	0	0
NS	0	0	3	7	10	7	3	0	0	0	0	0	0	0
NM	3	7	10	7	3	0	0	0	0	0	0	0	0	0
NB	10	7	3	0	0	0	0	0	0	0	0	0	0	0

Change in error (C)

c	-6	-5	-4	-3	-2	-1	0	+1	+2	+3	+4	+5	+6
PB	0	0	0	0	0	0	0	0	0	0	3	7	10
PM	0	0	0	0	0	0	0	0	3	7	10	7	3
PS	0	0	0	0	0	0	3	7	10	7	3	0	0
ZO	0	0	0	0	3	7	10	7	3	0	0	0	0
NS	0	0	3	7	10	7	3	0	0	0	0	0	0
NM	3	7	10	7	3	0	0	0	0	0	0	0	0
NB	10	7	3	0	0	0	0	0	0	0	0	0	0

Additional change in procesess input (P) and change in process input (U)

u and p	-6	-5	-4	-3	-2	-1	0	+1	+2	+3	+4	+5	+6
PB	0	0	0	0	0	0	0	0	0	0	3	7	10
PM	0	0	0	0	0	0	0	0	3	7	10	7	3
PS	0	0	0	0	0	0	3	7	10	7	3	0	0
ZO	0	0	0	0	3	7	10	7	3	0	0	0	0
NS	0	0	3	7	10	7	3	0	0	0	0	0	0
NM	3	7	10	7	3	0	0	0	0	0	0	0	0
NB	10	7	3	0	0	0	0	0	0	0	0	0	0

[a] The linguistic names are abbreviated to: PB, Positive big; PM, Positive medium; PS, Positive small; PO, Positive Zero; NB, Negative big; NM, Negative medium; NS, Negative small; NO, Negative zero; ZO, zero.

Thus

$$\mu_R(u, v, w) = f_{ALSO} \left(\mu_{R_k}(u, v, w) \right)$$
$$\forall_k$$

The alternative approaches used in implementing the rules then depend upon the choice of functions $f_{\rightarrow}$, $f_{\wedge}$ and f_{ALSO} described above. In fact, the way $f_{\rightarrow}$ is interpreted also defines how f_{ALSO} should be interpreted; while the form of $f_{\wedge}$ is not in doubt, this being the function *min* as mentioned already.

Alternative 1: Any one of the three forms can be used to implement $f_{\rightarrow}$. Whichever form one uses, f_{ALSO} must be interpreted as AND. This is because it is necessary to use the mathematical operation "minimum" to combine the relation R_k for the individual rules to form the overall relation R. The reason is that each rule will determine a different narrow region in the relation R_k with membership values that are less than 1 (note that R_k with membership is an array of the dimension of $U \times V \times W$). Outside this region the membership values will all be 1.

Now form (b) for $f_{\rightarrow}$ gives as good as results as any of the other forms and is easier to implement. Hence the rules can be implemented mathematically by using the following equations:

$$\mu_{R_k}(u, v, w) = f_{\rightarrow}[\min\{\mu_{A_k}(u), \mu_{B_k}(v)\}, \mu_{C_k}(w)]$$

Noting that the antecedent in $f_{\rightarrow}$ is complemented

$$\mu_{R_k}(u, v, w) = \max[\{1 - \min(\mu_{A_k}(u), \mu_{B_k}(v))\}, \mu_{C_k}(w)]$$

and

$$\mu_R(u, v, w) = \min_k \mu_{R_k}(u, v, w)$$

Alternative 2: This is derived by taking certain liberties with the interpretation of form (c) for $f_{\rightarrow}$. Historically, form (c) was the one originally proposed by Zadeh (1973); the other forms came much later in the development of fuzzy subset theory. In that work Zadeh expresses "*A* implies *B*" as:

If A then B else if not A then anything

Taking   If A then B as $\min(A, B)$ or $A \wedge B$
                ELSE as   max   or OR
and   anything as   1
one obtains the form (c), i.e. $(A \wedge B) \vee (\bar{A} \wedge 1)$.

When more than one rule is given, such as

A_1 implies B_1 also A_2 implies B_2

one can reinterpret Zadeh's form and write this as:

If A_1 then B_1 else If A_2 then B_2 else if neither then anything.

This will result mathematically in

$$(A_1 \wedge B_1) \vee (A_2 \wedge B_2) \vee ((\bar{A}_1 \vee \bar{B}_1) \wedge 1)$$

One can then omit the final term if the rules are complete, i.e. if they span the state-space completely. In fact, one can do this even if they are almost complete. This would tantamount to interpreting $f_{\rightarrow}$ simply as min giving it the same form of f; and interpreting f_{ALSO} as f_V, i.e. ALSO as OR.

The collection of rules now appear as a disjunctive form in which each rule is a conjunctive term

$$(A_1 \wedge B_1 \wedge C_1) \vee (A_2 \wedge B_2 \wedge C_2) \vee (\ldots\ldots) \vee (A_n \wedge B_n \wedge C_n)$$

Mathematically R_k is given as

$$\mu_{R_k}(u, v, w) = \min\{\mu_{C_k}(w), \min(\mu_{A_k}(u), \mu_{B_k}k(v))\}$$

and

$$\mu_R(u, v, w) = \max_k \mu_{R_k}(u, v, w)$$

OR

$$\mu_R(u, v, w) = \max_k [\min\{\mu_{C_k}(w), \mu_{A_k}(u), \mu_{B_k}(v)\}]$$

Here, it should be noticed that f_{ALSO} gets interpreted as OR. This is perfectly in order because the arrays for R_k will now be made up of clusters of non-zero values in the space of mostly 0 membership values. Thus in forming R from the individual R_k's the maximum operation (which stands for logical OR) will properly combine the various clusters.

Alternative 2, while hard to justify semantically has been widely used in process control applications—see Mamdani (1976). This is partly a derivative of Zadeh's original proposals and partly because the form of R_k that results for each rule (all 0 values except in the cluster relating to the rule) has a certain intuitive appeal.

III. Decision making using fuzzy rules

The above discussion simply shows how the rules can be expressed mathematically. One can now consider how to obtain a decision from these rules once an actual situation or an antecedent is given. Logically, this is the process of *modus ponens*. In fuzzy logic *modus ponens* is expressed through what Zadeh has termed "the compositional rule of inference".

The procedure in question is depicted in Fig. 8. If one has an implication $A \to B$ (this may be of a more complex form $A \wedge B \to C$, and may in fact be not just a single rule but a collection of them), and one is now given an antecedent A' which is a fuzzy subset of U, then the decision process amounts to computing the consequent B' which is a fuzzy subset of V.

The compositional rule of inference is expressed as

$$B' = A' \circ R_{A \to B}$$

This is implemented as a max–min operation between the "vector" A' and the "matrix" R and is shown in Fig. 8. Its effect is to use A' to reduce R to the dimensionality and the order of the universe of discourse of B or B'.

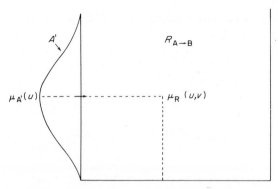

Rule of inference:
    Given: $R_{A \to B}$; A', the antecedent
           Calculate B' the consequent
    $B' = A' \circ R_{A \to B}$
    $\circ$ is the compositional rule of inference

Mathematically:
    $\mu_B(v) = \max_u \{\min(\mu_R(u, v), \mu_{A'}(u))\}$

Fig. 8. The rule of inference.

With the rules of Fig. 2 R will of course be 3-dimensional $(U \times V \times W)$ and the antecedent will be 2-dimensional $(U \times V)$ giving a decision as a fuzzy subset of W(HC).

As has already been shown above, the collection of control rules which are of the form $A_k \wedge B_k \to C_k$ will be represented by the relation R.

$$R \text{ then is } \mu_R(u, v, w) \quad \text{for all } u \in U, \ v \in V, \ w \in W$$

When a decision has to be made, two antecedents

$$A': \mu_{A'}(u) \qquad \forall u \in U$$

and

$$B': \mu_{B'}(v) \qquad \forall v \in V$$

will also be given. From this information the consequent C' is to be computed where

$$C': \mu_{C'}(w) \qquad \forall w \in W$$

This is done using the compositional rule of inference so that $C' = A' \circ (B' \circ R)$. Mathematically this gets expressed as

$$\mu_{C'}(w) = \max_u \min \left[\mu_{A'}(u), \left\{ \max_v \min \Big((\mu_{B'}(v), \mu_R(u, v, w) \Big) \right\} \right]$$

The inner bracket { } composes B' with R giving the "matrix", for example, S (S: $\mu_S(u, w)$ $\forall u \in U$, $\forall w \in W$). S is a fuzzy subset of $U \times W$ and the variable V has been composed out. The second stage composes S with A' leaving C' as the consequent. Because the operations involved are commutative one has:

$$C' = A' \circ (B' \circ R) = B' \circ (A' \circ R) = (A' \wedge B') \circ R$$

$$\therefore \mu_{C'}(w) = \max_{u} \max_{v} \min(\mu_A(u), \mu_B(v), \mu_R(u, v, w))$$

It should be noted that this computation is irrespective of how *implication* is interpreted; the mathematical form of $f_{\rightarrow}$ having already been taken into account when computing $\mu_R(u, v, w)$.

The mathematical discourse given this far is complete in every detail and can be implemented on a computer. However, it is cumbersome for this purpose and in practical applications the formulae were rearranged and simplified as discussed in the next section.

IV. Computer implementation of fuzzy rule-based decision making

The relation R, given as $\mu_R(u, v, w)$, can be computed when the decision is required, i.e. as the computation for the consequent C' progresses. This can be time consuming. However, precomputing $\mu_R(u, v, w)$ from the rules has the disadvantage that if the rules change then additional time must be set aside for calculating the new $\mu_R(u, v, w)$.

The other major difficulty with the mathematical formulae given so far is that they can only be used if the rules have a small number of variables (such as U, V and W, etc.). Suppose that each universe of discourse has ten elements; the universe of discourse of R then will have 10^3 elements. This rapidly grows, with the number of variables so that with ten variables the size of R becomes 10^{10}. Thus the problem of storing R can be the limiting factor in the application of this method. The only way out is to avoid the computation of $\mu_R(u, v, w)$ altogether. This, in fact, is of key importance if the method is to be applied at all.

The problem of avoiding the computation of $\mu_R(u, v, w)$ is relatively straightforward if all the antecedents are assumed to be crisp subsets of a particular kind. Figure 9 shows that when an implication $A \rightarrow B$ is given and the antecedent A' is such that $\mu_A(u)$ is 1 for only one element u_o of U and is 0 for all other elements of U, then applying the compositional rule of inference is equivalent to picking out the row of the matrix R at u_o.

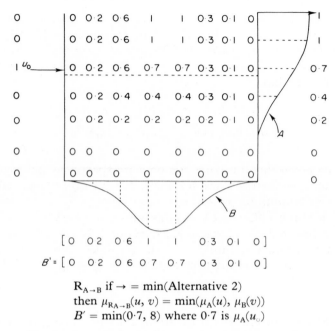

$$B' = \begin{bmatrix} 0 & 0.2 & 0.6 & 1 & 1 & 0.3 & 0.1 & 0 \end{bmatrix}$$
$$B' = \begin{bmatrix} 0 & 0.2 & 0.6 & 0.7 & 0.7 & 0.3 & 0.1 & 0 \end{bmatrix}$$

$R_{A \to B}$ if $\to$ = min(Alternative 2)
then $\mu_{R_{A \to B}}(u, v) = \min(\mu_A(u), \mu_B(v))$
$B' = \min(0.7, 8)$ where 0.7 is $\mu_A(u_o)$

Fig. 9. An example of inference using singular antecedent.

Mathematically,

$$\mu_{B'}(v) = \max_u \min(\mu_{A'}(u), \mu_R(u, v))$$

If A' is such that $\mu_{A'}(u_o) = 1$ for some one $u_o \in U$

and $\mu_{A'}(u) = 0$ for all $u \neq u_o$

then $\mu_{B'}(v) = \mu_R(u_o, v)$.

Now $\mu_R(u_o, v) = f_{\to}(\mu_A(u_o), \mu_B(v))$.

If $f_{\to}$ is min as in alternative 2 discussed above, then $\mu_{B'}(v)$ is simply the min of $\mu_A(u_o)$ and $\mu_B(v)$.

For each rule $A_k \to B_k$, one simply looks up the value $\mu_{A_k}(u_o)$ at u_o and forms the subset B' as the subset B whose largest value does not exceed $\mu_{A_k}(u_o)$.

In the general case when one is given:

  (i) Many rules of the type $A_k \wedge B_k \to C_k$.
 (ii) All the fuzzy subsets used in the rules, i.e. all A_k's, B_k's and C_k's.
(iii) Antecedents A' and B' as u_o and v_o at which the membership value
      is 1.

Then for each rule k, find

$$\mu_{A_k}(u_o) \quad \text{and} \quad \mu_{B_k}(v_o)$$

then

$$\mu_{C_k}(w) = f_{\rightarrow}[f_{\wedge}(\mu_{A_k}(u_o), \mu_{B_k}(v_o)), \mu_{C_k}(w)]$$

and

$$\mu_{C'}(w) = f_{\text{ALSO}} \, \mu_{C_k}(w). \qquad \forall k$$

In the two alternatives discussed above, these forms will appear mathematically as

Alternative 1: $f_{\rightarrow}: \overline{A} \vee B \quad f_{\wedge} = \min \quad f_{\text{ALSO}} = \min$

$$\mu_{C'}(w) = \min_k \max[\{1 - \min(\mu_{A_k}(u_o), \mu_{B_k}(v_o))\}, \mu_{C_k}(w)]$$

Alternative 2: $f_{\rightarrow} = f_{\wedge} = \min \quad f_{\text{ALSO}} = \max$

$$\mu_{C'}(w) = \max_k \min[\min\{\mu_{A_k}(u_o), \mu_{B_k}(v_o)\}, \mu_{C_k}(w)]$$

There are several factors to note here. First, in both alternative implementations, the computation $\min\{\mu_{A_k}(u_o), \mu_{B_k}(v_o)\}$ is involved. Let us call this λ_k. λ_k will determine the extent to which C_k or the kth rule contributes to the decision when the antecedents are as given. For any point of the state-space $U \times V$, there will be a small set (probably none) of the rules that will have $\lambda_k \neq 0$. These are the rules that apply. Thus the rules that apply in each given situation can be identified and if necessary altered.

Secondly, the decision C' is a fuzzy subset and as such may not be usable in a given application. For example, in the control application, one wants to know what input to apply to the process. From the fuzzy subset of C', $\mu_{C'}(w)$, one value w_o must be chosen as the representative value. Various heuristics may be used to select w_o, such as the value at which $\mu_{C'}(w)$ achieves the maximum value, or the point which is the "centre of gravity" of the fuzzy subset. Use any such heuristic means so that for any state u_o, v_o, the action w_o is deterministic. Thus one can reduce the rules to a decision table and refer to it when a decision is required. However, this approach cannot be used if the rules are to be changed in between decisions. More important, it cannot be used if the rules have many variables (unless the table is stored as a sparse array). For more complex systems (i.e. one with many variables) it is possible that one may cover only a small region of the state-space, the rest being not important, with a relatively small number of rules. Figure 10 gives a schematic diagram of the computer implementation of the procedures just described. The decision table obtained by using the rules of Fig. 2 with the fuzzy subsets of Table II, is given in Table III.

Finally, it is worth noting again that the simplified mathematical form which avoids the computation of $\mu_R(u, v, w)$ has been achieved only when the antecedents are all particular types of crisp subsets. If one or more of the antecedents have to be fuzzy subsets then other forms of simplifications and approximations may be necessary. Furthermore, all the mathematical forms discussed here assume that the universes of discourse are discrete sets and that fuzzy subsets can be represented as vectors. It is possible to use continuous universes of discourse and represent the fuzzy subsets as simple mathematical functions. In that case, the mathematical formulae, in particular those that can be effectively implemented on a computer, will differ substantially from those given here.

V. The need for a self-organizing controller

The fuzzy logic controller has in practice been found to be surprisingly effective. That is to say it works and achieves "good" performance with

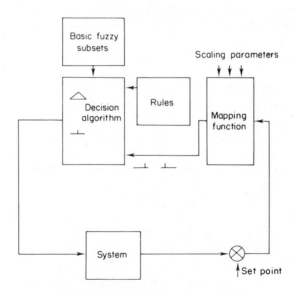

Fig. 10.   Simple fuzzy logic controller.

only very little effort being spent on adjusting the rules. The "surprise" element is due entirely to the fact that it works. Conventional wisdom in control engineering simply does not lead one to expect that such "rule-of-thumb" techniques would, or could actually work in practice. The conclusion then is that fuzzy logic as proposed by Zadeh is sound when used for interpreting linguistic rules of the type used in the process control work. A more important conclusion is that rule-based decision making is a powerful technique with potentially many applications yet to be investigated. Thus the question of acquiring the rules to be used in decision making is of great concern. So far it has not received the kind of attention it deserves.

In the steam-engine controller, the initial set of rules took some time to specify (after one had acquired some skill at controlling the steam-engine). These were not perfect and required further modifications. It can be seen from Fig. 10 that the controller needs three pieces of initial data for the mathematical procedures to be applied. These are

(a) The scaling parameters to be used to map actual measured and calculated values (of pressure error (PE), change in pressure error (CPE) and heat change (HC)) onto a normalized universe of discourse. Knowledge of the design of the process and its instrumentation can provide adequate information to select these scaling factors effectively. Subsequent tuning of these parameters is also possible and can have an effect on the performance of the controller.

Table III

The decision table for the rules in Fig. 2 using fuzzy subsets of Table II (using the mathematical forms of Alternative 2)

Error	Change in error												
	−6	−5	−4	−3	−2	−1	0	1	2	3	4	5	6
−6	0	0	4	4	4	5	6	6	6	6	6	6	6
−5	0	0	4	4	4	5	6	6	6	6	6	6	6
−4	−2	−2	0	4	4	5	6	6	6	6	6	6	6
−3	−2	−2	−2	0	0	0	5	5	5	5	6	6	6
−2	−2	−2	−2	−1	0	0	4	4	4	5	6	6	6
−1	−3	−3	−3	0	−1	0	0	0	4	5	5	5	5
0	−4	−4	−4	−3	−2	−1	0	0	0	4	4	4	4
0	4	4	4	3	2	1	0	0	0	−4	−4	−4	−4
1	3	3	3	0	1	0	0	0	−4	−5	−5	−5	−5
2	2	2	2	1	0	0	−4	−4	−4	−5	−5	−5	−5
3	2	2	2	0	0	0	−5	−5	−5	−5	−5	−6	−6
4	2	2	0	−4	−4	−5	−5	−5	−5	−5	−0	−6	−6
5	0	0	−4	−4	−4	−5	−5	−6	−6	−6	−6	−6	−6
6	0	0	−4	−4	−4	−5	−5	−6	−6	−6	−6	−6	−6

(b) The fuzzy subsets that are used in the rules (i.e. the information given in Table II). This is where one gets the actual numerical membership values to be used in the calculations. The initial assignment of these numerical values is arbitrary. Their function is to define an approximate meaning of the linguistic terms and as such cannot be used for subsequent tuning of the performance of the controller.

(c) The rules themselves, are the most meaningful way of effecting the performance of the controller.

Any initial set of rules will almost invariably need further modifications after noting how they perform in practice. As has been described earlier, the λ_k values for each rule at each decision point (u, v) provide useful information about which rules to modify. The algorithm of the controller can be written in such a way that rules can be edited on-line while the controller is being used.

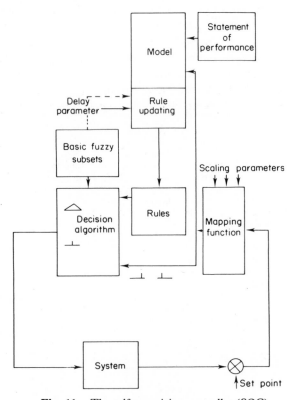

Fig. 11. The self-organizing controller (SOC).

Instead of this editing procedure, which would delete rules and insert new ones, it is possible to develop the controller algorithm that implements some form of training procedure. Figure 11 shows a schematic diagram of such a controller. The performance measure in this scheme is a means of judging if the state of the system just observed is adequate or not, and if not, then to what extent it is inadequate. The model in the scheme is a crude means of translating the judgement about the state into the amount of improvement to effect in the action taken by the controller.

If the performance measure is specified by the operator who monitors the performance then one has a supervised training scheme. If, on the other hand, the monitoring can be carried out by the algorithm itself, then one has a self-organizing controller. The self-organizing form of a fuzzy logic controller has been implemented and can be described without going into mathematical details. Such details can be found in Procyk and Mamdani (1979).

Table IV shows the table which gives the performance measure taking into account a crude model of the process. The implied model here is simply that there is a monotomic relationship between the input and the output of the process. That is to say, if the desired value is higher than required then this is because some responsible action or actions in the past were high and should be reduced. Such responsible past actions will not necessarily be the immediate last action but some more distant action or a set of them depending on the delays and the assumed dynamics of the process. The values in Table IV give the extent to which such past actions

Table IV
Table of reinforcements used in a single SOC

Error	Change in error												
	−6	−5	−4	−3	−2	−1	0	+1	+2	+3	+4	+5	+6
−6	0	0	0	0	0	0	6	6	6	6	6	6	6
−5	0	0	0	2	2	3	6	6	6	6	6	6	6
−4	0	0	0	2	4	5	6	6	6	6	6	6	6
−3	0	0	0	2	2	3	4	4	4	4	5	5	5
−2	0	0	0	0	0	0	2	2	2	3	4	5	6
−1	0	0	0	0	0	0	1	1	1	2	3	4	5
0	0	0	0	0	0	0	0	0	0	1	2	3	4
0	0	0	0	0	0	0	0	0	0	−1	−2	−3	−4
1	0	0	0	0	0	0	−1	−1	−1	−2	−3	−3	−4
2	0	0	0	0	0	0	−2	−2	−2	−3	−4	−4	−6
3	0	0	0	−2	−2	−2	−3	−3	−3	−3	−4	−4	−5
4	0	0	0	−2	−4	−4	−6	−5	−6	−5	−6	−5	−6
5	0	0	0	−2	−2	−2	−5	−5	−5	−5	−5	−5	−5
6	0	0	0	0	0	0	−6	−5	−6	−5	−6	−5	−6

should be increased or decreased for each present monitored state of the process. Whether this change would require creating a new rule or modifying an existing one, is the task achieved by a procedure that evaluates each existing rule in turn to examine its effect. Mathematical details of this procedure, as mentioned already, can be found in Procyk and Mamdani (1979). This paper also describes how such a self-organizing controller performs in practice. In broad terms, such a controller converges to a stable set of rules even when started initially without any control rules. Because these rules are in a linguistic form it is always possible to prime the controller with an initial set of rules which can ensure safe behaviour while the training is taking place.

The self-organizing control method of acquiring the rules has been described here in connection with engineering systems. These are relatively simple systems to deal with. Rule-based decision making has wider applications, in some of which the self-organizing approach may not be applicable. This is because one needs a procedure for evaluating each state locally on its own. Furthermore, a model, however crude, is required for determining to what extent the responsible action needs to be altered. (The reason that only a crude model suffices is that any inaccuracy in it will be removed because the training procedure is iterative.)

The supervised form of training, however, offers more promise. Here the judgement of the supervisor can take the place of both the performance measure and the model. If his internal model of the process is accurate only one training pass may be necessary; if not, then several passes will be required before satisfactory performance will be obtained from the controller. If, however, the internal model is faulty and full of inconsistencies then convergence to satisfactory performance will never take place. It has been found with other supervised training schemes that one wrong action by the operator in an otherwise good training can have a devastating effect on a learning algorithm. This is because it is very difficult indeed to design algorithms that cannot only be trained but which are also able to evaluate the quality of training that is being given to them by a supposedly expert trainer.

To summarize then, a careful design of initial rules is the best way to proceed. This can be an extensive task but is by no means impossible. Some research has gone into the job of protocol analysis which would give a formal approach to the design of linguistic rules. However, much more work needs to be done. Once a good initial set of rules is available, interactive control algorithms can be used for further tuning. Training schemes, both supervised and automatic, may be applicable in particular instances of the application of rule-based decision making, but these too require careful design.

VI. Conversational programs using fuzzy logic

This chapter has discussed the application of rule-based decision making using fuzzy logic in the particular area of control of industrial processes. Here the input to the decision-making algorithm is linguistic but its output is a fuzzy subset from which, furthermore, a particular element of the universe of discourse is selected. It is obvious that this method can have many other applications as well. In some of these applications it may be desirable to have the answer from the algorithm also coming out in a linguistic form. This means that in order to make the decision-making algorithm described here fully conversational, it is necessary to find a linguistic label which best describes the fuzzy subset that results from the operation of the algorithm. This process has been called Linguistic Approximation (LA) by Zadeh. Wenstoep (1976) has used a linguistic approximation procedure and shown how it can be used in management decision making. Recently, Eshragh and Mamdani (1978) have developed an algorithm for linguistic approximation that is more general. Below, only the problem is explained, leaving the reader to find out about the details of the algorithms used in its solutions from the references cited.

To start with some terms have to be defined in an informal manner:

A primary fuzzy phrase is a linguistic term whose meaning is obtained directly as a given fuzzy subset. The primary phrases are the atomic elements of a compound phrase. The fuzzy subsets may be specified as membership functions of the universe of discourse or where possible as vectors of membership values. Examples are: **large, medium** and **small** height.

A simple phrase is a primary phrase preceded by certain allowed adjectives or hedges. An example of a simple phrase is "**not very small**", where **small** is the primary phrase for which a fuzzy subset is given; **not** and **very** are allowed hedges for which there are functions specified which modify the membership values of the subset they precede. From the definitions already given:

$$\mu_{\text{very small}}(u) = \{\mu_{\text{small}}(u)\}^2$$

and

$$\mu_{\text{not very small}}(u) = \{1 - \mu_{\text{small}}(u)\}^2$$

Two other hedges that can be introduced in linguistic approximation are "**Above** x" and "**Below** x". Their form is shown in Fig. 12. They are designed to have the following interesting properties:

Above x **OR Below** x = **Not** x
not above x **AND not below** x = x

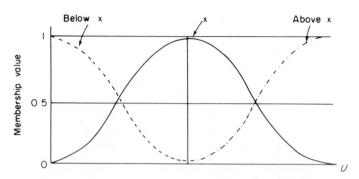

Fig. 12. The hedges **Above** x and **Below** x for a given x.

From above, it is worth noting that while mathematically one can compute a subset for the phrase "**very not small**", linguistically it does not carry any meaning. Similarly, while **very very small** is acceptable, **more or less, more or less small** is not.

$$[\mu_{\text{more or less small}}(u) = \{\mu_{\text{small}}(u)\}^{1/2}]$$

This means that it is necessary in linguistic approximation to also have a grammar which only generates linguistically acceptable phrases.

A compound phrase is one which is obtained by combining several simple phrases by the logical connectives **AND** and **OR**. An example of this would be the phrase "**not above medium AND not below more or less small**". Again the grammar mentioned above has to be extended to generate only linguistically acceptable compound phrases.

When a decision-making algorithm is used it results in a fuzzy subset. Now the operations in fuzzy logic are such that the logic is not closed to all linguistic compound phrases. It certainly is not closed to all acceptable or meaningful compound phrases. It is necessary therefore to resort to some linguistic approximation procedure which will use a grammar and a matching algorithm to find a compound phrase that has a fuzzy subset most like the fuzzy subset which results from decision-making algorithms. The result of this combined procedure is a conversational program.

The decision making in such a conversational program can involve more complex operations than have been described in this chapter. In particular, it is possible to have fuzzy arithmetic operations beside the fuzzy logic operations given above. It will be noticed that the universes of discourse in all examples cited in this chapter are ordered sets. There are applications in which one may wish to calculate "distances" between fuzzy subsets and express the result linguistically. As an example, consider a program which is able to express that the difference between "**more or less medium** x" and "**not very small** x" is "**more or less medium**". This would require the use of some form of fuzzy difference operation. Zadeh proposes the following mathematical way of achieving it:

Given two fuzzy subsets, A and B, on the universe of discourse U, the membership values for their difference can be computed as:

$$\mu_{|A-B|}(|u_A - u_B|) = \max_{\forall |u_A - u_B|} \min\{\mu_A(u_A), \mu_B(u_B)\}$$

For example, suppose A is "**about five**" and B is "**about three**". The fuzzy subsets defining the meaning of A and B are as given in the following table:

about 5	0	0	0	0·2	0·8	1	0·8	0·2
about 3	0	0·2	0·8	1	0·8	0·2	0	0
$|A - B|$	0·8	0·8	1	0·8	0·2	0·2	0·2	0
universe	0	1	2	3	4	5	6	7

The difference between A and B as computed by the form defined is also shown in the table. It can be seen that the result is more fuzzy than both A and B and the peak value occurs at 2. The resulting fuzzy set can be expressed linguistically using LA and maybe something like "**more or less 2**".

It can be seen that conversational programs extend the power of fuzzy logic. Alternatively, it can be argued that if fuzzy logic is the logic which deals with linguistic terms having approximate meanings (expressed as fuzzy subsets), then fuzzy algorithms must be conversational. If so, then Linguistic Approximation is not merely a procedure "tagged on" at the end of a fuzzy decision-making algorithm, but an integral part of fuzzy mathematics.

VII. Conclusion

In describing the process control application of fuzzy logic, this chapter has dealt with, in detail, the aspects of fuzzy mathematics employed in that application. This chapter has also tried to show that the application is essentially one of rule-based decision-making in which fuzzy logic has been employed as a tool for computer implementation. As a method of decision making the power of this approach has yet to be fully realized by other application studies, possibly in areas dealing with soft or humanistic systems. For such applications, the method of acquiring the rules requires a great deal of careful attention.

Fuzzy logic, the theory of which is still being developed further by many research workers, is extremely sound as a tool. With linguistic approximation it is possible to develop conversational programs in which not only are the inputs linguistic but which produce the answers also in a linguistic form. Such programs offer exciting possibilities in extending the interaction between man and the computer.

VIII. References

Buchanan, B. G. and Lederberg, J. (1971). The Heuristic DENDRIL Program for Explaining Emperical Data. *Proceedings of the IFIP-1971 Congress.*

Eshragh, F. and Mamdani, E. H. (1979). A general approach to linguistic approximation. *Int. J. Man–Machine Studies* **11**, 4, 501–519.

Mamdani, E. H. (1976). Advances in the linguistic synthesis of fuzzy logic controllers. *Int. J. Man–Machine Studies* **8**, 669–678.

Peray, K. E. and Waddell, J. J. (1972). *The Rotary Cement Kiln.* The Chemical Publishing Co., New York.

Procyk, T. J. and Mamdani, E. H. (1979). A linguistic self-organising process controller. *Automatica* **15**, 15–30.

Watermann, D. A. (1970). Generalisation learning techniques for automating the learning of heuristics. *Artificial Intelligence* **1**, 121–170.

Wenstoep, F. (1976). Deductive verbal models of organisations. *Int. J. Man–Machine Studies* **8**.

Zadeh, L. A. (1973). Outline of a New Approach to the Analysis of Complex systems and decision processes. *IEEE Trans. SMC-3* **1**, 28–44.

Subject index